NOLO *and* USA TODAY

NOLO
YOUR LEGAL COMPANION

For more than 35 years, Nolo has been helping ordinary folks who want to answer their legal questions, create their own documents, or work with a lawyer more efficiently. Nolo.com provides quick information about wills, house buying, credit repair, starting a business—and just about anything else that's affected by the law. It's packed with free articles, legal updates, resources, and a complete catalog of Nolo books and software.

To find out about any important legal or other changes to this book's contents, sign up for our free update service at nolo.com/legalupdater or go to nolo.com/updates. And to make sure that you've got the most recent edition of this book, check Nolo's website or give us a call at 800-728-3555.

USA TODAY
The Nation's Newspaper

USA TODAY, the nation's largest circulation newspaper, was founded in 1982. It has nearly 3.9 million readers daily, making it the most widely read newspaper in the country.

USATODAY.com adds blogs, interactive graphics, games, travel resources, and trailblazing network journalism, allowing readers to comment on every story.

1ST EDITION

The Essential Guide
for First-Time Homeowners

Maximize Your Investment & Enjoy Your New Home

by Ilona Bray & Alayna Schroeder

First Edition   SEPTEMBER 2008

Cover & Book Design   SUSAN PUTNEY

Proofreading   ROBERT WELLS

Index   SONGBIRD INDEXING

Printing   DELTA PRINTING SOLUTIONS, INC.

USA TODAY CONTRIBUTORS

Book Editor   BEN NUSSBAUM

Contributing Editors   JIM HENDERSON, FRED MONYAK,
                       AND GERI TUCKER

Special thanks to   JULIE SNIDER

Bray, Ilona M., 1962-
   The essential guide for first-time homeowners : maximize your investment & enjoy your
new home / by Ilona Bray & Alayna Schroeder. -- 1st ed.
     p. cm.
   ISBN-13: 978-1-4133-0895-2 (pbk.)
   ISBN-10: 1-4133-0895-3 (pbk.)
   1. Home ownership. I. Schroeder, Alayna, 1975- II. Title.
HD7287.8.B73 2008
643'.1--dc22
                             2008012908

For information on bulk purchases or corporate premium sales, please contact Nolo's Sales
Department. For academic sales or textbook adoptions, ask for Academic Sales. Call 800-955-4775
or write to Nolo, 950 Parker Street, Berkeley, CA 94710.

Acknowledgments

Every book is a team effort, and this one even more so, with all the topics it brings within one cover. We'd like to thank the following people in particular:

For substantive input: Paul Grucza, author, TV show host, and faculty member of the Community Associations Institute (CAI), based in Coppell, Texas (www.caionline.org), for help with issues concerning new home construction; Shae Irving, for demonstrating how much you can learn from buying one sofa; Willow Liroff, a savvy first-time homeowner, for sharing her eBay and Craigslist wisdom; Mike Mansell of Argo Insurance in Pleasant Hill, California (www.argoinsurance.com), for insights on homeowners' insurance; Janet Portman, Nolo editor and author, for practical advice on working with contractors, dealing with mold, bringing in tenants, and more; and Norma Vally, the "Toolbelt Diva," for sharing her list of tools every homeowner should have.

For making it all look good, Nolo's Production Department, including Jaleh Doane, Emma Cofod, and Susan Putney. And special thanks to Marcia Stewart and Mary Randolph, for ongoing editorial advice.

Finally, we'd like to thank the late, great Robert Bruss, syndicated columnist, for a lifetime of real estate wisdom.

About the Authors

Ilona Bray is an attorney, author, and legal editor at Nolo. Her working background includes solo practice, nonprofit, and corporate stints. She spends many weekends pruning her apple trees and trying to undo the effects of time on her 1917 Arts and Crafts bungalow. Her favorite homeownership responsibility is refilling the backyard fountain every day, and watching as it's visited by local hummingbirds, finches, and California towhees.

Alayna Schroeder is a member of Nolo's editorial staff whose legal career has taken her from corporate law firm to consulting to a stint in the Peace Corps. According to *Sacramento Magazine*, the home she shares with her husband and their Bolivian-born dog, Luna, is in one of the Sacramento area's ten Great Neighborhoods—a fact Alayna tries to remember as she redoes the aging plaster and labors over the new patio.

Table of Contents

Your Homeowning Companion_____1

It's Really Yours! What to Do First_____3

Getting the Word Out: You've Moved!_____4

At Your Fingertips: Organizing Your Records_____7

Now Where Did I Put...? Organizing Your Worldly Goods_____11

Making Sure Your Home Is Safe and Secure_____15

First-Year Finances: Living on Spaghetti_____21

Eyes on the Prize: Set Your Goals_____22

See Whatcha Got: Your Current Financial State_____25

Save or Spend? Putting Your Priorities in Order_____33

**Of Mice and Maintenance: Keeping Up Your
Property's Value**_____45

Regular Maintenance, Whether You See Problems or Not_____48

Do You Hear Munching? Know Your Pests_____53

In the Garden: First, Do No Harm_____56

Reviewing and Renewing Your Homeowners' Insurance Policy___58

Greening Your Home—On a Budget_____67

Easy Changes Anyone Can Make_____68

Life Inside: Greening Your Home's Interior_____72

The Green Garden_____77

Eating Green_____80

Driving Green (Without a Hybrid)_____84

Maintaining and Upgrading Responsibly_____86

5 Hey, Neighbors: Getting Acquainted and
Resolving Disputes_____91

Meet and Greet: Introducing Yourself to Neighbors_____93

Drawing the Line: Knowing Where Your Property Ends_____95

Other Basic Property Rights: Nuisances, Fences, Trees,
   Noise, and Pets_____99

Getting Neighbor Buy-In on Your Remodel Plans_____108

Creating Peaceable Solutions to Neighbor Issues_____110

6 Keeping Up With Your Mortgage_____115

It All Looks Like Fine Print! What's in Your Mortgage_____116

Keeping Your Mortgage Costs Down_____123

Troubled Times: What to Do If You Can't Pay_____128

7 Is It Time to Refinance?_____143

Why Refinance?_____144

Calculating the Costs and Benefits of Refinancing_____148

Choosing the Right Loan_____154

Qualifying for Your New Loan_____158

Alternatives to Refinancing_____162

8 Tax Breaks for Homeownership_____167

Are You a First-Time Itemizer?_____169

Tax Deductions for Homeowners_____172

Tax Credits for Homeowners_____177

In Case You Sell: Plan Ahead to Avoid Capital Gains Taxes_____180

Your Property Tax Bill: Keeping It Low_____183

9 **Sweat Equity: Home Renovation Projects That Pay Off** _____189

How Renovations Can Increase Resale Value_____190

What You Can Do ... And What to Leave to the Pros_____195

Before You Leap: Learning More About the Project_____197

Scheduling Your Project_____204

Hiring Extra Hands_____206

10 **Remodeling Your Home With a Contractor's Help**_____211

Blueprints and Rock Piles: Planning Your Remodel _____212

Who's Going to Help? Hiring Contractors _____221

Negotiating a Written Contract_____227

Figuring Out Where the Money Will Come From_____234

Living Through a Remodel_____238

11 **After Damage: Who Pays?**_____241

Look What Happened! What to Do First_____242

Making a Homeowners' Insurance Claim_____245

Making a Home Warranty Claim_____253

How Long Has This Been Going On? Liability for Existing Defects_____254

Built to Last? Liability for Defects in New Homes_____258

Should You Sue? Deciding to Go to Court_____262

12 **Movin' on Up: Planning for Your Next House**_____265

Ready to Go? Deciding When to Move_____266

Another Paint Job!? Your Selling and Moving Costs_____267

Financial Strategies for Moving Up_____269

Maximizing Profits on Your Home Sale _____276

How to Buy and Sell Simultaneously—Without Getting Stuck_____282

Index_____285

Your Homeowning Companion

You've done it! Planned, dreamed, worked hard, and probably endured a few anxious moments to buy your first home.

The question on your mind now may be, what's next? Your house probably didn't come with an owner's manual. And having raided your cash supply to buy the place, you're probably not in a position to lavish money on it. So how do you take care of your big new investment, but also turn it into a place you really want to live in—without going overboard or, at worst, losing it to damage or foreclosure?

Consider this book as your new owner's manual. It's full of practical advice that will help you not only cope with, but enjoy your exciting new role as a homeowner. We'll show you how to:

- settle in and deal with practical tasks like change-of-address notifications, getting organized, and making your home safe and secure
- take stock of your new financial situation, create a new spending plan, and find good deals on furnishings and other home purchases
- maintain your property, guard it from pests, and make sure it's adequately insured
- develop good relations with your neighbors and understand your legal rights regarding boundaries, trees, and more
- keep up with your mortgage, and get back on track if you have trouble making payments
- refinance, if and when the time is right
- take advantage of tax breaks for homeowners

- plan and budget for do-it-yourself renovations and major remodels
- claim compensation from your homeowner's insurance company and others if your house is damaged or contains defects, and
- look to the future, making sure you'll earn the greatest possible profit when you sell.

As coauthors of *Nolo's Essential Guide to Buying Your First Home*, the authors of this book, Ilona Bray and Alayna Schroeder, know a little about what you've been through to get here. And now we'll tell you a little about where you're headed. As homeowners, we've seen our share of burst pipes, termites, and intruders. We've logged many miles to home and hardware stores, trying our hands at do-it-yourself projects and learning when it's time to call in the pros. And we've loved turning our respective homes into welcoming gathering places for families and friends. We know you will, too.

It's Really Yours!
What to Do First

Getting the Word Out: You've Moved!_____4

At Your Fingertips: Organizing Your Records_____7

    Your purchase and ownership records_____8

    Your tax records_____9

    Your maintenance records_____10

Now Where Did I Put...? Organizing Your Worldly Goods___11

    Setting up your home_____12

    Inventory your goods_____14

Making Sure Your Home Is Safe and Secure_____15

    Preventing crime_____15

    Preventing damage from disasters, big and small_____18

Congratulations! It's exciting to enter the world of homeownership for the first time. And with that excitement comes possibilities, like buying new curtains, throwing a housewarming party, remodeling the kitchen—the list only seems to grow.

Whether you're about to move in or have already spent some months getting settled, sit down for a minute and realize one thing: You can't do everything at once. And if you don't do some of the boring, sensible stuff now, it may never get done, which could cost you money later. So let this chapter help you cover some basic tasks, like:

- advising people of your new address and phone number
- organizing your records and home so you'll be able to claim insurance proceeds, tax deductions, and more, and
- making sure your home is safe and secure.

Don't worry, we'll take this step by step. And in later chapters, we'll get into some of the details, like budgeting, maintaining your home, and dealing with neighbors.

TIP

Haven't moved in yet? Think before you set the date. It's easiest to do many fix-ups (like painting, or replacing floors) in an empty house.

Getting the Word Out: You've Moved!

You've probably told your friends and family about your new location ten times over, but those who most need to know are those easiest to forget. If you haven't done so already, fill out a Change of Address form with the U.S. Postal Service—you can do it online at www.usps.gov or at a local post office. Your regular mail will be forwarded for 12 months, and your periodicals for 60 days. But the post office doesn't advise senders about your new address, so whoever is living in your old place will eventually start receiving your mail. It's best to get in touch with everyone you can think of now.

If you haven't moved in yet, make sure local service companies know that it's time to turn on your power and water and transfer these services to your name. (The former homeowner probably had everything turned off.) You don't want to get stuck in the dark, or hassle over dividing a bill with the former owner.

Here's a handy checklist of the most important places to notify of your new contact information. Make sure you can check them all off.

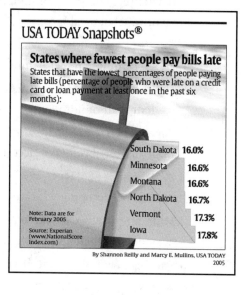

USA TODAY Snapshots®

States where fewest people pay bills late

States that have the lowest percentages of people paying late bills (percentage of people who were late on a credit card or loan payment at least once in the past six months):

State	Percentage
South Dakota	16.0%
Minnesota	16.6%
Montana	16.6%
North Dakota	16.7%
Vermont	17.3%
Iowa	17.8%

Note: Data are for February 2005

Source: Experian (www.NationalScoreindex.com)

By Shannon Reilly and Marcy E. Mullins, USA TODAY 2005

❑ **Electricity, water, and gas companies.** Call your local providers and arrange for a new account. If the seller hasn't told you who to contact, search for "utilities" in a directory like Yahoo!'s (http://dir.yahoo.com).

❑ **Trash collectors.** Find the local waste management provider through the Environmental Protection Agency (www.epa.gov/msw/states.htm). If you're in a condo or co-op, this may be included in your monthly fee—check with the association.

❑ **Telephone, Internet, and TV provider (cable/satellite).** It may be economical to subscribe through one provider for phone, Web, and cable TV, or now may be a good time to check out the latest satellite deals. If you're interested in forwarding phone calls from your previous number, contact your previous provider to find out your options.

❑ **Cell phone provider.** Don't create any delays in disputing your next exorbitant bill!

❑ **Subscriptions.** You can probably update your address at the periodical's website. Don't forget to contact alumni magazines or newsletters you get from nonprofits, too. And what about your favorite retail catalogues?

❑ **Credit card companies.** Make sure creditors know where you are—you'd hate to get behind on a payment now.

❑ **Other creditors.** Also contact any other creditors, like your student loan or auto lender.

❑ **Bank or investment account managers.** You really don't want information about your accounts going to your former address.

❑ **Department of Motor Vehicles.** Go to www.dmv.org to get information on updating your car registration and driver's license.

❑ **Your auto insurer.** If you've moved to a ZIP code with fewer accidents or thefts, the insurer may even lower your rates.

❑ **Parking permit provider.** If you need a residential parking permit, let the appropriate permit-issuing entity know. Try your city's website.

❑ **Registrar of voters.** Go to www.nased.org/membership.htm for links to your state's elections offices, which should give you a change of address form online.

❑ **Other service providers.** Call your doctor, dentist, chiropractor, and anyone else likely to call or write to you—perhaps with a discount coupon or appointment reminder.

Where do earthquakes happen?

The top five earthquake-prone states include Alaska, California, Hawaii, Nevada, and Washington. And scientists think some other states may be overdue for major quaking, including Arkansas, Missouri, Kentucky, Illinois, and Tennessee.

If you have children, make sure they know how to get home. Have them memorize their new address and telephone number and your full name, and ensure that the school has the correct contact information.

Tips for a Low-Cost Housewarming Party

Throwing a party is a great way to stay connected with old friends and introduce yourself to new neighbors. But if your cash flow is at an all-time low, try any of these tactics:

- Set the party for a logically alcohol-free time of day like a mid-morning brunch or afternoon tea.
- Make it a potluck. A theme, like food of the 1950s, can spur creativity. And if you specify "no gifts," people will put more effort into the food.
- For invitations, use Evite or search online for free, printable invitations (as well as party hats, napkin rings, and more).
- Show your joy at owning a home by playing house-related tunes like "Our House" (by Madness), or "Home" (by Bonnie Raitt).
- Clip plants and greens from your own yard instead of buying flowers.
- If you're uncomfortable with the current state of your décor, lower the lights and set out candles.

At Your Fingertips: Organizing Your Records

Keeping good house-related and financial records can save you money, period, end of story. Well, not quite the end of the story. As a new homeowner, you've probably never had to keep track of so many documents, so it's important to set up a good filing system at the beginning. Later when, for example, you're wondering how much you can deduct in mortgage interest or are ready to sell and want to show potential buyers how your energy-saving improvements cut your gas bill, you'll love being able to go right to the appropriate file. In this section, we'll suggest categories for your files, and explain why keeping them up to date is important.

But first, a basic word on storing these documents. It's best to buy a locking file cabinet and keep the key somewhere secure. Or if you live in a flood zone, choose airtight, waterproof plastic containers, and store them well above ground level. Create folders with relevant titles such as "Closing Documents," "Repair and Improvement Receipts," "Product Manuals," "Homeowners' Insurance," and more, according to the topics below. If you're not sure which file a document should go in, make copies and keep it in more than one.

USA TODAY Snapshots®

Home sweet home
Highest and lowest homeownership rates, by state:

Highest

West Virginia — 81.3%

Lowest

New York — 55.9%

Source: Census Bureau

By David Stuckey and Adrienne Lewis, USA TODAY
2008

Also find a location outside your house in which to keep copies of critical papers, including your house deed, loan documents, and car and homeowners' insurance policy. If a fire or other disaster makes your house temporarily uninhabitable, easy access to these will make your life much easier. A safe deposit box is good, as is a secure place at a trusted friend's house (for weekend access).

Your purchase and ownership records

Below are the basics: documents that prove you own the house and contain information about its ongoing financing and insurance.

- **Closing documents.** These include all the paperwork that was flying around at your closing, such as your purchase agreement, deed, disclosure forms you received from the seller, title insurance commitment, and more. They prove your ownership (a top priority), and can be useful to refer back to, for example to see how your property boundaries are shown on the title report.

- **Home loan documents.** These include all documents associated with your mortgage—such as your promissory note, HUD-1

Settlement Statement (listing all the services and charges to you and the seller), and payment schedule.

- **Inspection reports.** Keep your home inspector's written report, along with any reports you received from the seller or from city inspectors. They may be handy for answering questions like, "When did our inspector say we should replace the roof by?"

- **Homeowners' insurance policy.** In an emergency, you'll want to know how to contact your insurance company and what you're covered for. Having the contract handy will make dealing with company representatives much easier.

- **Community association records.** If your condo or home is governed by a homeowners' or community association, keep all the relevant documents, like the CC&Rs, so you can check on such things as whether you can put up a clothesline or must really pay a special assessment fee.

Your tax records

At last, you can claim those big-ticket tax deductions that come with homeownership (which we'll discuss more in Chapter 8), and itemize a few other deductions, to boot. But no fair guessing on the numbers—you never know when you'll be audited. Here are some of the most important pieces of information to keep:

- **Mortgage interest and points.** The interest you pay on your mortgage or home equity loan is generally tax deductible, as are points you paid up front. Your lender (or lenders) should send you a post-year-end statement totaling your interest payments.

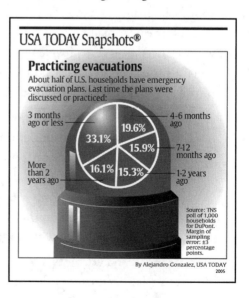

USA TODAY Snapshots®

Practicing evacuations

About half of U.S. households have emergency evacuation plans. Last time the plans were discussed or practiced:

3 months ago or less — 33.1%
19.6% — 4-6 months ago
15.9% — 7-12 months ago
More than 2 years ago — 16.1%
15.3% — 1-2 years ago

Source: TNS poll of 1,000 households for DuPont. Margin of sampling error: ±3 percentage points.

By Alejandro Gonzalez, USA TODAY
2005

- **Property tax.** State property taxes are deductible from your federal taxes. Keep a copy of every tax statement you receive, with notes on how you paid the bill (for example, a personal check number). If your property tax bill is paid out of a lender's escrow account, this will also appear on the annual statement the lender sends.

- **Private mortgage insurance (PMI).** If you took out your mortgage between 2007 and 2010, any PMI premiums you're paying are tax deductible as long as you make less than $100,000 (after that, the deduction is phased out). Keep a copy of your billing statements.

- **Charitable contributions.** If you've donated to any 501(c)(3) charities, the donation is probably tax deductible. Charities must send you receipts for donations over certain amounts, but for others, you'll need to keep your own proof (such as a cancelled check).

- **Home business records.** If you run a business from your home, your taxes are going to be more complicated than the average Joe's. However, that can also translate into more deductions, for a portion of your home maintenance and utilities, office supplies, and more.

Your maintenance records

All homes require upkeep, and upkeep costs money. Keeping track of your maintenance and improvement efforts and costs will help you anticipate regular maintenance costs (such as when you might need a new water heater), as well as provide information to later potential buyers. You'll also be able to contact the appropriate manufacturers or service providers if something goes wrong. Here are some documents to save:

- **Professional service records.** Careful notes on or records of who has been unclogging your plumbing, updating your electricity, landscaping your garden, and more—and how much you paid them—will help you if you decide you want to use (or avoid) them again. These records can also be turned over to prospective buyers when you sell, so they can see what's been done and hire professionals familiar with the property.

- **Manuals and warranty information.** Keep all the info you'll need to replace, return, or otherwise deal with your house's furnace, air conditioning system, and appliances. Hopefully the seller left you relevant manuals and warranties; most warranties carry over to subsequent homeowners.

- **Repair and improvement receipts.** Keep records of and receipts for your repairs and improvements to the house. When you sell, you can figure out which projects qualify as improvements that lower your capital gains tax liability (discussed in Chapter 8).

- **Utility bills.** When and if you sell your home, buyers will most likely want to see about two years' worth of utility bills, to estimate their average expenses. (You can shred the older bills.)

- **Permits and plans.** If you add a room, remodel a bathroom, or knock out a wall, and need to get plans or permits, hold on to them. Again, when you sell you can pass these on to the new buyer.

Now Where Did I Put ... ? Organizing Your Worldly Goods

Moving into a new home is like being given a blank slate, a chance to set things up the way you want them—free of all that stuff you sold at your premoving garage sale. With a little initial planning, you'll know exactly where to find what you need when you need it—the winter jacket you store during the summer, or those martini glasses for your first cocktail party. And with everything in its place you can make an inventory of your most valuable items, important if your home is struck by a burglary, fire, flood, earthquake, or other disaster.

> **TIP**
>
> **While you're walking around, check the moving parts.** Your house is a web of mechanical systems, some of which require your attention. For example a garden irrigation system may need periodic adjustment, to reduce the flow during the rainy season. Also get to know where all the light switches are, and whether things like outdoor motion-sensor lights are still working.

Setting up your home

As soon as you can—even before you've unpacked your toothbrush, if possible—give yourself a complete tour of your house. Open every cabinet and closet and measure the areas where you might place your larger items of furniture. Then plan for what should go where, using the following tips:

- **Design multiuse spaces.** Some rooms may have more than one use—in fact, you can create zones within rooms by arranging the furniture appropriately (for example, not lining it up around the walls.) Picture household daily activities, then figure out the most logical, accessible places to place furniture and store accessories to support those activities.

- **Store the largest things first.** There are only so many places within a house that will fit your camping equipment or 20-quart electric turkey roaster.

- **Watch for light, heat, and moisture in storage areas.** Putting linens into a humid closet (perhaps created by a hot pipe running through it) can lead to mildew or discoloration. And in the kitchen, avoid storing oils in hot or sunlit cabinets.

- **Put breakables in safe places.** Particularly if you live in earthquake territory—which is wider than you'd imagine—don't put heavy or breakable objects where they might tumble down. Bottled foods, glass objects, and your dinnerware should ideally be kept in low, closed cabinets with latches. Also hang heavy items such as pictures and mirrors away from beds, couches, and places people sleep or sit.

RESOURCE

For more organizing tips: *Real Simple* magazine and organizing guru Julie Morgenstern both have useful books to keep your place decluttered. And if you want to hire a pro, check out the National Association of Professional Organizers at www.napo.net.

Got a Front Porch? Don't Waste That Space!

Homeowners, weary of deserted-looking neighborhoods, are moving back to the front porch, as USA TODAY's Mary Thurman Yuhas found. In fact, more than half (53%) of the 1.6 million new single-family homes built in the USA in 2005 included them.

Danny Seo, host of *Simply Green* on cable's Lime TV, moved into a 1921 bungalow in Bucks County, Pennsylvania. The porch that runs across the front of the home was a big selling point.

A bonus: "The porch has become a third bedroom for houseguests who don't like air conditioning." His tips for cozying up the space:

- Painting a wall, or part of it, with chalkboard paint gives children a place to make masterpieces. "I leave messages for delivery people, write welcoming words to guests, or write the menu for a party on it," Seo says.
- Hang solar lanterns in trees that surround the porch to create a romantic setting. They slowly dim as the night grows darker.
- A vase filled with water and fresh flowers from the garden placed in an old boot or a row of tattered children's sneakers serves as outdoor art.
- If architecture or cost prohibits a front porch, fake it with a free-form space marked off with rocks or pavers. Add an Adirondack chair or two, sit back and enjoy.
- A tree stump can be a beautiful stool.

 "Moving back to front porch does a body good; A neighborly tradition catches on," by Mary Thurman Yuhas, September 8, 2006.

Inventory your goods

If your home is struck by a burglary, fire, flood, earthquake, or other disaster, an up-to-date home inventory will make it easier to deal with police and your insurance company. Without one, you'll have to create a list of all your missing or damaged property from memory—no small task. Many people go several months before figuring out everything that a burglar stole. And as USA TODAY's Christine Dugas notes, "The burden of proof is on homeowners to document their losses. Without some kind of inventory, your insurer may dispute your assessment of the damage."

After you've unpacked, walk through your entire house with a pad of paper and a camera. Don't forget to visit the garage, attic, and basement. Look for any items worth more than around $50. You'll most likely find them among your jewelry, clothing, collectibles, CD and record collections, silver, tools, sporting or outdoor equipment, and electronic equipment.

USA TODAY Snapshots®

Property crime rates dip

Property crimes per 1,000 households, by region: 1994 2004

436.1 204 West

295.2 168.8 Midwest

236.6 107.1 Northeast

288.6 158.3 South

Source: Bureau of Justice Statistics

By David Stuckey and Dave Merrill, USA TODAY 2005

Take pictures of each item you identify as valuable (or of groups of items, such as your jewelry). Also write down a brief description of each, complete with the make, model, and serial number, if any. If you usually keep the item in one part of your house, for example the garage or bedroom, write the location down, too. This will help you identify what you've lost if only one area, such as the garage, is hit. And if possible, note each item's purchase price, current value, and replacement cost.

You may want to mark expensive items with an ID number such as your driver's license number. (Electric engraving pens cost about $50.) The ID and serial numbers help police identify stolen goods.

Finally, take a little time to formalize your inventory. Your insurance company can probably give you an inventory form, or you can get software online from the Insurance Information Institute, www.iii.org (click "home," then "Know Your Stuff"). And don't forget to update your inventory if you buy or receive something new.

Making Sure Your Home Is Safe and Secure

Your house can be your fortress, your retreat from the outside world, and a place to cozy up and be yourself. Too bad this fortress isn't made of solid stone and didn't come with a moat—you'll need to take some different protective measures.

Preventing crime

Thankfully, most people live in their house for years without it being broken into. Here are some quick and easy ways to prevent uninvited guests.

- **Change the locks.** If you don't bring in a locksmith or visit a hardware store, you won't know who has keys to your front door (the seller's wacky houseguest from two years ago and several neighbors, perhaps).

- **Add deadbolts.** If your exterior doors have only regular, pushbutton locks or something similar, you could probably break into them yourself with a swift kick. Every exterior door should have a deadbolt. Call a locksmith or follow the instructions on a site like www.diynetwork.com.

- **Prevent sliding doors from being forced open.** Even with a lock, putting a dowel or bar in the tracks of sliding glass doors offers backup security.

- **Reset the alarm code.** If the house came with an alarm system, choose a new number you'll remember, share it on a "need to know" basis, and keep the owners' manual on hand in case of false alarms, dead batteries, and other issues.

- **Consider buying an alarm system.** Even the warning signs from the alarm company are a deterrent—burglars are looking for an easy mark, not to break into Fort Knox. There's a wide array of choices at different price points, from systems that simply make a loud noise to those that are monitored by a professional company. With more advanced systems, company representatives should help you with customized design—speak up if, for example, you plan to leave certain windows cracked open at night or get a pet—and they'll likely do the installation, too. Tell your homeowners' insurance company once the system is installed, which will probably lower your rates.

- **Make a habit of locking your interior garage door.** You don't want a thief to gain entry to your garage and then have easy, hidden access to your house.

- **Talk to the neighbors.** Ask what security measures they've found useful or necessary, and whether a neighborhood watch group is in place. Even without formally creating such a group (in which you register with the city and it puts up signs warning criminals away) many neighbors find it useful to exchange daytime and evening phone numbers, so that you can call each other if you see something strange going on.

When do most burglaries happen?
During the day, says the FBI. And the average value of goods stolen is nearly $2,000.

- **Evaluate the need for additional changes.** Take a walk around your house to see what should go on your longer-term to-do list. Pretend you're a burglar, and think about how you'd break in and how easily you'd be seen by others doing so. Make sure the outside of your property is well-lit at night and doesn't contain obvious hiding places or trees whose branches can be used to climb in through windows. Planting holly, roses, and other prickly or thorny plants is also a recommended burglar deterrent.

That's No Burglar, It's a Bear!

As more and more homes are built near forests or wild areas, conflicts have arisen between people and wild animals including wolves, bears, mountain lions, and even deer (who love to dine on flowers). Steve Zawistowski, a scientist with the American Society for the Prevention of Cruelty to Animals (ASPCA) in New York City, assured USA TODAY's Anita Manning that suburbanites can coexist with wild animals, with a little planning.

Experts suggest:

- Don't leave pet food outside.
- Don't feed wild animals. It's not good for them, and it reduces their natural wariness of humans.
- Keep barbecue grills clean. The grease can attract bears.
- Secure trash can lids or keep cans in the garage. Garbage and dirty diapers attract animals.
- Remove thick brush or tall grass that could provide cover for snakes.
- Try to make your garden unappetizing to deer by planting flowers and shrubs that they don't like, such as holly, lilac, yarrow and daylilies.

Source: Florida Fish and Wildlife Conservation Commission; USA TODAY research.

 "Wildlife wanders into urban, suburban landscapes; Problems are increasing as human-animal contact rises," by Anita Manning, September 22, 2003.

Preventing damage from disasters, big and small

Natural disasters don't strike homes nearly as often as the TV news would have you believe. And even when a true disaster strikes, many homes and their inhabitants come through just fine. But it's not all due to sheer luck. Some advance preparation will help your house and family successfully deal with a storm, fire, or earthquake. Here are your first steps:

- **Check smoke detectors and sprinkler systems.** Even though your home inspector should have told you whether your smoke detection or sprinkler system meet local codes, it's up to you to keep them in good working order. All smoke detectors have a test button, which, when pressed, should cause a shrill, obnoxious noise or a flashing light that tells you it's working. The battery normally lasts no more than a year. If the unit has no battery, it's wired into your home's electrical or fire alarm system, so you'll need to check the circuits or get a new unit. In addition, no matter what the codes say, consider installing smoke detectors in every bedroom or in hallways that lead to bedrooms. And if you've bought a condo or co-op in a building with a sprinkler system, make sure you know how it works and where your unit's sprinkler heads are.

USA TODAY Snapshots®

Fire starter
Percentage of home fires originating in these rooms:

Kitchen — 34%
Bedroom — 12%
Living room, family room or den — 6%

Source: National Fire Protection Association

By David Stuckey and Robert W. Ahrens, USA TODAY 2007

- **Learn where your shutoff valves are.** Every member of your family should learn how to shut off the gas, water, and electricity in case of pipe leaks after a disaster, or in situations where electricity may either come into contact with water or spark gas fires. Your home inspector may have pointed out your gas and water shutoff valves, or you may need to ask your utility company to help you locate them. (Don't turn the gas off for practice—only a professional can turn it back on.) Your main electrical panel may be inside the house or on an outside wall. It's best to shut off the individual circuits before the main breaker. Unplug appliances before you turn the power back on, to avoid a surge.

USA TODAY Snapshots®

Haunted houses, anyone?
In the USA, 37.2% agree or strongly agree that places can be haunted. By gender:

Female **45.5%**

Male **32.2%**

Source: The Baylor Religion Survey, a mailed survey of 1,721 Americans statistically representing a sampling of the USA by age, gender and race conducted in fall 2005 by the Gallup Organization; margin of error is ±4 percentage points.

By Tracey Wong Briggs and Alejandro Gonzalez, USA TODAY 2006

- **Clear dead brush.** To reduce the impact of fires, it's wise to create "defensible space" around your home by clearing away brush and keeping your roof clean of dead leaves and pine needles.

- **Plan an escape route.** In a panicked situation, your halls might feel like a labyrinth—especially for children. Make sure every family member knows all entrances and exits, how to get out from the second floor, and where to meet up or who to call (preferably someone who lives far away and wouldn't be affected by a local disaster) if separated.

- **Childproof everything.** If you're a parent, you've probably done this before. Put chemicals and cleaning supplies out of reach, and add child safety locks to all cabinets. Also put important phone numbers (your cell phone, police, fire department, health care providers, and more) as well as your address on a bulletin board or refrigerator for babysitters.

- **Read the directions on your fire extinguisher.** If you don't have one, buy one right away.

- **Evaluate the need for additional changes.** For example, if your house has a swimming pool, make sure it has child-protective gates.

Hearing Spooky Bumps in the Night?

You wouldn't be the first homeowner to wonder whether odd sounds or cold spots in your house are signs that it's haunted. There's probably an ordinary explanation—but to check out "real" haunted houses, here's a list from Dennis William Hauck, author of *Haunted Places: The National Directory* (Penguin Putnam).

Shirley Plantation, Charles City, Virginia

Of note: a first-floor bedroom where a painting of early resident Martha Pratt reportedly raises a ruckus whenever it's moved from a spot facing the ancestral graveyard.

Fort Warren, Boston

The Civil War fort on George's Island in Boston Harbor reputedly is haunted by "The Lady in Black," a devoted wife who was hanged for attempting to break her husband out of the Confederate prison.

The White House, Washington, DC

The Executive Mansion is "one of the most haunted places in the United States," Hauck says. Among the apparitions: William Henry Harrison in the attic and Dolley Madison in the Rose Garden, and most frequently, Abraham Lincoln in his namesake bedroom.

Whaley House, San Diego

Even before Thomas Whaley completed his house in 1857, the execution by hanging of "Yankee" Jim Robinson on the site presumably primed future ghostly scenarios. Robinson's footfalls are believed to be heard in the house.

Winchester Mystery House, San Jose, California

The house was built by Winchester rifle heiress Sarah Winchester with direction from designing spirits, Hauck says. Starting with an eight-room ranch house, Winchester added on continuously for 38 years, resulting in an unfinished 160-room Victorian mansion.

 "10 great places to get spooked by your surroundings," by Jayne Clark, October 26, 2007.

First-Year Finances: Living on Spaghetti

Eyes on the Prize: Set Your Goals_____22

See Whatcha Got: Your Current Financial State_____25
   How much money is coming in_____25
   How much money is going out_____27
   What's left over_____32
   Changing your spending habits_____32
   Tracking your ongoing expenses_____33

Save or Spend? Putting Your Priorities in Order_____33
   Making a list, checking it twice_____35
   Buying home furnishings on a budget_____38
   Buying appliances on a budget_____41

R ight after closing on your new home, your financial reserves may be lower than they've been in awhile. At the same time, you're probably confronted with some new expenses, which may add up to more than your rent ever did. Rest assured that this sense of having no money is, if you play your cards right, only temporary. As one homeowner told us, "We were nervous, but our agent told us, 'You'll just need to eat spaghetti for about a year, and then things will even out.' In fact, that's about the way it worked."

You probably won't have to go to the extreme of a spaghetti-only diet, but it's a good idea to create a plan for getting back on track financially. The planning process described in this chapter will help you answer questions like whether you should make home improvements and which to make, how to start replenishing your savings account, whether to contribute to your 401(k), or whether you'll ever be able to take a vacation again.

So although you may have run some numbers when you arranged your financing, it's time to take a fresh look. Your first step will be to set your priorities. Next. you'll evaluate where you are, by looking at your income, then your expenses. Finally, if there isn't enough left over to accomplish the tasks you think are important, you'll have to figure out what to prioritize.

Eyes on the Prize: Set Your Goals

To get started, think about your goals for the coming year. For now, think big. Include everything you might need or want this year, house-related or otherwise. You can pare the list down and decide what might be pushed to subsequent years later.

Some goals to consider are:

- **Saving for taxes and insurance.** Unless you pay these out of an escrow account through your lender, check your records: You might need to write checks for several thousand dollars at a time.

Think Twice Before Relying on Credit Cards

If you're thinking, "Well, I'll just let my credit card absorb the extra house expenses," think again. Owning a house often involves bigger expenses than you've dealt with before, and credit card interest rates can drive those numbers into the stratosphere. Unless you're disciplined enough to pay off balances quickly, you could find yourself in real trouble. The worst part is, if your payments are small, you may not even feel the long-term hurt, so you won't realize how much it's really costing you.

Look at the chart of likely home purchases below: If you make the minimum, 2.5% payment on a credit card with 18% interest, you'll see that you significantly drag out your payment and end up paying a lot more over the long term.

Paying off debt at 18% with 2.5% minimum payments			
Item	Price	Total you'll pay (with interest)	Approximate length of time to pay off debt
Rug	$500	$865	7 years
Sofa	$1,000	$2,115	Nearly 13 years
Granite countertops	$5,000	$12,115	26 years

To run more personalized calculations, go to www.bankrate.com and, under "Credit Card Calculators," choose "The true cost of paying the minimum."

- **Saving for emergencies.** It's wise—and could prove essential—to set aside money for unexpected medical expenses or basic living expenses if you lost your job. At an absolute minimum, try to save enough to cover your family's daily living expenses for three months. Six months or more would be wiser, unless you have another income source, such as parents who could back you up in a financial jam.

TIP

Where should you stash your savings? You might need to get to your emergency fund in a hurry, so store it somewhere that's both easy to access and safe. A savings or money market account would be good, as opposed to a long-term CD or stocks (the value of which could go down just when you need the money).

- **Retirement savings.** This may not be the year to make huge strides in your retirement savings—in fact, you may have borrowed from or stopped paying into your 401(k) to swing your purchase. But at very least, put enough into your 401(k) to get any employer match (free money!).

USA TODAY Snapshots®

Many Americans unprepared
How long could you cover household living expenses with your current liquid savings?

Less than one week	One week to less than one month	One month to less than three months	Three months to less than six months	Six months or more	Declined to answer
17%	14%	24%	10%	19%	17%

Note: Total doesn't add up to 100 due to rounding
Source: LexisNexis Martindale-Hubbell's Lawyers.com survey of 2,318 adults 18 and older. Margin of error ±3 percentage points.

By Jae Yang and Marcy E. Mullins, USA TODAY 2006

- **Home improvements.** Sit down with members of your household and list the first things you need or want to do to furnish, fix up, and improve your house and garden. Include everything you can imagine, from new built-in shelving to a birdbath to a studio over the garage.

- **Children and education.** Perhaps you're considering starting a family. If so, consider your increased expenses and possibly decreased income. Or, if you already have children, you might be thinking about saving for college.

Here's a sample of what your goals list might look like. For now, leave the "Priority" and "Cost" columns blank.

Sample List of This Year's Financial Goals		
Goal	Cost	Priority
Replenish savings (at least for taxes, insurance, and emergencies)	$	
Increase 401(k) contributions	$	
Home improvements:	$	
Refinish hardwood floors	$	
Replace windows	$	
Buy dining room furniture	$	
Soil amendments/plant seedlings	$	
Total annual cost:	$	
÷ 12 = Total monthly cost:	$	

Keep this list handy. Next, you're going to look at your actual income and expenses. Once you understand those, you can see how much you can spend, evaluate how much each of your goals will cost, and choose what to prioritize. Goals that can't be completed this year can be shifted to the next.

See Whatcha Got: Your Current Financial State

Let's take a look at what's coming in and going out of your household till.

How much money is coming in

First, get a handle on your income. We recommend creating a worksheet like the sample Household Spending Plan below. Budgeting software (by *Quicken*, for example) or a spreadsheet like *Excel* can make this task easy. The benefit of a program like *Quicken* is that you can download your bank and investment account information directly from the Internet. Another alternative is to upload your information to an online site like Moneycenter.yodlee.com, Wesabe.com, or Mint.com (the last two are both free), which offer basic tracking programs.

Whatever method you use, start by adding up your household's gross income. That's the amount before deductions like taxes, flexible spending accounts, and 401(k) withdrawals. Even though this isn't the amount of money you can spend each month, you'll want to know where it's all going. And while some of the categories are fixed, others aren't. For example, you may be able to reduce your federal tax withholding to account for the interest and property tax deductions you'll now be eligible for. For more on that, see Chapter 8.

Next, move to your household's monthly net income—what comes home. Likely your main source of income is a paycheck or self-employment, so you can look at your pay stub or business records to find the net amount. But your income may also include tips, royalties, rental income, dividends, regular gifts from family, disability payments, child support, and the like.

TIP

Perturbed at how little money is coming in? Consider renting out a room in your new home, particularly if you live in a college town. You can often charge almost as much as what renters would pay for an apartment (plus utilities), and set down rules regarding which rooms the renters can use, kitchen cleanliness, and more—it's still your place. Of course, you'll want to protect yourself with good tenant screening and a written rental agreement. Get help from:

- *Every Landlord's Legal Guide*, by Marcia Stewart, Ralph Warner, and Janet Portman (Nolo). Although aimed primarily at off-site landlords, this book will help you find and screen tenants and draft your rental agreement.
- *Every Landlord's Tax Deduction Guide*, by Stephen Fishman (Nolo). Find out how to save even more money by taking advantage of favorable tax laws.

How much money is going out

To get a picture of your spending patterns, fill in all your regular or predictable expenses on your Household Spending Plan, such as mortgage payments, other debt, food, transportation, entertainment, child care, and more. Create the smallest categories you can (mortgage, homeowners' association dues, and property taxes, for example, rather than "home expenses"). This will help avoid forgetting things.

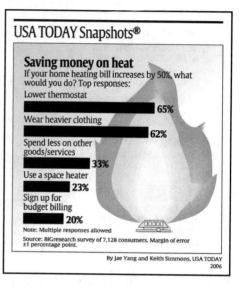

USA TODAY Snapshots®

Saving money on heat
If your home heating bill increases by 50%, what would you do? Top responses:

Lower thermostat — **65%**
Wear heavier clothing — **62%**
Spend less on other goods/services — **33%**
Use a space heater — **23%**
Sign up for budget billing — **20%**

Note: Multiple responses allowed
Source: BIGresearch survey of 7,128 consumers. Margin of error ±1 percentage point.

By Jae Yang and Keith Simmons, USA TODAY 2006

Some of your most significant expenses may be yearly, such as your homeowners' insurance and property taxes (unless you already pay these from an escrow account with your mortgage payment). Divide such yearly expenses by 12. Other expenses may occur weekly, irregularly, or as a single lump sum, so you'll need to play with the numbers to put them into monthly terms.

Regular bills and debt payments will be the easiest to figure out—though, for house-related expenses, it will help if the previous homeowner gave you some idea of the house's average monthly electric, garbage, and other utility bills. And keep in mind that some of these expenses change over the course of the year, for example, heating and cooling costs, which fluctuate by season. For energy-saving tips, see Chapter 4.

An open fireplace damper can let out 8% of your home's heat. Unless you've lit a fire, close the damper.

For non-house expenses, look over your old receipts, credit card statements, and bank statement. Try to figure out averages, for example how much you spend each month on restaurant meals or clothes. (Some software programs will do this for you.) Don't forget any automatic monthly withdrawals, such as for your DSL line, DVD rental service, or gym membership.

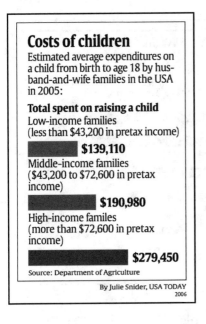

Costs of children

Estimated average expenditures on a child from birth to age 18 by husband-and-wife families in the USA in 2005:

Total spent on raising a child
Low-income families
(less than $43,200 in pretax income)

$139,110

Middle-income families
($43,200 to $72,600 in pretax income)

$190,980

High-income familes
(more than $72,600 in pretax income)

$279,450

Source: Department of Agriculture

By Julie Snider, USA TODAY
2006

Cash spending can be the hardest to track. As Jean Chatzky, author of *Pay It Down! From Debt to Wealth on $10 a Day*, told USA TODAY, "Most people pull out $100 or $200 from the ATM and lump it as 'cash,' but they don't know where it goes." Track your cash spending for a week or two and write it down.

Also include on your chart any regular deposits you already make into savings or retirement plans such as your 401(k). And for your outstanding credit card balance, enter the minimum payment. (However, recognize that you'll want to work toward paying this off before too long, to avoid high-interest payments.) Finally, estimate how much you plan to spend on the remaining items on your goals list, including new furniture, necessary repairs, or other expenses related to your new home.

CAUTION

Don't just multiply weekly expenses by four. Technically, there are 52 weeks in a year, and that makes a difference. If you pay a gardener $60 a week, you might think that you're spending $240 per month (4 × $60), or $2,880 per year (4 × $60 × 12). But your true annual spending is 52 × $60 = $3,120, or $240 more. The accurate way to average monthly spending on weekly activities is to calculate the annual figure and then divide it by 12 ($3,120 ÷ 12 = $260).

Household Spending Plan	
MONTHLY INCOME	
Household gross income:	$8,500
Federal tax withholding	– $1,200
State tax withholding	– $400
OASDI/Medicare/State SDI	– $640
FSA Withholdings	– $100
401(k)/403(b)/elective retirement withholding	– $300
Disability insurance	– $10
Household net income:	$5,850
MONTHLY EXPENSES	
Household expenses	
Mortgage(s)	$1,500
Homeowners' association dues	$150
Insurance (homeowners', life)	$80
Property tax	$250
Utilities	
Water	$20
Garbage	$15
Gas	$45
Sewer	$20
Electric	$70
Home renovations/remodeling	
Household furnishing (furniture)	$100
Household decorating (art, bedding, etc.)	$75
Household maintenance expenses	
Appliances	$0
Cleaning supplies	$15
Maintenance supplies	$45
Garden care/supplies	$40
Home office supplies (computer and printer, paper, file cabinets and folders, postage stamps)	$55
Other: water heater	$35
Household services	

Household Spending Plan, continued	
Cleaning	
Lawn and garden care	
Other: pool maintenance	$80
Phone and TV (including cell phone, cable, and DSL/Internet)	
Cell phone	$75
Cable	$40
Home phone/DSL	$60
Other	
Total monthly household expenses:	**$2,770**
Personal expenses	
Groceries (not including meals out)	$550
Health and dental expenses	
Insurance	$0
Prescriptions	$30
Copays	$30
Glasses	$10
Clothing and shoes	$250
Personal care (dry cleaning, haircuts, makeup, massage)	$150
Personal fitness and sports (gym membership, yoga classes, children's activities and equipment)	$100
Pets (food, walking, grooming and boarding services, veterinary care)	$85
Total monthly personal expenses:	**$1,205**
Transportation expenses	
Car payment	$350
Gas and tolls	$250
Car registration and insurance (annual payment divided by 12), roadside assistance coverage	$160
Maintenance/repairs	$60
Public transportation	$0
Total monthly transportation expenses:	**$820**
Entertainment	
Eating out	$200
Events (concerts, museums, shows)	$100

Household Spending Plan, continued	
Books, newpapers, magazines, DVD rentals, software, and games	$25
Vacation	$150
Gifts	$100
Hobbies (photography, quilting)	$40
Total monthly entertainment expenses:	**$615**
Child-related expenses	
Preschool, private school, college tuition, or college savings	$100
School expenses	$0
Classes/activities	$100
Day care	$400
Allowance	$0
Support payments	$0
Total monthly child-related expenses:	**$600**
Regular savings	
Rainy day/special event savings	$75
Other savings	$0
Total monthly savings:	**$75**
Miscellaneous expenses	
Legal or accounting fees	$30
Gifts to charity	$40
Other	
Total monthly miscellaneous expenses:	**$70**
Other monthly debts	
Credit card minimum payment	$0
Student loans	$350
Unpaid bills on repayment plans	$0
Other	$0
Total monthly debts:	**$350**
Total of expenses and debts:	$6,505
Total net income:	$5,850
Difference between income and expenses:	−$655

What's left over

The drum roll, please: Subtract your total monthly expenses from your total income. Is the result a positive number? Great, you're in a perfect position to start prioritizing your goals, discussed further below.

Still, there's always more you can do, and this budget exercise may turn up spending patterns that you want to change. We're not here to lecture you, but to remind you, that with some trimming and shifting in your spending, you may be able to reach more of your goals, or reach them a little faster.

What if—like most Americans —you're getting a negative number, meaning you're building up debt? Having created a picture of your monthly spending, you're in a great position to critically evaluate your habits and make changes to discretionary spending, and then get back to fulfilling those goals you've set. We'll explain how to do that in the next section.

Changing your spending habits

Whether you're coming out ahead or behind each month, carefully scan your worksheet for expenditures that are higher than you realized or are going to things you don't really need. Start by examining purely discretionary expenses—those which you don't have to pay. For example, the person in our sample worksheet might be able to cut back on those $200 a month "eating out" expenses. Your first year in a new home is a good time to explore dining in, library books and DVDs, and other low-cost ways to have fun.

> **TIP**
> **Are you paying for stuff that's going to your old address?**
> Check your monthly bills for newspaper subscriptions, magazines, and the like, just in case you (or the provider) forgot to change your address.

Many people can shave a lot off what they spend on consumer goods like electronics or clothes. Impulse shopping is the death of many a household budget. And we're not talking only about luxury items. Spending money at discount stores or garage sales can add up, too. As financial planner Alice Bullwinkle of North Star Financial Direction in Lakewood, Colorado, told USA TODAY, "The spontaneous purchases really hurt. People shop for fun, and they don't want to go home without something." As you approach the cash register, remind yourself that $20 spent on a sweater—even if it was originally $120—is $20 less to spend on fixing your doorbell.

Of course, you can drive yourself crazy trying to control every dollar, so be realistic. If you know that every few weeks you're going to hit a sale, focus on buying things that improve your home's look or value— costs you can potentially recoup when you sell. For more advice, see "USA TODAY's Financial Diet Tips," later in this chapter.

Tracking your ongoing expenses

After trimming where you can, draw up a new Household Spending Plan to use as a tracking tool. Continue to shift and revise it as needed. This will also help you see the costs of home ownership more realistically over time. And your Plan lets you carefully decide how to spend extra cash that comes your way later, like unexpected bonuses, gifts, or pay increases.

Save or Spend? Putting Your Priorities in Order

Now that you've figured out what you're currently spending your cash on and how much you're left with at month's end, revisit your goals list. Estimate the cost of the different items—for example, of adding $9,000 to your emergency fund, or paying $2,000 for new dining room furniture. Then rank their order of importance.

Saving for certain necessities should be first, beginning with basics like a refrigerator if the past owner didn't leave you one. Move quickly to saving for your property taxes and insurance (unless these are paid from an escrow account). If you fail to pay property taxes, the taxing authorities can put a lien on your house and eventually force a sale. If you fail to pay your homeowners' insurance premium, your mortgage lender can foreclose, because you've violated a term of the loan. And, of course, you won't be covered for damage to the house, nor for your personal liability if someone is injured there.

Next, focus on replenishing your emergency account with three to six months of living expenses. As USA TODAY's John Waggoner advises, "Don't count on yourself to write a check each week to your savings account. Set up an automatic deduction program, from your checking account to your savings. Even better, see if you can arrange to have money shifted directly from your paycheck to a savings account."

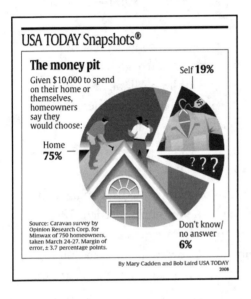

USA TODAY Snapshots®

The money pit

Given $10,000 to spend on their home or themselves, homeowners say they would choose:

Self **19%**

Home **75%**

Don't know/ no answer **6%**

Source: Caravan survey by Opinion Research Corp. for Minwax of 750 homeowners, taken March 24-27. Margin of error, ± 3.7 percentage points.

By Mary Cadden and Bob Laird USA TODAY 2008

Now consider your other savings goals. As mentioned, make sure you get any employer match on your 401(k), and if saving aggressively for retirement is important to you, mark it next.

On the other hand, if you're hoping to take time off to start a family, plan to set aside cash to cover expenses, or to reduce current debts (like car or student loan payments) so you'll have more disposable income when the time comes.

As you'll see, you may have to reset your overall goals to accommodate more than one. For example, if you'd like to increase your 401(k) savings by $300 a month, but you know you're going to need to update the wiring at an average cost of $100 a month, you could increase your monthly 401(k) savings by only $200 this year, and increase it after the wiring is paid for or next year, perhaps when you get a raise.

Making a list, checking it twice

Next, factor in the estimated cost of home improvement projects. The biggest mistake many new homeowners make is to plunge into debt within a few weeks or months trying to make their new home not only livable, but beautiful. Yes, it's no fun sitting in folding chairs around a card table in your spacious new dining room. But a few more weeks hunting for a good find on Craigslist, eBay, or at a sale can pay off big in the long run. Plus, waiting will help you get more familiar with the space—you may decide that the dining room can't really accommodate the formal dining table you'd always dreamed of, for example.

As with your overall goals, the key to home improvement goals is prioritize, prioritize, prioritize. Go back to the "home improvement" section of your first year goals list. If you still have any available cash left, or if you've adjusted savings or other goals to leave room for some home improvement, continue to rank the home improvement items on your list. At the very top should go all items that affect your family's health and safety or your home's longevity—for example, patching a potentially leaky roof or trimming trees before winter. For more information on prioritizing these goals, see Chapter 9.

> **TIP**
> **Tell your homeowners' insurance carrier what you've changed.** Added security features such as an alarm system may actually lower your premium. Other improvements may raise your premium a bit, but are important to mention so that you'll receive coverage if they're damaged.

Next on your list should go any items that will fill important gaps in your furnishings and appliances. For example, you may need a table to fill the first dining room you've ever had. Also high on your list should be items that save you money immediately, such as new attic insulation. (Check with your utility company—you may even get a rebate against what you spend.)

CROSS REFERENCE
Need to make some changes, but don't have the cash?
Consider a home equity loan or line of credit, discussed in Chapter 7.

Further down in your ranking, you can categorize items that you both want and can probably afford without going into further debt. This might include new light fixtures, throw rugs, side tables, accessories, outdoor and indoor plants, and more. Even on a very tight budget, you may want to sprinkle a few of these items in—they go a long way toward making a house feel like home. And if you like decorating, you'll never reach the end of your wish list.

Finally, at the very bottom of your list, put the expensive and not immediately necessary items: perhaps newer furniture that fits the scale and style of different rooms, higher-quality appliances, updated kitchen cabinets, major landscaping, and room remodels and additions. We'll discuss handling these later in this book.

TIP
Keep an eye on resale value. While your first priority may be to make your home livable, your property is also an investment. Changes you make to it can either raise its value so you'll eventually recoup your costs—or not. We'll discuss this more in later chapters, but for your current sense of prioritizing, check out RemodelingOnline's "Cost vs. Value Report," at http://remodeling.hw.net (click "Resale value of your project").

But first, plan to start attacking your goals list, item by item. If the first and most important thing on your list will be a budget buster— a new roof, for example—you may need to borrow cash. (For more information, see Chapter 7.) If it's a small-scale repair or renovation— the kind you can do yourself—see Chapter 9 for advice and help setting a more specific budget and plan. For larger repairs or remodeling, see Chapter 10 for tips on making it affordable. And for everyday expenses, keep reading.

Decorating If You've Got Kids or Pets

Is it worth trying to make your house "magazine perfect" if you share it with pets, children, or others whose aesthetic sensibilities range toward slob-dom? Debbie Wiener of Designing Solutions in Silver Spring, Maryland, gave USA TODAY's Craig Wilson some compromise suggestions, below. (Find more at mydesigningsolutions.com.)

Q: Did the fact that you married a slob spur this easy decorating style?

A: He is the man behind my success. Before him, I was just another interior designer. There was a lot of chintz, flowing curtains, elegant traditional homes. And then he went about ruining them. We have two boys, and he encourages them to participate in the demolition. I couldn't see myself yelling and screaming anymore. I gave in.

Q: How do you go about finding high-quality, fuss-free styles that don't require special care?

A: There are some things you just have to rule out. If you've got kids or a black lab, white upholstery is no longer an option. Beige carpeting is an endangered species, too. Skirts vs. no skirts on chairs and sofas? I go for no skirt. If you've got pets rubbing up against it, you get hair. And I strongly advise, if you think your family belongs in an institution, get institutional fabrics. Get Crypton fabrics. You can sit down with wet bathing suits, and the chlorine won't hurt the fabric. And use color! It's better at camouflaging everyday life.

Q: You follow what you call WWE (World Wrestling Entertainment) guidelines. What are they?

A: Be prepared for whatever life throws at or on your furniture. A spitting-up baby, a sick cat, my husband. If you anticipate the worst-case scenario, like in wrestling, you're going to make better decisions. A sisal rug, for instance. If you spill or vomit on it, it's going to get ruined. It's very simple. Just don't do it.

 "Keep the 'slob' from overrunning your house," by Craig Wilson, April 5, 2007.

Buying home furnishings on a budget

Let's look first at buying furniture, artwork, and home accessories. Here are our top tips for getting great stuff on a budget:

- **Make the quest half the fun.** Your personal creativity won't get much exercise if you simply walk into a store and buy a houseful of furniture and home décor. If you like secondhand shopping, go to garage sales, flea markets, the Salvation Army, and Goodwill; accept castoffs from friends; and even find the occasional treasure on the curb. If you're looking for something specific—perhaps to replicate the perfect living room you saw in a magazine—bargain hunt, piece by piece, from online and local retailers.

- **Choose a unifying look or theme.** Some homeowners go wrong by buying a scattering of decorative items that look pretty by themselves, but don't add up to anything—ultimately wasting money. Homeowner Willow Liroff, of Oakland, California, instead planned ahead, by painting the walls of her new living room a rich coffee brown, then searching online for used framed black-and-white photographs. She notes, "By going to the 'for sale' area of Craigslist and searching for the word 'framed,' I pulled up entries from all the various categories where sellers might list artwork (arts/crafts, collectibles, furniture, and more). I had a fantastic range of choices, and made my living room look great for next to nothing."

- **Buy high quality.** If you concentrate your resources on buying one eye-catching piece of furniture—like a dining room table or an antique cabinet for your living room—you'll set the tone for your house's eventual look, but give yourself time to fill in the rest with high-quality pieces you won't need to replace anytime soon. In the meantime, spend as little as possible on the remaining furniture or use what you already have, and plan to slowly replace it.

- **Buy used wood furniture.** With a single wipedown, you won't need to worry about what's been spilled on it in the past. The same can't be said of couches or upholstered furniture. (Thrift stores may steam clean furniture—ask or look for labels.)

Hardwoods (like oak, cherry, or walnut) are the longest lasting. And before you plan to reupholster, check out prices—it can be more expensive than buying new.

- **Buy from furniture liquidators.** For good deals, furniture liquidators carry one-off pieces in new or like-new condition. You may not be able to customize color or size, but the prices are hard to beat and you might bargain them down further. If you plan to buy from a major retailer, wait for a sale (sign up for their email alerts) or hunt for coupons.

USA TODAY Snapshots®

Watch where you lay things
Top five possessions dog owners said their dogs damaged because of chewing habits:

Shoes	39%
Furniture	38%
Clothing	26%
Kids' toys	20%
Electronic equipment	15%

Source: TheHealthyChew.com   By David Stuckey and Dave Merrill, USA TODAY 2006

RESOURCE

Bargain-hunting websites. PriceGrabber.com is a great place to comparison shop. Go to SlickDeals.net to look for additional coupons. And if you register with Ebates.com, you can get a small percentage of cash back on online purchases through certain merchants.

- **Tell other people what you're looking for.** A quick email to the people who know you best will add eyes and ears to your search. And if you're willing to go public with your needs, post a "wanted" notice in the "for sale" section of Craigslist.
- **Make regular visits to online sites.** Look for high-quality items on Craigslist or eBay. Excellent deals often go lightning fast, however, so check often and don't be slow or flake out on picking up anything you've purchased: The seller probably had plenty of backup offers.

- **Consider shipping costs.** Home furnishings can be expensive to ship; an online bargain will quickly lose its luster if the seller charges you top-rate shipping and handling. You can avoid this by shopping locally (online or off) and finding a friend with a pickup truck, looking for ads where the seller offers delivery, or asking about fees ahead of time. Also check out www.overstock.com, where all shipping (as of this book's printing) is $2.95.

- **Sell your old stuff.** There's a market out there for almost anything, so get cash where you can. Willow Liroff of Oakland, California, describes selling a huge 1970s, mustard-yellow refrigerator: "I put an ad on Craigslist and within a day, a group of college students came to take a look. They loved the retro look and the size, and they'd brought their own truck, so we completed the sale right there."

- **Consider what will happen if you don't like what you've bought.** To minimize returns or dissatisfaction, measure your spaces before you go shopping and take photos of other pieces in the room to make sure everything matches. Bring a tape measure, photos, and any relevant color swatches with you to the store or seller's house. If you're buying from individual sellers, expect the sale to be final. In other cases, familiarize yourself with return/exchange policies. If, for example, you've custom-ordered a couch in fabric of your own choosing, it may not be returnable.

USA TODAY Snapshots®

Convenient return policy important

If a retailer's return policy is not convenient, would you continue to shop there?

No 82%
Yes 16%
Don't know 2%

Source: Newgistics survey of 1,061 adults 18 and older. Margin of error ±3 percentage points.

By Jae Yang and Steve Conley, USA TODAY 2006

Buying appliances on a budget

Your house's seller may have left behind a refrigerator, stove, dishwasher, and other appliances. But if not—or if their quality is subpar—appliances may be among your first home purchases. Here are some tips to help you shop:

- **Check product ratings and reviews.** An online search for "customer reviews" and the name of the product is a good bet.

- **Look for the Energy Star rating.** Energy Star is a program run by the EPA and the Department of Energy that recognizes energy-efficient appliances. As Jill Notini of the Association of Home Appliance Manufacturers told USA TODAY, overall, Energy Star appliances are about 10% to 20% more efficient than their unrated counterparts. Also, you can sometimes get a rebate from your utility company for installing these appliances.

- **See the tips for buying individual appliances at www.consumer reports.org.** For ratings, however, you'll need to subscribe to the magazine (but your local library probably has it).

- **Visit manufacturer's discount stores.** These may offer items that have nicks, scratches, or dents, were separated from a group set, or were returned without having been used. If no such stores exist in your area, ask your local retail store whether it has similar bargains in the back room.

- **Just say no to extended warranties on new appliances.** They're often a clever way for the manufacturer to boost its profits without offering you any real benefits. Most of them run out after three years, which is less time than it takes the typical product to break. Besides, you're likely to pay as much for the extended warranty as you would have for repairs.

- **Use store financing wisely.** Some stores, like Lowe's or Home Depot, have been known to offer 0% financing for the first year on large purchases. This may be a good option if you're sure to have the cash soon, but part of the deal is normally that you apply for and pay for the item with their store credit card, on which the eventual interest rates may be unusually high.

- **Furnish in proportion.** Unless you're a professional chef or have 12 children, you might actually find the newly chic industrial-size kitchen equipment inconvenient, oversized, and hard to use. Don't buy more than you need.

- **Buy local.** While you're not likely to get a special deal from a large, chain retailer, a local shop may be willing to offer special discounts if you ask—especially if you buy more than one appliance at a time.

- **Find out whether delivery and installation are included.** If so, this can decrease the comparative cost substantially, especially if you're dealing with heavy or difficult items, such as a front-loading, stackable washer and dryer.

- **Buy last year's model.** Especially toward December, stores are trying to get rid of old inventory. You can easily research the difference between one year's model and the next. If they're not significantly different, get the older model for less.

- **When buying used appliances, ask for a complete demonstration.** Make sure every button and function works before you plunk down your money.

USA TODAY Snapshots®

Dining out is hardest to give up

What would you be least willing to give up or cut back on each month to save more for retirement? Top categories:

Dining out — 31%
Travel — 18%
Clothes — 17%
Entertainment — 15%
Sporting event — 10%

Source: ShareBuilder survey of 2,033 adults 21 and older. Margin of error±2 percentage points.

By Jae Yang and Robert W. Ahrens, USA TODAY 2008

USA TODAY's Financial Diet Tips

To help people cut spending and build up their savings, USA TODAY developed a set of "fiscal exercises" with the help of Elissa Buie, a Falls Church, Virginia, financial planner. Here are some of our favorites:

- Pick one luxury item that you pay for each month and eliminate or reduce it. Skip a massage/facial/manicure/car wash/maid service.
- Look for some service you can trade. Join a babysitting co-op or cat/dog/house sit for a neighbor in exchange for the same.
- Take your lunch to work for a week instead of buying it out.
- If you're not using all your cell phone minutes each month (putting you among the 40% of people who pay for minutes they don't use), renegotiate your cell phone contract or switch providers.
- Cable TV, satellite TV, TiVo, on-demand movies—you might not be using all these services enough to justify what you're spending for them.
- Have the house cleaned every three weeks instead of every two.
- Cut your own grass for a few months.

 "Kids college fund can wait, but your future security can't," by Sandra Block, May 13, 2005; "Financial diet tip #1: Carve up your expenses," by Mindy Fetterman, April 22, 2005; and "Must-have expenses can be cut with a little effort," by Mindy Fetterman, April 22, 2005.

Of Mice and Maintenance: Keeping Up Your Property's Value

Regular Maintenance, Whether You See Problems or Not____48

Do You Hear Munching? Know Your Pests_____53

In the Garden: First, Do No Harm_____56

Reviewing and Renewing Your Homeowners'
  Insurance Policy_____58

  What you should find in a homeowners' policy_____58

  Are you at risk for particular damage your hazard
    insurance won't cover?_____59

  Would your hazard coverage pay to rebuild your house?__60

  Would your living costs be covered while your house
    is being rebuilt?_____61

  Will your coverage be enough to replace personal
    possessions?_____62

  Got expensive items needing separate coverage?_____62

  Will your liability coverage be enough if someone
    is injured?_____63

  Is your deductible too low?_____64

A well-kept home can last for centuries. You can, for example, still visit Abraham Lincoln's home in Springfield, Illinois, or Emily Dickinson's home in Amherst, Massachusetts. But no house is immortal. "I can't tell you how many people who live in an expensive house, that they spent a significant amount of money on, assume it doesn't require ongoing maintenance," Ron Phipps of Phipps Realty in Warwick, Rhode Island, told USA TODAY's Noelle Knox. "They pay the electric bill and get the grass cut, but they don't do maintenance."

All houses require ongoing upkeep, from patching minor cracks to replacing major structural components to repelling pest invasions. And if you wait too long to deal with these issues, you'll find yourself faced with some very expensive remedial work. To help secure your home's place in history, follow these steps:

- perform regular mini-inspections and maintenance
- prevent, recognize, and deal with termites, rodents, and other pests
- learn what's growing in your garden, and how to keep it healthy, and
- update your homeowners' insurance company regarding certain changes to your property.

TIP

How much will maintenance cost? USA TODAY's Noelle Knox found that the average homeowner should budget 1% to 3% of the home's value for annual maintenance, depending on the age and size of the home and area climate. Some years it might cost more, other years less.

Tools Every Homeowner Should Have

Are you still using your Swiss Army knife for home repairs? Might be time to expand your tool kit, suggests Norma Vally, also known as the Toolbelt Diva. According to her website, www.chixcanfix.com, you shouldn't be without these six tools:

Tools Every Homeowner Should Have, continued

- **13-oz. curved claw hammer.** This is the perfect all purpose hammer. It's light enough, so it won't strain your wrist, yet it's heavy enough to get the job done. The curved claw is great for "rocking" out nails without marring a surface.

- **16-foot /1-inch-wide tape measure.** I love this tape measure because it's fat, an inch wide. This allows you to read the numbers more easily. It also has great "throw"—which means it can be extended several feet without the tape bending.

- **6.5-inch tongue & groove pliers.** These pliers are adjustable and versatile. They will fit around various sized fittings, nuts, and bolts. Whether it's assembling furniture or a plumbing project, because of their shape, they're easy to maneuver.

- **Retractable utility knife (with blade storage in handle).** You will use this knife for cutting everything from to carpet to vinyl tiles, stripping wires to cutting drywall. It's also easy to replace the blade, especially with extra blade storage right in the handle!

- **Ratcheting screwdriver with multiple bits.** The multiple bits change out easily whether you need a Phillips, slotted head, or square drive. The ratcheting action allows you to keep steady pressure in the head of the screw while simply twisting the handle in place, thus giving you more turning power.

- **Torpedo level with magnetic strip.** Let's get things straight—and there's no better way to do that than with this handy little level! Whether it's a picture frame or shelf, making it plumb and level is easy with this tool. The magnetic strip leaves you two free hands when working with metal and its small size gets in tight spaces.

For further tips on tools and home projects, see Norma's books, including *Norma Vally's Bathroom Fix-Ups* (Wiley), *Norma Vally's Kitchen Fix-Ups* (Wiley), and *Chix Can Fix: 100 Home-Improvement Projects* and *True Tales from the Diva of Do-It-Yourself* (Penguin).

Reprinted with permission

RESOURCE

Beyond maintenance: For an unbelievably comprehensive treatment of homeowner how-tos, from cleaning stone floors to testing for lead in your china, caring for books, and cleaning your pet, see *Home Comforts: The Art & Science of Keeping House,* by Cheryl Mendelson (Scribner).

Regular Maintenance, Whether You See Problems or Not

USA TODAY's Noelle Knox asks, "When was the last time you changed the filter in your air conditioner or put a battery in your fire alarm? Tested the pressure valve on your water heater? Or are you thinking, 'Uh … there's a valve?'"

Don't wait until an emergency to realize your house needs some attention. Knox explains, "All it takes is an unchecked leak under the upstairs bathroom sink, and instead of replacing a $30 valve, you're spending your vacation fund on home repairs."

"It's not just the wood under the sink; the water can quickly spread into the downstairs ceiling," explains Gil Engler of Master Home Inspectors in Bethesda, Maryland. "And that's a $500 repair."

If you're in the "what valve?" camp, see the handy month-by-month list of maintenance tasks, below (created by Noelle Knox,

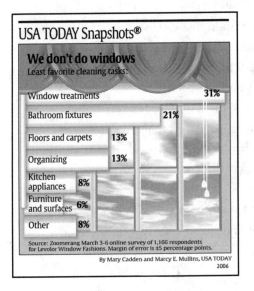

USA TODAY Snapshots®

We don't do windows
Least favorite cleaning tasks:

Window treatments	31%
Bathroom fixtures	21%
Floors and carpets	13%
Organizing	13%
Kitchen appliances	8%
Furniture and surfaces	6%
Other	8%

Source: Zoomerang March 3-6 online survey of 1,166 respondents for Levolor Window Fashions. Margin of error is ±5 percentage points.

By Mary Cadden and Marcy E. Mullins, USA TODAY 2006

with help from the National Association of Realtors®). Following it will help keep your house in excellent shape, minimizing your long-term costs.

January

❑ Dig out warranties and product manuals from under that stack of restaurant-delivery menus and check on recommended maintenance for furnaces, equipment, appliances, and tools. Mark your calendar to track scheduled upkeep and service.

❑ Make a room-by-room inventory of everything in your house. This will be important, in case of fire, flood, or any of the Ten Plagues covered by your insurance policy, in filing an insurance claim.

❑ Don't close vents to crawl spaces. If you live where pipes can freeze and the floors become very cold, you should either move to San Diego or insulate pipes under the floor. Double-check insulation around exterior pipes that are exposed to freezing weather to be sure water can't seep under the insulation.

February

❑ Remove drain traps under sinks and clean them thoroughly. Inspect grout and caulk around tubs, sinks, and showers. Chip out cracked grout and replace. Stained, discolored, and mildewed caulk should be cleaned with household cleaner.

❑ Musty closet odors can be reduced or eliminated by removing the closet's contents and washing walls with a diluted solution of chlorine bleach.

❑ To keep valves from sticking and to check for leaks, turn all water valves off and on. That includes outdoor faucets and valves to toilets, bathroom and kitchen sinks, laundry, bar, etc.

March

❑ After heavy rain, inspect your basement walls for signs of moisture or, worse, swimming sharks. If you detect wetness, first try running a portable dehumidifier. Check the downspouts and the grading around the foundation.

❑ Check to make sure your sump pump works properly by pouring water into the pump silo to raise the float and activate the motor.

❑ Test the pressure and temperature relief valve on your water heater by opening it and allowing some water to flow out. Bad valves can cause explosions. Remember that office building in *The Matrix Reloaded?*

April

❑ Replace batteries in smoke detectors. Battery: $2. Your life: priceless.

❑ Inspect screens for tears and bent frames. Check outdoor structures for deterioration—especially signs of rot. Also inspect the crawl space or basement after rain for water accumulation or excessive moisture. Look for signs of water damage on the sub floor and joists beneath bathrooms, the kitchen, and laundry.

❑ Check fire extinguishers to make sure they're not outdated, have lost pressure, or are damaged.

❑ Check all weatherstripping around doors and windows for wear, damage, or loss of flexibility.

May

❑ Clean gutters. Make sure downspouts or splash backs direct water at least six feet from the foundation.

❑ Have central air-conditioning unit checked. Replace the filter in the forced-air system. Clean debris from condenser or heat pump outside.

❑ Remove mineral deposits from faucet aerators and shower heads by soaking parts in white vinegar and scrubbing with an old toothbrush.

❑ Have swimming pool cleaned. Inspect and service pool liners and filters.

June

❑ Clean and seal decks, using ultraviolet-resistant sealer.

❑ Hire a certified chimney sweep to inspect and clean chimneys and watch *Mary Poppins* with the kids.

❑ Clean lint from the entire clothes dryer vent system, from the dryer to the exterior vent cap.

July

❑ Check all exterior walls for peeling or cracked paint. Carefully inspect brick or masonry siding for cracks or missing mortar.

❏ Inspect roofing material for cracks and loose or missing shingles and repair as necessary.

❏ Prune trees and shrubs so branches do not come in contact with exterior siding.

❏ Clean and repair cracks in concrete driveways using epoxy patching material. Repair asphalt driveways using asphalt patching material. Seal asphalt driveways every other year.

❏ Inspect foundation walls for signs of termites—tunnels or dirt bridges.

USA TODAY Snapshots®

A clean sweep through the house

Rooms taking top priority during spring cleaning:

Kitchen 37%

Living room 19%

Bedrooms 14%

Bathrooms 12%

Family room 8%

Source: International Communications Research (ICR) Omnibus telephone survey for the Soap and Detergent Association of 1,014 adults from March 1-5. Margin of error, ±3.1 percentage points.

By Mary Cadden and Marcy E. Mullins, USA TODAY
2008

August

❏ Use a vacuum with a narrow nozzle to clean condenser coils on the back or underneath your refrigerator—for the first time in your life.

❏ Check faucets for leaks and replace washers or repair the faucet as necessary.

❏ Clean underneath range hood. Remove and clean or replace range hood filters. Yes, they can be changed.

September

❏ Paint interior rooms while it's still warm enough to leave windows open.

❏ Check heating system, including filters, pilot lights, and burners, and have the system serviced by a qualified professional. Read: This is dangerous.

❏ Survey the outside of your house to make sure soil around the foundation is properly graded. Soil should slope three to six inches for a distance of three feet out from the foundation walls.

October

❑ Detach hoses in case of freezing temperatures. Ask yourself why you didn't move to San Diego.

❑ Inspect weatherstripping around doors and windows and repair or replace if necessary.

❑ Clean gutters after leaves have fallen. Make sure downspouts are in good condition.

❑ Change batteries in smoke and carbon monoxide detectors. Check gauges on home fire extinguishers to ensure a full charge.

November

❑ Inspect automatic garage-door opener and lubricate according to the manufacturer's directions.

❑ Check for leaks around washing machine. Prime suspects for leaks are the water supply hose washers.

December

❑ Check the operation of all circuit interrupters in your ground outlets by pushing the "test" button. The "reset" button should pop out, indicating the receptacle is operating properly. Press in the reset button.

❑ Check inside bathroom vanities and kitchen-sink cabinets for moisture and other signs of leaks. Carefully inspect pipes for condensation or slow drips.

Don't panic!

Most pests work slowly. It takes a termite colony of 60,000 workers around four months to consume a one-foot length of two by four.

Once you've done all this, Noelle Knox says, you can gloat, knowing that "Your home's value is rising faster than your neighbor's."

TIP

Timely maintenance also helps you get the maximum coverage from your homeowners' insurance. Most homeowners' policies require you to make reasonable and necessary repairs to protect your property. Failure to do so could lead to your claim for damage being denied or your policy not being renewed. For example, USA TODAY's Christine Dugas explains, "If water seeps from the ground into your basement and damages your foundation, it's considered a maintenance problem and generally won't be covered."

Do You Hear Munching? Know Your Pests

Despite a clean inspection report when you bought your house, termites, mice, rats, ants, and other pests may subsequently decide that your home looks like a warm refuge or a tasty treat—and can create major damage before you realize it. Take a look at the chart below, which details the most likely pests to pose a threat to your home, and how to prevent, detect, and deal with them.

USA TODAY Snapshots

What scares women most?

29% Heights
22% Spiders
16% Being seen in public in my bathing suit
10% Flying in an airplane
22% None of these things scared me at all

Source: Harris Interactive QuickQuery study of 1,224 U.S. women for Marshalls (Jan. 27-31). Margin of error ± 4 percentage points.

By Mary Cadden and Frank Pompa, USA TODAY
2006

Once you've spotted signs of a problem, you will most likely want to call in a pest control professional. Get recommendations from your friends and real estate agent, and compare estimates. Check that the person has complied with any licensing requirements (you don't want a nonexpert playing around with chemicals in your home). Balance the price with the scope of service and the length of time the professional will guarantee results.

Common Destructive Pests

Pest	Appearance	Signs	Damage
Termites	Winged, ant-like insects that may appear in your house, likely in springtime, when "swarmers" search for mates.	Termite tubes, about pencil-width, most likely leading up walls; damaged areas in walls or ceilings. Check basement, crawl space, patio, garage, and attic, and anywhere plumbing or utility pipes enter the foundation or flooring.	Termites eat wood and other cellulose-containing material (like paper or dried leaves) and tunnel through nonwood (like foam insulation or plaster board) in search of wood.
Rodents	Rats and mice—furry, long-tailed, and hopefully smaller than your cat.	Look for droppings or urine stains; sounds of scrabbling and scratching in walls.	They may chew through walls, wiring (potentially causing fires), and your personal possessions; leave droppings and bacteria.
Carpenter ants	Big red or black ants, from 1/4" to 5/8" long.	Look for small piles of sawdust, insulation, and insect body parts under a hole in a wooden part of your house.	They drill through wood or foam to hollow out Swiss-cheese-like nest galleries.
Powder-post beetles	The beetles are reddish-brown, with narrow, flat bodies between 1/8" and 1/4" long. They may fly around at night, especially near lights.	Check wood surfaces in your home for pinhead-sized, round exit holes and powder.	Beetles make tunnels in unwaxed, unvarnished wood or bamboo to lay their eggs.
Carpenter bees	Large bees with stomachs more black than yellow.	Look for near-perfect holes, about 1/2" in diameter, in wooden portions of your home exterior.	They drill through wood to create nesting galleries, usually in eaves, siding, soffits, decks, overhangs, fence posts, window frames.
Dry rot (a fungus)	May be powdery white and dusty, cottony, or like the skin atop a mushroom.	Look in dark areas for weak, brittle, cracked, and chunky looking wood (a sign that the fungus is digesting the parts of it that give it strength).	Left untreated, dry rot can cause your home to become structurally unstable or even collapse.

Prevention	Solutions
Get rid of any wood that touches both soil and your foundation (such as mulch, trellises, firewood, or debris); don't let moisture accumulate near your foundation (most termites need water for survival); don't let humidity build up in your crawl space. You need at least one square foot of vent opening per 150 square feet of crawl space. Cut away plants covering the vents.	Brush down tunnels, remove debris and other likely food sources, then call a structural pest control specialist. For larger infestations, the specialist may recommend fumigation or heating the entire house (heating avoids chemical exposure)—but get more than one opinion. For a swarm, get out your vacuum cleaner, and remove and dispose of the bag when you're done.
Seal up holes or cracks in floors, walls, and areas under built-in cabinets, using wood sealant, nailed-down mesh, and steel wool. Some mice can crawl through a space as small as a pencil. Don't leave pet food bowls outdoors, and don't leave food on counters overnight.	Lay traps or poison, and double-check that all entry points to your house are sealed off. Snap traps are the least cruel, most environmentally friendly option. If self-help doesn't work, call a pest control professional. Some will come and remove the trapped or dead rodents, too.
Close entry points to your home by following prevention methods for termites and rodents, keeping wet wood away from your house, and trimming back tree limbs that touch your home.	You'll have to find the nest and kill the queen (not just ants you see), most likely with pesticides. It's best to call a professional; though if you want some do-it-yourself advice, see the University of Wisconsin's website at www.entomology.wisc.edu/ppants.html.
Examine wood before you let it in the door—especially wood less than five years old.	For minor, localized infestations, replace the board or wooden item. After cleaning up, keep an eye out for new powder. For slightly larger infestations, a pest control professional can treat the wood surface with virtually nontoxic borate formulations. If beetles have spread into your walls or floors, you may have to have your property fumigated.
There's not much you can do to prevent these bees. Because they prefer weathered and unpainted woods, keeping up your exterior paint job may offer some protection.	Call a professional: The extermination requires injecting pesticide into each individual bee gallery, usually from a high ladder.
As with termites, reduce or eliminate excess moisture around wood, and remove wood that touches both soil and your home.	Small areas of rot can be cut out and filled with wood putty or Bondo. For larger problems, call a pest control professional.

> **RESOURCE**
> For more information on the topics covered below, and for help finding pest control professionals, see the website of the National Pest Management Association at www.pestworld.org.

In the Garden: First, Do No Harm

Did your house come with some land? If so, what's growing there and how do you take care of it? Maintaining or creating a thriving garden is a great way to boost your house's resale value, and not something best done at the last minute, because plants need time to mature and fill out. (Don't be discouraged if a few die, despite your best efforts.) Also, planting your own fruits, vegetables, and herbs can be economical and save you trips to the grocery store.

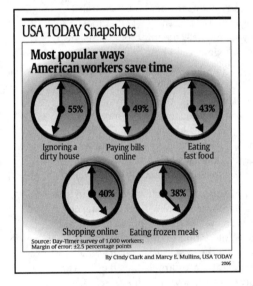

USA TODAY Snapshots

Most popular ways American workers save time

55% Ignoring a dirty house

49% Paying bills online

43% Eating fast food

40% Shopping online

38% Eating frozen meals

Source: Day-Timer survey of 1,000 workers; Margin of error: ±2.5 percentage points

By Cindy Clark and Marcy E. Mullins, USA TODAY 2006

At the risk of insulting any readers with green thumbs, here are the absolute first steps you should take:

- **Look around.** To identify both plants and pests in your garden, take clippings and samples to your local nursery. They'll be glad to help a potential new customer. While you're there, ask for general advice on each plant's care, watering, and eventual size. Peruse local bookstores for regional guides like the *Sunset* series (mostly Western) or the *Southern Living Landscape Book*, or visit regional Internet chat rooms and advice sites to find out what grows well where you live.

- **Watch what you weed.** We know someone who had always dreamed of planting foxgloves, so she ripped up the "weeds" in her new garden and planted seeds. As she watched them grow, she realized that what she had ripped up earlier were—you guessed it—foxgloves. Once you know what's what, try to weed while plants are small, and after a rain, when they're easiest to pull up.

- **Figure out how you'll water.** An irrigation system is a convenient, efficient way to handle your plants' need for water. For information on these systems, check out www.irrigationtutorials.com and www.epa.gov/watersense. Also research how much water each plant needs, because overwatering can kill certain plants (citrus trees, for example).

- **Buy basic tools.** Gardening gloves (protection against scratches and insect bites), a dandelion weeder (useful for getting at the roots of other weeds, too), a pruner, and a small handsaw (for branches up to four inches thick) are the crucial ones. If you've got hedges, add a hedge trimmer. Pay a little extra for the high quality tools, which will last longer and be easier to use.

  ### Want to lose weight or de-stress?

  "Over five months, a person gardening for 20 to 30 minutes a day would burn 15,000 calories and lose four pounds," says James Hill, cofounder of America on the Move, quoted in USA TODAY. Studies also show that strolling through a garden or even seeing one out your window can lower blood pressure, reduce stress, and ease pain.

- **Before buying plants, read their specs!** Find out as much as you can about a plant before buying—including how much sunshine and water it needs, so a cute two-inch flower doesn't either die in the shade or shoot up to a six-foot, invasive shrub.

- **Enjoy the learning process.** Garden questions are a great way to bond with neighbors. You might also join a local gardening club, take a class, and check out books at your local library.

Reviewing and Renewing Your Homeowners' Insurance Policy

Not all maintenance requires crawling around in dark spaces. Another important way to protect your property's value is to keep your homeowners' insurance current and appropriate for the costs of unexpected damage. The most obvious time to do this is when you get your annual renewal paperwork. Your homeowners' insurance company probably won't ask you to revisit the assumptions behind your policy (though it might raise your premium, particularly if you made a lot of claims last year).

Which common garden flowers are edible?

According to www.thenibble.com, you can eat the petals of roses, clover, chrysanthemum, chamomile, calendula (pot marigold), dandelions, nasturtiums, borage, pansies or Johnny Jump-ups, and lavender. Most are rather spicy and best used as garnish or in salads.

But first, make sure you know what your policy covers. You were in the midst of closing on your house purchase when you first reviewed and signed the paperwork, not exactly prime time for concentrating. No wonder many homeowners are shocked, after the fact, to find that their policy doesn't cover them for certain types of major damage, or pays an insufficient portion of their losses.

Use the guidance below to give your policy a good looking over. Talk to your insurance rep about any needed changes, or shop around for better or cheaper insurance. No one says you have to keep the same policy forever. For consumer ratings of different policies, go to www.jdpower.com (click "Homes," then "Homeowners Insurance Company Ratings").

What you should find in a homeowners' policy

The standard homeowners' insurance policy includes:

- **hazard insurance**, to cover physical damage or loss involving your property and possessions, and

- **liability insurance,** to cover injuries to people on your property or caused by members of your household (including pets).

In addition, your policy is no doubt customized to your home and possessions, perhaps with extra coverage (in the form of "riders" or "endorsements") to cover any nonstandard structures (such as a boathouse or cottage) or particularly valuable items. And every policy contains exclusions, or types of damage that the policy won't cover.

Are you at risk for particular damage your hazard insurance won't cover?

Your hazard insurance probably compensates you (and your lender) for physical damage to your property and its contents caused by everything from fire and smoke to wind, hail, lightning, explosions, volcanoes, riots and vandalism, theft, water damage, and similar events. Despite the seemingly exhaustive list, the following types of damage probably won't be covered: flooding, earthquakes, mudslides, police activity, power outages, sewer backups, dry rot, vermin, war, nuclear perils, losses if your house is vacant for 60 days or more, or losses caused by your own poor maintenance or failure to preserve or protect the property after it's been damaged.

Most of these exclusions you'll just have to live with. However, there are cases in which you can buy extra coverage from your insurance company or from another source, as is common with flood and earthquake insurance. Your top priority is to buy added coverage for hazards that can cause huge damage (like sewer backups), or are big risks in the area where you live (like earthquakes, hurricanes, or sinkholes).

> CAUTION
>
> **Did your lender tell you that you don't need flood insurance?** That just means you're not in a federally recognized flood zone. As USA TODAY's Kathy Chu explains, "By law, homeowners in flood-prone areas—such as along the coast—must buy such a policy if they get a mortgage from a federally regulated lender." But that's based on general (and sometimes outdated) maps, not local conditions and realities. Check recent, local statistics and other information and make your own decision about buying flood insurance.

Would your hazard coverage pay to rebuild your house?

When thinking about how to deal with a home destroyed by fire or another hazard, many people immediately start visualizing using the insurance money to rebuild the place just as it was, or even bigger or better. Before you imagine that, reexamine your policy. "Inadequate insurance coverage plagues homeowners across the USA," explain USA TODAY's Kathy Chu and Elizabeth Weise. "Nationally, 58% of homes were underinsured in 2006, by an average of 21%, according to Marshall & Swift/Boeckh, which supplies building-cost information to insurers and government agencies." Here are the different types of coverage, and what they're likely to mean if disaster strikes.

The norm: replacement cost coverage. Most policies give you what's called "replacement cost" coverage. Despite its name, it doesn't mean you'll get a blank check with which to rebuild. Instead, you'll receive a set dollar amount, written in your policy contract. That amount was calculated back when you first got the policy, most likely after you had a phone conversation with the insurance rep or filled out a questionnaire (they rarely visit in person). You were probably asked about your house's size, location, number and type of rooms, building materials, amenities, and more.

But as Kathy Chu and Elizabeth Weise found, "In each of the past three years [2004 to 2006], the cost of building materials has climbed 6% to 6.5%, far above overall inflation. Prices of construction materials can rise even more after natural disasters." Increased demand for home contractors after a disaster may also cause them to raise their prices. And if your house has historical features that are hard to recreate, rebuilding is especially likely to cost more than your homeowners' policy covers.

For a reality check, ask a local contractor how much a house like yours would cost to build today. If that's less than the amount offered by your insurance, work with your insurance rep to raise your replacement cost figure. Another worthwhile option is buying an "inflation guard," which raises the stated value of your house by a set percentage each year.

The ideal: guaranteed replacement coverage. With some searching, you may find a policy that guarantees 100% payment of your repair or rebuilding costs, without limits. This is known as a "guaranteed replacement cost" policy. If your house has unique historical features, finding such a policy will be especially difficult—and expensive.

To be avoided: actual cash value coverage. If your insurance policy pays the "actual cash value" of your house, start shopping for new coverage. If the house were destroyed, you'd get its replacement cost minus any depreciation or wear and tear that's occurred since it was built. For example, USA TODAY's Kathy Chu explains, the insurer might deduct for a roof that needed to be replaced. You could end up with too little to rebuild at all.

> **TIP**
> **Tell your insurance company about any remodels or upgrades.** USA TODAY's Sandra Block discovered (in 2006) that, "Nearly 40% of Americans who have made significant home improvements since 2003, such as adding a room or deck, said they hadn't updated their home- owners' insurance, or weren't sure if they had. That could be disastrous if your home is destroyed, according to Madelyn Flannagan, a spokeswoman for Trusted Choice (a network of insurance agencies). If your policy is based on the value of your home before you remodeled, you may not recoup the money you spent to add a bathroom or update your kitchen."

Would your living costs be covered while your house is being rebuilt?

Where will you live if your house needs major repairs? Standard policies include a "loss of use" provision, to cover hotel bills, restaurant meals, and other living expenses, usually for up to one year. You can pay a little more and get two years' of coverage, worth it in case of a major flood or fire, when contractors and architects will be busy and difficult to hire.

Some policies place a dollar limit (instead of a time limit) on your living expenses, often 20% of the total insurance on your house. If that's true of your policy, calculate the average rental and utility costs in your area and figure out whether the amount will be enough.

Will your coverage be enough to replace personal possessions?

Most people don't think too hard about personal possessions when buying their homeowners' coverage. Nevertheless, the stuff inside your house—jewelry, television, refrigerator, and more—can be worth a lot. Look for the words "replacement value" in the relevant section of your policy. This is good: It means you'll get the actual cost of buying a new item. The alternative, "actual cash value," isn't so good. You'll get the amount your stuff would sell for used—like on eBay—after depreciation has been taken into account.

Got expensive items needing separate coverage?

What did you get for your last birthday—or buy for your new home? As Jeff McCollum, a spokesman for State Farm told USA TODAY's Kathy Chu, "If you've added a big-screen TV or furniture, you may have items in your home worth way more than you're covered for" under your homeowners' policy.

In particular, big-ticket items such as jewelry, cameras, sports equipment, musical instruments, electronics, furs, firearms, coins, or silver may need separate coverage. That's because the standard policy has separate limits for these categories, usually between $1,000 and $2,000 in total.

You'll need to pay more for endorsements insuring each such item for what it's worth—but the risks make it well worth it, thefts being among your most likely losses. The extra coverage will also take care of "accidental disappearance," such as losing your diamond bracelet while jet skiing.

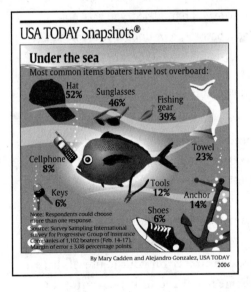

USA TODAY Snapshots®

Under the sea

Most common items boaters have lost overboard:

Hat 52%
Sunglasses 46%
Fishing gear 39%
Towel 23%
Cellphone 8%
Tools 12%
Anchor 14%
Keys 6%
Shoes 6%

Note: Respondents could choose more than one response.
Source: Survey Sampling International survey for Progressive Group of Insurance Companies of 1,102 boaters (Feb. 14-17). Margin of error ± 3.08 percentage points.

By Mary Cadden and Alejandro Gonzalez, USA TODAY 2006

Will your liability coverage be enough if someone is injured?

Liability insurance compensates you and the people who visit your property for both:

- **Medical payments to others.** This pays the medical bills of people from outside your household who are accidentally injured while on your property. It includes the classic slips and falls, as well as accidents directly caused by you, a household member, or even a pet. This coverage also pays medical costs of people you or your pet injure while off your property (except if the incident is covered by auto insurance).

- **Personal liability.** If you're sued, this covers your legal fees and any amounts a court orders you to pay to someone who was injured or whose property was damaged by you or someone in your household (human or animal). For example, the court might order you to pay medical expenses and lost wages.

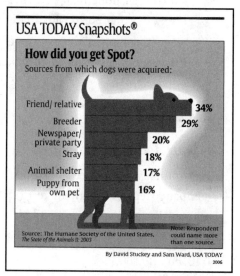

USA TODAY Snapshots®

How did you get Spot?
Sources from which dogs were acquired:

Friend/ relative — **34%**
Breeder — **29%**
Newspaper/ private party — **20%**
Stray — **18%**
Animal shelter — **17%**
Puppy from own pet — **16%**

Source: The Humane Society of the United States, *The State of the Animals II: 2003*

Note: Respondent could name more than one source.

By David Stuckey and Sam Ward, USA TODAY 2006

Standard homeowners' policies have traditionally provided around $100,000 in liability coverage. However, that amount is going up, because one person's medical bills these days could easily top $100,000. And if you're sued, you could end up paying even more. Don't put your house at risk of being sold to pay a court judgment. Instead, set your liability coverage at a realistic level, between $500,000 and $1 million.

Check Your Insurance Before Choosing a Dog

Dog bites and other pet-related injuries are normally covered under the liability portion of your homeowners' insurance. However, if you bring home a dog with a history of aggressive behavior, or whose breed the company (fairly or unfairly) considers likely to bite, your company might refuse coverage if the dog causes an injury. And some companies will then raise your premium or cancel the entire policy.

So check with your insurance company before you bring home a rottweiler, doberman, german shepherd, chow chow, pit bull, husky, or other breed with an iffy reputation.

Also be prepared to pay extra or have your liability coverage cancelled if you've got a pet snake, alligator, spider, or exotic bird.

Is your deductible too low?

How much will you need to pay after a loss before your insurance company steps in to pay the rest (up to the policy limits)? That amount is called your "deductible." Most homeowners agree to a $500 deductible (for the hazard portion of their insurance; liability insurance doesn't normally carry a deductible).

However, raising your deductible can save you big bucks, in both the short and long term. First, you'll be able to significantly reduce your premium costs. And later, you won't be tempted to call your insurer for every little bit of damage—a good thing, because

USA TODAY Snapshots®

Safety precautions at home
Percentage of adults in the USA who have:

Smoke alarms
96%
Fire extinguishers
80%
Carbon monoxide detectors
46%

Source: 2006 Fire Safety Census, a telephone survey of 1,005 adults 25 and older conducted in August 2006 by KRC Research for Liberty Mutual and International Association of Fire Fighters. Margin of error ±3.1 percentage points.

By Tracey Wong Briggs and Veronica Salazar, USA TODAY
2008

the more claims you make, the more likely the insurer is to raise your premiums or cancel your policy. Some people even continue paying for minor losses out-of-pocket after reaching their deductible, just to avoid having their premiums raised.

Greening Your Home— On a Budget

Easy Changes Anyone Can Make_____68

Life Inside: Greening Your Home's Interior_____72
   Green clean: Healthy cleaning products_____72
   Stylin' green: Healthy personal care products_____75

The Green Garden_____77

Eating Green_____80

Driving Green (Without a Hybrid)_____84

Maintaining and Upgrading Responsibly_____86

Maybe buying a home has made you more eco-conscious, or maybe you just want to save a few bucks and steer clear of toxic chemicals. Either way, now is a good time to pick up some new habits that can help your wallet, help the planet, or keep your little part of the world green.

We'll cover some basic, affordable ways to go green, including:

- a few easy steps anyone can take
- choosing eco-friendly products for your home
- using and caring for outdoor areas in an environmentally friendly way
- eating and driving responsibly, and
- maintaining and updating your home in a way that conserves energy and resources.

> **TIP**
> **Wonder what your household's environmental impact is?** Go to the U.S. Environmental Protection Agency (EPA) website for calculators that help you tally up your household emissions (www.epa.gov/climatechange/emissions/individual.html) and learn how these emissions affect the environment.

Easy Changes Anyone Can Make

In a USA TODAY poll, 78% of respondents said spending several thousand dollars to make their homes more energy-efficient would be a good idea. But there are many energy—and environment—saving steps you can take that cost nothing or very little, including:

- **Hang laundry.** Who doesn't love the smell of sheets dried in the sun? And hanging the laundry has the additional benefit of going easy on the dryer. Cost: approximately $5 for a clothesline.

CAUTION

If you're governed by community association rules, make sure they don't prohibit visible clotheslines. If they do and you want to change things, visit Project Laundry List (www.laundrylist.org) to find like-minded souls.

- **Wash your clothes in cold water.** About 90% of the energy used for washing clothes is used to heat the water. Modern detergents don't need hot water to work, and stains that won't come out in cold water probably aren't going to come out in hot water either—in fact, the hot water may make them set. As with other household products, choose biodegradable and earth-friendly detergents— traditional ones contain many earth-harming and potentially toxic substances. For more information,

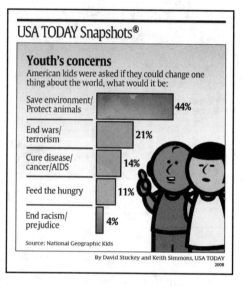

USA TODAY Snapshots®

Youth's concerns
American kids were asked if they could change one thing about the world, what would it be:

Save environment/ Protect animals	44%
End wars/ terrorism	21%
Cure disease/ cancer/AIDS	14%
Feed the hungry	11%
End racism/ prejudice	4%

Source: National Geographic Kids

By David Stuckey and Keith Simmons, USA TODAY 2008

check out www.sixwise.com (search for "laundry detergent"). For maximum environmental benefit, skip fabric softener, choose one that's soy based, or throw vinegar into the rinse cycle to soften your clothes. Cost: $0 extra.

- **Put on a sweater.** Lower your central air temperature two degrees in the winter and let it go up by two degrees in the summer and you could save up to 2,000 pounds of carbon dioxide per year. Cost: $0 (and your energy bill may go down).

- **Clean or replace furnace and air conditioning filters.** Keeping your furnace and air conditioning filters clean will help them function efficiently. An electrostatic filter will cost more up front than a paper or fiberglass one, but can be cleaned and reused. Cost: $0 to clean, $5–$50 to replace.

- **Turn down the water heater.** Most people find 120 degrees to be warm enough. While you're at it, wrap an insulating water heater blanket around your unit to help reduce heat loss by 25%–40% (unless it came with built-in insulation, or the manual says to not use an insulating blanket, as is the case with some newer units). Turn off the heater entirely when you're out of town (but don't forget to turn it back on when you return, or the cold shower will remind you). Cost of blanket: around $10–$20.

- **Add a water heater timer.** If you have an electric water heater, install a timer that will shut it off when it's not being used—for example, in the middle of the night. Cost: around $60 (should pay for itself within a year).

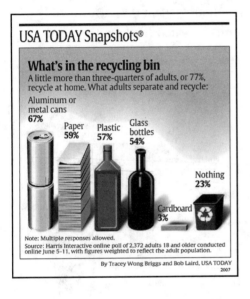

USA TODAY Snapshots®

What's in the recycling bin
A little more than three-quarters of adults, or 77%, recycle at home. What adults separate and recycle:

Aluminum or metal cans **67%**
Paper **59%**
Plastic **57%**
Glass bottles **54%**
Nothing **23%**
Cardboard **3%**

Note: Multiple responses allowed.
Source: Harris Interactive online poll of 2,372 adults 18 and older conducted online June 5–11, with figures weighted to reflect the adult population.
By Tracey Wong Briggs and Bob Laird, USA TODAY 2007

- **Use the dishwasher.** Modern dishwashers tend to be more efficient than handwashing, since they use less than ten gallons of water per load. And they're effective enough that you can feel justified in not prerinsing your dishes, which wastes water. Wait to run the dishwasher until it is completely full, and let dishes air dry if you can. Cost: $0 extra if you have a dishwasher ($300–$1,000 for a new one).

- **Recycle.** If you don't already have curbside recycling, find out about local programs to recycle paper, cans, bottles, plastic, and more by visiting www.earth911.org. Cost: possibly $0—you may even make money!

- **Limit paper consumption.** Buy cloth napkins and reuse them. Purchase recycled, unbleached toilet paper, paper towels, and printer paper. And of course, don't use more than you need—a sponge or rag often works better than a paper towel anyway. Cost: small increase in price, which you can make up for by using less.

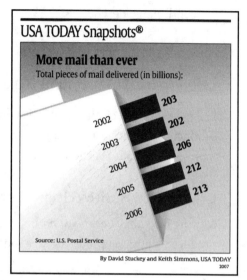

- **Get a low-flow showerhead.** It will still have good water pressure, but will release (and waste) a lot less water. While you're at it, shorten your showers and avoid water-hogging baths altogether. An even better (but pricier) option is to get a low-flow toilet. (You can make an adjustment to your current toilet, though, by putting a gallon milk jug with rocks into the tank to displace the water.) Cost of showerhead: about $20. Cost of new toilet: $300–$400.

- **Get rid of the junk mail.** Cancel catalogues you don't need at www .catalogchoice.org. Pay your bills—and get your statements—online. Cost: $0 (and you'll save a little in postage).

- **Use power strips.** Anything plugged into an electrical outlet sucks energy even when not in use. Plug everything into power strips that you can turn off easily. Cost: $10–$20 per strip.

Follow these easy steps, and you'll make a positive environmental impact. Moreover, you'll see your minimal investment come back to you in lower energy bills.

> **TIP**
> **Get other easy ideas from a checklist created by the American Council for an Energy-Efficient Economy** (www.aceee.org/ consumerguide/checklist).

Life Inside: Greening Your Home's Interior

From cleaning to clothing, we all spend a fair bit of cash on consumer products. Here are ways to protect the environment and your health with smart consumer choices.

Green clean: Healthy cleaning products

Moving into a new home often involves buying a slew of new cleaning products. But these products are a source of possible environmental and personal harm. According to the EPA, the air inside the typical home is on average two to five times more polluted than the air just outside, largely because of household cleaners and pesticides.

USA TODAY Snapshots®

Asthma: A day in the life

Every day in the USA:

▸ **40,000** people miss work because of asthma

▸ **30,000** people have an asthma attack

▸ **5,000** people visit the emergency room because of asthma

▸ **1,000** people are admitted to the hospital

▸ **11** people die from asthma

Source: Asthma and Allergy Foundation of America

By David Stuckey and Robert W. Ahrens, USA TODAY 2007

You can reduce your family's exposure and protect the environment by using nontoxic products. But don't fall for every green ad claim. As USA TODAY's Laura Petrecca discovered, "There are no universally recognized label rules for 'green' cleaners." Read the labels—many conventional cleaners won't list their ingredients—and buy from reliable companies: Seventh Generation (www.seventhgeneration.com), Method (www .methodhome.com), and Ecover (www.ecover.com) are a few examples.

Alternatively, you can make your own cleaning products. Some common household supplies—like vinegar, baking soda, and lemons—

work wonders. If you don't like the smell of these natural cleaners, add a few drops of essential oil, like lavender or cedar. For do-it-yourself options, go to www.care2.com (search for "cleaning products").

Household Products: More Harm Than Good?

You can't see them. There's no way to tell from a product label whether they've been used. And they don't appear in every variation of the same kind of product. Scientists are not always sure how they are transmitted from product to person.

These man-made chemicals are endocrine mimics. By sheer chance, their molecules are perfectly shaped to form keys that open the hormonal locks that control the proper development and function of our bodies.

They may do little harm to adults, but evidence mounts that they can wreak havoc in the development of fetuses and children.

Ana Soto, a professor of cell biology at Tufts University School of Medicine in Boston, found that exposure to bisphenol A, a common ingredient in plastics such as reusable water bottles and the housing of laptop computers and in resins that line some food cans and dental sealants, can change the course of fetal development.

Exposure to phthalates (pronounced THAL-ates) comes from direct contact with products that contain them, such as vinyl flooring, detergents, automotive plastics, soap, shampoo, deodorants, fragrances, hair spray, nail polish, plastic bags, food packaging, garden hoses, inflatable toys, blood-storage bags, and intravenous medical tubing, according to the Centers for Disease Control and Prevention.

Research published in the journal *Environmental Health Perspectives* by epidemiologist Shanna Swan at the University of Rochester in New York found an association between higher phthalate levels in pregnant women and changes in the genitals in their infant sons that suggest lower concentrations of male hormones and can lead to incomplete testicular descent.

Household Products: More Harm Than Good?, continued

Environmental groups and researchers maintain that it's possible to have modern conveniences without all the health risks.

If the chemicals that make plastics soft are endocrine disruptors, chemists now have the ability to design them without that side effect. It just takes convincing industry that the result is going to be cheaper in the long run, says Mary Ellen Weber, director of the EPA's pollutions and toxics research group. "When you can replace a known toxic chemical with sugar or cornstarch or sunlight, you know you've got an environmentally preferable product."

While scientists do their research, what can consumers do to limit exposure to these hormone look-alikes?

- **Cut down on personal-care items,** such as hair products, deodorants, and fragrances. They often contain endocrine disruptors, and some of them can be absorbed through the skin. The website www.nottoopretty.org lists alternatives.

- **Eat fewer fatty meat and dairy products.** When animals take in endocrine disruptors, the chemicals accumulate in fat. This is a big source of human exposure.

- **Avoid buying new clothes that are coated with stain-resisting chemicals.** Look for words such as "stain shield," "stain resistant" or "stain protected." These coatings often contain perfluorooctanoic acid (PFOA), which an EPA panel recently named a likely carcinogen. Forgo optional stain treatments on furniture, upholstery, and cars for the same reason.

- **Reduce consumption of prepackaged foods, which often have grease-resistant coatings that contain PFOA.** These include popcorn and french fry boxes, fast-food packaging, the paper that protects the pizza box, and butter boxes.

 "Are our products our enemy?; Chemicals in everyday goods disrupt hormones," by Elizabeth Weise, August 3, 2005.

Stylin' green: Healthy personal care products

Most of us want to be environmentally responsible without wearing all hemp and no deodorant. Thankfully, there are many options, and they don't mean dumping everything we own and going out to buy the more eco-friendly model. (Consuming less is always eco-friendlier.) When you do need to buy new things, here are some guidelines.

Clothing. Moving into a new home may mean a bigger closet, and you may be tempted to fill it. But one easy way to be green is to avoid buying things you really don't need. Every item in your closet was made somewhere, and whether fabricated from cotton, rayon, polyester, or something else, behind it may lurk an energy-sucking, toxin-producing process. Finally, that item also had to be transported to where you are, another energy-drainer.

But hey—we all need clothes. Focus on buying fewer items that will last longer. If you really want to get into the green spirit, buying vintage or used clothing also reduces environmental impact (and you'd be surprised how many new or almost-new clothes end up in thrift stores). Finally, if you buy clothing that needs to be dry cleaned, go to www .greenearthcleaning.com to find a cleaner that doesn't use conventional harsh solvents containing percholoethylene (sometimes called "perc"), a toxic contaminant. (Silicone-based solvents are a friendlier alternative.)

TIP
Don't just recycle, free cycle. At www.freecycle.org, you can connect with others in your community who have goods to give away—and give away goods of your own.

Health and beauty products. Lucky consumers that we are, there's now a wide range of "natural" choices in personal care products like toothpaste, deodorant, shampoo, and cosmetics. For a list of companies that have pledged to not use harmful chemicals in their products, go to the website for the Campaign for Safe Cosmetics (www.safecosmetics .org). Again, be skeptical: The U.S. Department of Agriculture (USDA) doesn't regulate the term "organic" as it applies to personal care products (it's more focused on food products). For more information, visit the website for the Organic Consumers Organization (www.oca.org, search for "Coming Clean Campaign"). And get toxicity ratings of specific products using the Environmental Working Group's database at www.cosmeticdatabase.com.

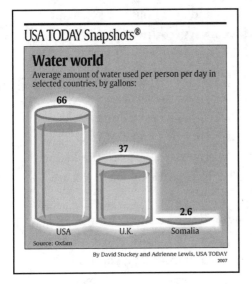

USA TODAY Snapshots®

Water world
Average amount of water used per person per day in selected countries, by gallons:

66 — USA
37 — U.K.
2.6 — Somalia

Source: Oxfam

By David Stuckey and Adrienne Lewis, USA TODAY 2007

Green kids. In addition to the options in personal care, clothing, and the like, carefully select toys that are not made with harmful plastics or lead paint. For ideas, visit www.treehugger.com, and type "kids' toys" in the search box.

> **TIP**
>
> **What about diapers?** The endless debate over cloth versus disposable diapers may be over: A 2005 study revealed there's not much difference between the two in environmental impact (one uses water and electricity, the other emits methane and clogs landfills). However, a relatively new product called G Diapers may be the happy medium: It includes washable outer "pants" and an interior snap-in, biodegradable, flushable insert. See www.gdiapers.com.

Green pets. Make sure your pets are spayed or neutered to prevent overpopulation. Choose food, products, and toys that meet the same criteria discussed above (organic, free of harmful chemicals), and keep things clean with biodegradable doggie-poo bags and eco-friendly kitty litter. For other ideas, check out www.grist.org (search for "green pets").

Furniture. Before buying new furniture, think about purchasing items made of reclaimed, reused, or recycled products. Consider also sustainable materials like cork. These products won't necessarily be cheaper, but they'll probably be high quality and last a good long time. If those don't fit your budget, try to buy used (see Chapter 2 for tips on this).

The Green Garden

Everyone wants a pleasing outdoor space—but it should complement, not destroy, the environment. Here are some ways to do that:

Lose the lawn. Watering lawns and gardens accounts for 50%–70% of home water use. Replace some of your grass with native plants to decrease your use. Native plants grow best without altering the natural conditions, so they'll thrive naturally on their own and help sustain native birds and wildlife.

Check out electric lawn mowers. They're quiet, cost less than some gas mowers, and don't use much energy. To avoid losing water to evaporation, water your lawn early in the morning and keep the grass three to four inches long. Finally, avoid using chemical pesticides; choose those made from natural sources like plants and minerals, as discussed on www.organicgardening.com (enter "lawn care" in the search box).

Plant trees. Trees can add beauty and color to your landscape, but they serve other important functions: They shade your home, reducing the temperature in warm spring and summer months; they produce oxygen; and they give songbirds a home. Deciduous trees will drop their leaves in the fall, too—letting sunlight in and potentially lowering the heating bill. Visit the Arbor Day Foundation's website at www.arborday .org—a $10 annual membership gets you ten free trees.

Skip the outdoor fireplace. To add ambience, choose a well-placed water feature instead. If the water feature catches prevailing winds, it can cool things off. On the other hand, an outdoor fireplace uses natural resources and reduces air quality by releasing soot.

Ignore the Map: Ask for Directions

Every gardener is familiar with the multicolor U.S. map of climate zones on the back of seed packets. It's the Department of Agriculture's indicator of whether a flower, bush, or tree will survive the winters in a given region.

It's also 18 years old. A growing number of meteorologists and horticulturists say that because of the warming climate, the 1990 map doesn't reflect a trend that home gardeners have noticed for more than a decade: a gradual shift northward of growing zones for many plants.

The map doesn't show, for example, that the Southern magnolia, once limited largely to growing zones ranging from Florida to Virginia, now can thrive as far north as Pennsylvania. Or that kiwis, long hardy only as far north as Oklahoma, now might give fruit in St. Louis.

USDA officials reject suggestions that the agency's resistance to changing the 1990 map reflects a reluctance to acknowledge the potential impact of climate change. They say the agency wants its next map to reflect a 30-year period that gives a fuller picture of the world's climate.

The recent pace of climate change—the U.N. Intergovernmental Panel on Climate Change says 11 of the 12 warmest years since 1850 came between 1995 and 2006—means gardeners must be more flexible, says Kelly Redmond, climatologist with the Desert Research Institute in Reno.

"We could be heading into a time where the temperature is always above 'normal,'" he says. "If a plant has a short lifetime, what are the odds of that plant being killed by a climate event? If it's a tree or something that you want to live longer, you're probably a little more conservative (in choosing your plants) because even if the (climate) zones are slowly migrating, that doesn't mean there won't be cold spells."

So what's a gardener supposed to do in the meantime?

Ignore the Map: Ask for Directions, continued

Sometimes, says the National Arboretum's Scott Aker, the best thing to do is talk to someone who's really down in your local dirt. Nurseries and public gardens are good resources, he says.

Aker says your neighbors can be a big help, too.

"Nobody is more familiar with soil and weather conditions in your yard than the person down the street with the beautiful garden," he says, "because usually what went into making that garden was a lot of mistakes and dead plants."

 "Warming climate makes gardeners' map out-of-date," by Elizabeth Weise, April 24, 2008.

Use a gas or propane grill. Charcoal grilling gives off more carbon monoxide, particulates, and soot than other barbeque methods. Consider using lump charcoal (made from wood) certified by Rainforest Alliance's Smart-Wood program instead of briquettes (made from scraps and sawdust from lumber mills, possibly with some coal dust and other unhealthy additives thrown in). To get things going, try a chimney starter (around $15, and reusable) instead of lighter fluid, which releases toxins.

Collect rainwater. When it rains, clean water is wasted when it goes straight down the gutter. But you can purchase large rain barrels and have your gutters feed into them (make sure the barrel is covered, so as not to attract mosquitoes). Use the rainwater to water plants. For more information, check out www.rainbarrelguide.com.

Mulch. Keep moisture in the soil with a layer of organic material, such as bark. Mulch will keep down weeds, and keep the ground cool in hot summer months. (Just keep it away from your foundation, as discussed in Chapter 3.)

Compost. Instead of throwing organic materials in the trash, make a natural soil amendment by composting. You'll reduce waste and enrich and improve soil for little or no cost. Find out more at www.epa.gov/compost.

Grow your own fruits, herbs, and vegetables. What better way to avoid shipping costs and know what you're getting is healthy and fresh? And if you convert lawn to garden space, you'll help reduce water waste, too.

Eating Green

Some people advocate buying local products first, so as to save energy (food travels an average of 1,500 miles to reach your plate, much longer in some cases) and enjoy fresher produce. Plus, you'll get the opportunity to support local growers. Look for farmer's markets in your neighborhood, or ask at your local grocery store where products came from.

Favorite Local Farmer's Markets

For markets that include organic growers, who better to ask for directions than Alice Waters, chef, author, co-owner of Chez Panisse in Berkeley, California, and food visionary credited with spearheading the sustainable and organic food movement in the USA?

Portland Farmers Market, Portland. "Produce is the backbone of this market, but you'll also find buffalo, wild salmon, oysters, clams, and artisan cheeses," Waters says. 503-241-0032; www.portland farmersmarket.org.

Crescent City Farmers Market, New Orleans. This downtown market near the French Quarter has fresh shrimp and fish, along with a huge variety of flowers and produce. The prices are good, and there's often free entertainment, from string quartets to jazz singers. www. crescentcityfarmersmarket.org.

Green City Market, Chicago. This market near Lake Michigan in Lincoln Park is noteworthy because it's a whole-day event with shopping, chef demonstrations, and local vendors selling prepared food from products sold at the market. 847-424-2486; www.chicagogreencitymarket.org.

Favorite Local Farmer's Markets, continued

Union Square Greenmarket, New York. "The Greenmarket connects New Yorkers to the natural world and to the people who grow their food," Waters says. 212-788-7476; www.cenyc.org.

Santa Monica Farmers Market, Santa Monica. The local Persian population favors the green pistachios, Oaxacans like the fresh shell beans, and flavorful greens will satisfy every culinary taste. www.smgov.net/farmers_market.

Coconut Grove Organic Farmers Market, Coconut Grove. Blue and white tents and shady live oaks provide a canopy for this Miami-area market. There's a raw-food salad bar, plus 40 kinds of juices and creamy nut milks. 305-238-7747; www.glaserorganicfarms.com.

Santa Fe Farmers Market, Santa Fe. "This market is huge, with lots of local, organic produce. You'll find every kind of dried and fresh chili imaginable," Waters says. www.santafefarmersmarket.com.

City Farmers Market, Wooster Square, New Haven. " Food stamps are accepted here, as are WIC coupons, enabling low-income women and children access to wholesome food," Waters says. www.cityseed.org.

Dane County Farmers Market, Madison. Organic farming is widely supported in Wisconsin, a major agricultural producer, and it really wouldn't be Wisconsin without cheese. But that's not all. Pick up wild mushrooms, squash and Brussels sprouts, as well as any kind of steaks, emu, elk, ostrich, pheasant, duck, goose, pork, bison, venison, rabbit. 608-455-1999; www.dcfm.org.

Ferry Plaza Farmers Market, San Francisco. "This is the place I go on Saturdays to meet many of my friends, selling extraordinary jams, bread, and organic produce," Waters says. www.cuesa.org/markets.

 "10 great markets to cultivate organic farmers," by Kathy Baruffi, September 21, 2007.

You might also join a community supported agriculture (CSA) project. In a traditional CSA, you buy a share in a farm or group of farms, and reap the rewards in fresh produce. Some CSAs will even deliver to your home or office. This may be a chance to get creative with new vegetables (Jerusalem artichokes or cardoons, anyone?). For recipe ideas, go to www.epicurious.com and type in a list of ingredients. To find a CSA near you, visit the USDA's website at www.nal.usda.gov (search for "community supported agriculture").

Other foodies focus on the importance of eating organic. What exactly does that mean? According to the USDA, "Organic food is produced by farmers who emphasize the use of renewable resources and the conservation of soil and water to enhance environmental quality for future generations. Organic meat, poultry, eggs, and dairy products come from animals that are given no antibiotics or growth hormones. Organic food is produced without using most conventional pesticides; fertilizers made with synthetic ingredients or sewage sludge; bioengineering; or ionizing radiation." In short, organic food reduces your exposure to and the environmental harm of pesticides and other bad substances.

> **TIP**
>
> **Some organic food doesn't say "organic."** Because official USDA organic certification requires an extensive review process, some local farms may not go through it. One of the benefits of buying local is that you can go right to the source to ask how the food is grown or animals are raised.

The biggest reason that many people don't buy local and organic is the cost (although, as Barbara Kingsolver points out in *Animal, Vegetable, Miracle*, food is a small percentage of most U.S. household budgets). Still, if you can't stomach paying $5 a pound for organic eggplant, here are some other ways to eat wisely and responsibly:

- **Buy selectively organic.** It's hardest to get rid of pesticides on fruits and vegetables with thinner skins (such as apples, peaches, and bell peppers). Print out a handy list of the top offenders at www.foodnews.org/walletguide.

- **Shop the edges.** An easy way to avoid buying processed foods—which tend to have the most packaging and chemical additives and the least nutrients—is to avoid the center aisles in most grocery stores, since most "natural" foods like fruits and vegetables, dairy products, and meat are usually along the edges.

- **Make less frequent trips to the store.** Make a list so you buy everything you need for a week in one trip. Alternatively, ride your bike, walk, or stop at a store that's on your way home from work so you don't make a special trip.

- **Buy in bulk.** Many grocery or health food stores sell products like spices, grains, and pastas in bulk. Others even carry liquids like olive oil, soy sauce, or vinegar, allowing you to reuse old bottles. Both reduce waste and usually cost less. Even for packaged products, buying the largest item you'll use is best, to reduce the packaging-to-waste ratio.

- **Eat seasonally.** You'll more easily find regional produce if you buy what's in season. After all, pineapples aren't grown in the fall in Maine—they take a long plane ride to get there, losing nutrients along the way.

- **Buy just enough.** You'll save money and resources if you don't buy more than you need. Don't force yourself to buy seasonal organic chard if it's going to rot in your refrigerator.

- **Eat out less.** For the cost of a restaurant meal, you can take home some fabulous organic salad greens, mushrooms, pasta, sausage, and wine.

- **Buy a reusable water bottle.** In both creation and shipping, plastic water bottles generate a lot of waste, even if they're recycled (and only about 20% are). They may also leach harmful chemicals into the water—and the water may have come from a tap anyway! Buy a reusable bottle, ideally one made of stainless steel or aluminum, and a filter for your home faucet. While you're at it, get a reusable coffee mug. Coffee shops can fill it just as easily as a paper cup, and you may even get a discount.

- **Bring your own bags.** When shopping, your best option is to invest in a set of canvas bags you can use again and again (try your local thrift shop for these, too). Some grocery stores give a small credit, like five or ten cents, for bringing your own bags. If you forget them at home, be sure to reuse the new bags. And avoid smaller bags too, for vegetables or fruits you plan to wash anyway or that have an external skin you won't eat, or for an item you can easily take home in your purse or pocket.

- **Choose meats wisely.** Conventionally raised animals are often fed or injected with hormones and antibiotics, which you may not want to be ingesting either. Consider buying higher-quality meats (hormone and antibiotic free, raised humanely) from local suppliers. You can offset the cost by experimenting with occasional meat-free meals.

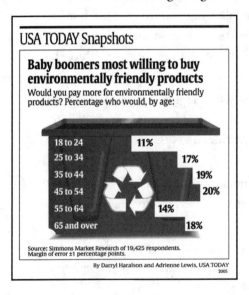

USA TODAY Snapshots

Baby boomers most willing to buy environmentally friendly products

Would you pay more for environmentally friendly products? Percentage who would, by age:

18 to 24	11%
25 to 34	17%
35 to 44	19%
45 to 54	20%
55 to 64	14%
65 and over	18%

Source: Simmons Market Research of 19,425 respondents. Margin of error ±1 percentage points.

By Darryl Haralson and Adrienne Lewis, USA TODAY
2005

Driving Green (Without a Hybrid)

Ask someone how drivers can help the environment, and they're likely to start by suggesting you buy a hybrid vehicle. But for most of us—especially after plunking down cash for a home—buying a new car isn't going to happen for a few years. In the meantime, here are some practical alternatives:

- **Walk!** The easiest way to ease the environmental impact of your car is to drive it less. Walking or riding a bike has great health benefits. While no one expects you to do this in the middle of a blizzard, do you have a good excuse if the store isn't far away and it's a beautiful, sunny day?

- **Use alternate transport.** Take the time to find alternative options —carpools, buses, trains—from your new home. Yes, they may take longer, but can you do some work while you're waiting or riding? You'll probably save money too. The IRS estimates it costs 50.5 cents per mile to operate a vehicle in 2008 (and with gas prices gone crazy, that's probably on the low side). If you can take a five-mile bus ride to work for $1 each way instead of driving, you'll help the environment and save yourself at least $3 a day. And as USA TODAY's Sandra Block advises, "If the price of gas has led you to join a car pool or to take the bus to work, talk with your auto insurer, because you may be eligible for a low-mileage discount."

- **Get rid of extra cars.** No one thinks of cars as "extra"—but many families have at least two. It's drastic, but even driving a hybrid isn't as environmentally friendly as not driving at all. When needed, take a cab or rent a car—you'll still be saving money overall.

- **Lighten your load.** Don't buy a bigger car than you need, don't fill it with things you aren't using, and don't leave storage or bike racks on when not in use. All these decrease your fuel economy.

- **Telecommute.** Saving the environment is a perfect excuse for finding out whether you can work at home instead of in your office. For advice on getting your boss to agree, see *The Work From Home Handbook*, by Diana Fitzpatrick and Stephen Fishman (Nolo and USA TODAY).

- **Avoid air.** Air conditioning isn't efficient, but neither is opening your windows, which causes drag and slows your car down. To keep things cool, try tinting your windows, parking in the shade, and getting a sunshade to reflect heat.

- **Inflate your tires.** You'll increase your gas mileage by about 3.3% if you have properly inflated tires.

- **Cruise.** Increase mileage by avoiding quick stops and starts. Don't drive at excessively high speeds.

- **Change the oil.** Or pay someone to do it—but make sure it gets done, because it will increase fuel efficiency (as will using the recommended oil weight). Make sure the used oil gets recycled. Stay on top of the air filter too: Replacing a clogged one can increase your efficiency by up to 10%.

- **Tune it up.** According to the EPA, you can increase gas mileage by an average of 4% by making sure your car is tuned up. (Most cars need a tune-up every two years or 30,000 miles.)

- **Drive through the car wash.** You'll use more water doing it at home, and you won't have any way to clean up the soap that will go pouring onto the lawn or into the storm drains (which often lead to places where fish swim).

Maintaining and Upgrading Responsibly

In Chapter 3, we showed you how to perform annual property maintenance to keep your property in top shape. As long as you're checking things out, think about your home's energy efficiency, safety, and environmental impact. Below are some ideas for basic upgrades. (If you're planning to do a major remodel, refer to Chapter 10.)

Before making any choices about what to do, get an energy audit. A professional will perform several tests and assess your current energy use. There are some up front costs—usually between $100 and $200—and your utility company may even offer these services or subsidize payment to an independent auditor. In any case, the audit may discover easily correctible problems like leaky doors and windows. Fixing these will reduce your home's energy consumption, saving you money in the long run. For more information, visit the Department of Energy's Energy Efficiency and Renewable Energy website (www.eere.energy.gov; type "energy audit" in the search box).

Revelations From an Energy Audit

In a time of environmental awareness, with its background hum of "green" advice emanating from everyone from Al Gore to the local utility company, it's not that easy to find a company that does full energy audits.

Just a few hundred firms in the USA do this in-depth, duct-testing, attic-scrambling, crawl-space-creeping work. The Environmental Protection Agency offers a way for consumers to find local auditors through its Home Performance with Energy Star program.

"We look a little like the Ghost Busters with all our weird buzzing, beeping equipment," says Matt Golden, president of Sustainable Spaces, a San Francisco based energy auditor.

Golden and two other staffers descended on the San Jose ranch house of Cliff and Monica Knudson. The couple and their two children live in a 1,300-square-foot, single-story home built in 1959. They've done a lot over the years to lower costs, from blowing insulation in the attic and walls to replacing windows, but their energy bill is still typically $450 a month, says Cliff, an engineer.

He and Golden went around the house plugging a Kill-A-Watt power meter into outlets and measuring how much electricity each appliance drew. Knudson was surprised to learn that the family's various cell phone and camera chargers draw as much energy when they don't have anything charging as when they do.

But the real eye-opener came when Golden crawled behind the family's home entertainment center and unplugged everything in it. Then he plugged it all back in through the wattage meter.

The total came to 800 watts when the family's plasma screen TV is turned on and a shocking 100 watts even when it isn't. The Comcast digital video recorder, TV, DVD and video players and sound system draw that much even when nothing is playing. "So you're paying $200 a year not to watch TV," Golden told Knudson.

Revelations From an Energy Audit, continued

In the kitchen, the ten recessed lights from the 1980s drew 650 watts of power when on. Changing them to compact fluorescent bulbs would save 25% of electricity costs, Golden said.

Up in the attic, staffer Pam Molsick was finding numerous problems. Unless insulation actually fits to the surface of the area it's supposed to be insulating, it doesn't really do anything, she said. As she clambered from one joist to the other in the stiflingly hot attic, she pointed out at least ten areas where the insulation was bunched up or had been shoved aside, making it ineffective.

Then Golden went to open the door from the kitchen into the garage, which had been carefully weather stripped.

"The key of weather stripping is when you have to give (the door) that extra little push. But most people hate having to do that. So most weather stripping doesn't do anything," he says. The Knudson's door failed the "extra little push test."

It may seem a minor problem, but those little items can add up when it comes to conservation.

Says Golden: "At the end of the day, if you're going to solve global warming, the vast majority is going to have to be efficiency."

USA TODAY usatoday.com "Homes get help to go green," by Elizabeth Weise, April 19, 2007.

Whether you're updating from the start or replacing current components after they've worn out, here are some changes with a positive environmental impact:

Switch to CFL light bulbs. Okay, you've heard this 200 times already. But seriously—compact fluorescent light bulbs have quite an impact. The EPA estimates that if every home in America replaced just one light bulb with a CFL bulb, the United States would save enough energy to light more than three million homes for a year and more than $600 million in annual energy costs. Yes, they cost a little more than regular bulbs (but last much longer and are cheaper in the long run) and no, they're not perfect (they don't tend to work well with dimmer switches, for example). But if you're replacing a light bulb anyway, there's little reason for not making such a simple change.

Get a tankless water heater. If you need to replace your water heater, consider a tankless one that heats water only as you need it. It usually costs about twice as much as a regular water heater, but it can lower your bills because you won't be heating water that sits around in a tank cooling off. The technology isn't yet perfect, however. Do your homework to make sure that the unit you choose will supply the amount of water you need for multiple uses like running the dishwasher and showering, at the speed that you'll need.

USA TODAY's 25th Anniversary Snapshots®

We salute the nation's generosity

One bright idea

Earth Day Network supports solutions for climate change. One is switching from inefficient incandescent bulbs to compact fluorescent lamps to cut energy use and greenhouse gas emissions.

	60-watt incandescent	Compact fluorescent lamp
Average life of bulb	875 hours[1]	8,000 hours[1]
Cost of energy	$48.38	$10.48

1 – hours of use
Source: The Earth Day Network (learn more at earthday.usatoday.com)

By Sam Ward, USA TODAY
2007

Insulate. There are many choices in modern insulation, but most can drastically increase the energy efficiency of your home by restricting the flow of heat, keeping cold air out in the winter, and warm air out in the summer. Some types of insulation, like cellulose fiber insulation, can be blown into available spaces like attics. Check the website of the Northern American Insulation Manufacturer's Association (www.naima.org) to learn whether your state, city, or local utility offers any rebate for adding insulation.

Windows and storm doors. Efficient windows can prevent heat from escaping in the winter and entering in the summer. Choose Energy Star windows or windows with low-E coatings, which typically cost 10% to 15% more than regular windows but save 30% to 50% of energy costs. For more information, go to www.energystar.gov and search for "windows."

Programmable thermostat. A programmable thermostat can help keep energy costs down by adjusting temperature according to the programming you set. So if you're at work all day, you can set the thermostat to turn down the heat or air conditioning during the day, then turn it back up in the evenings when you're at home. (A lower-tech alternative is to remember to turn your system off when you leave and at night.)

Install ceiling fans. Installing a ceiling fan can save up to 40% of summer cooling costs and 10% during the winter heating season. Warm air is drawn upward in the summer, pushed down in the winter. Curtains also help block out heat in the summer, and retain it in the winter.

Go solar. Okay, not everyone is ready to spend thousands of dollars to install solar panels—especially if this is your starter home, or you don't have the option (maybe because you're in a multiunit building). But if it's even a remote possibility, keep a few options in mind. One is a power purchase agreement (PPA), in which a solar company will install and maintain solar panels for you and you'll pay an up-front fee but won't buy the panels yourself. (These agreements aren't available everywhere.) Also, check with your city—some California cities are planning to fund home systems with tax-free bonds. Finally, don't give up on the idea, even if it means waiting for your next house. Solar panel prices are projected to drop 50% in a few years, so your timing may be perfect.

Choose alternate power. Contact your utility company to find out whether it offers any green power programs (around 750 U.S. utility companies do). For a small premium, you can buy power generated from renewable sources like wind and solar power. Find out about national programs at The Green Power Network (www.eere.energy.gov/greenpower).

Research rebates and other benefits. See Chapter 8 for certain tax benefits to going green. Also look into whether your local utilities offer special treatment, such as a rebate for buying Energy Star appliances or installing insulation. Start with the list at the Database of State Incentives for Renewable Energy's website (www.dsireusa.org).

Hey, Neighbors: Getting Acquainted and Resolving Disputes

Meet and Greet: Introducing Yourself to Neighbors_____93

Drawing the Line: Knowing Where Your Property Ends_____95

    Look at a map_____96

    Getting help from surveyors_____96

    Dealing with boundary issues_____97

    Getting or granting permission to use land_____97

    When neighbors can temporarily access your property___98

Other Basic Property Rights: Nuisances, Fences, Trees,
  Noise, and Pets_____99

    Laws against nuisance_____100

    Laws against excessive noise_____101

    Laws regarding fences_____102

    Laws regarding trees_____103

    Laws regarding views_____105

    Laws against blighted or trash-covered property_____106

    Laws regarding animals_____106

    Your rights in a planned community_____107

Getting Neighbor Buy-In on Your Remodel Plans_____108

Creating Peaceable Solutions to Neighbor Issues_____110

Welcome to the neighborhood! If you've been bouncing from rental to rental over the last few years, this may be your first opportunity to develop more than a passing relationship with the people who live near you. And, because you may be dealing with each other for quite a while, it's best to get things off on the right foot—you don't want neighbors to remember only that your moving truck noisily arrived at 6 a.m. the day you moved in, or that your dog barked incessantly for the first week.

USA TODAY Snapshots®

The grass is greener ...
Who would you say has the best lawn on your block?

A neighbor **64%**

Yourself **28%**

Don't know **3%**

Source: *Consumer Reports* National Research Center

By David Stuckey and Veronica Salazar, USA TODAY
2008

Implanting some happier memories will help you avoid neighbor disputes, which at their worst, lead to lawsuits and devaluation of your property. To that end, this chapter will address:

- getting to know your neighbors
- knowing your property boundaries
- understanding your basic rights and responsibilities as a landowner
- making sure remodeling plans work in your neighborhood, and
- preventing and dealing with common neighbor disputes.

RESOURCE

For more information on the topics in this chapter, see *Neighbor Law: Fences, Trees, Boundaries & Noise,* by Cora Jordan (Nolo). It also contains lists of relevant laws, and covers additional topics such as water rights and dealing with dangers to children.

Meet and Greet:
Introducing Yourself to Neighbors

It's hard to be the new kid in town—but making the rounds and introducing yourself to the neighbors can be surprisingly satisfying. Aside from its heartwarming aspects, developing good neighbor relations can save everyone time and money as you trade pet care, plant cuttings, and eggs, and get on the phone when you see smoke rising from each others' roofs. Here are some ideas for how to avoid social awkwardness.

- **Have a housewarming party.** While a housewarming party is a great way to thank the people who helped you find, purchase, and move into your home, it's also a good opportunity to get to know the neighbors.

- **Have a neighbors-only party.** A smaller gathering, like a weekend barbecue or a dessert evening, may create a more relaxed and intimate atmosphere.

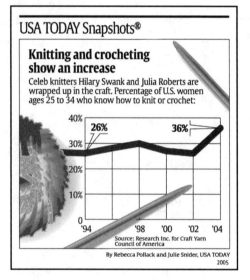

USA TODAY Snapshots®

Knitting and crocheting show an increase

Celeb knitters Hilary Swank and Julia Roberts are wrapped up in the craft. Percentage of U.S. women ages 25 to 34 who know how to knit or crochet:

26% 36%

'94 '98 '00 '02 '04

Source: Research Inc. for Craft Yarn Council of America

By Rebecca Pollack and Julie Snider, USA TODAY 2005

- **Knock on doors.** Don't wait for the neighbors to come to you! Bring cookies or another small gift, like a bar of handmade soap or a coupon for "one emergency cup of sugar or equivalent."

- **Look for community activities.** You may have just moved in, but you'll also want to get out sometimes. Whatever your interests (knitting, tennis, reading, cooking, or gardening), there's probably a local group that fits. Check out the local paper, ask your neighbors, search online, or visit the community center (if any).

Should You Regift Unwanted Housewarming Presents?

You're short on cash to buy holiday and other gifts, and you may have received some wild and wacky housewarming presents. What to do? According to USA TODAY's Olivia Barker, "Regifting—recycling new or (gasp!) used presents and passing them off as new—is a practice as old as, well, a brick of fruitcake."

For example, "Betsy Clarke stashes trivet sets and soap baskets on an emergency gift shelf, alongside the 'misguided gifts that were given to you by people who had their heart in the right place but possibly not their brain,' such as the hot-dog toaster she promptly regifted to a friend.

"The contents of the gift closet, though, 'should be tagged and tracked like wildlife on a nature show,' warns Clarke. She and her husband once received an electric ice-cream maker as a housewarming gift; tucked inside was a receipt from Macy's dated approximately the time of the gift-giver's wedding."

 "Sagging economy brings an upturn in recycled gifts," by Olivia Barker, December 14, 2001.

Also, if you have children, keep in mind that they may need additional help integrating. Here are a few ideas to help them adjust:

- **Volunteer at school.** You can participate by becoming a room parent, going on field trips, and generally helping out in the classroom (unless of course your kids are teens, who might prefer that you stay miles away).
- **Join a carpool, playgroup, or babysitting co-op.** If your kids' school isn't within walking distance, start or join a carpool with nearby parents. Playgroups and babysitting co-ops are also great ways to meet and get to know other families. Check out www.babycenter.com for ideas.

- **Have a kids' party.** Just because no one's having a birthday doesn't mean you can't have a party. Decorate the house, serve up some kiddie treats, and play a few games.

While it takes time to establish relationships in a new community, these tips should get you off on the right foot.

Drawing the Line: Knowing Where Your Property Ends

Not all properties are neat squares bordered by a white picket fence. And even white picket fences are sometimes in the wrong place. No wonder boundary disputes are such common sources of neighbor anxiety—and lawsuits.

Particularly if you're planning on doing any construction such as widening you driveway, erecting a play structure, or even planting a tree, you'll want to make sure not to encroach on your neighbor's property. Or if your neighbor is considering a similar move— hopefully your relationship will be such that you know about it before the construction team arrives—you may want to make sure it won't spill onto your side of the property line.

USA TODAY Snapshots®

Hot on the grill

Most popular foods for barbecuing:

Hamburgers 87%
Steak 83%
Chicken 78%
Hot dogs 76%

Source: Hearth, Patio & Barbecue Association

By David Stuckey and Karl Gelles, USA TODAY 2008

Even if the two of you agree that an encroachment in one direction or another is not a problem, a subsequent owner (of either property) might not. At very least, you'll want to make the encroachment official—more likely, you'll want to work together to avoid it.

Look at a map

As preparation for any future changes, it's worth taking a quick peek at a map showing your property lines. When you bought your home, you probably got title insurance. Included in your title report should be a handy little drawing called a plat map. This map shows your property's boundaries, location, and size, as created when the neighborhood or area was first subdivided. Find your plat map, walk outside, and see whether your property looks like the map. In particular, look for any inconsistencies between the map and what you see in person—perhaps fences in the wrong place, or a row of hedges you thought divided the property but is clearly on the neighbor's side. Also look for things that just don't make sense, such as your property narrowing toward the back when the plat lines show it as a perfect square.

Getting help from surveyors

The plat map does not, unfortunately, provide the last word on your property lines. (If the plat map is wrong, however, your title insurer should provide coverage.) If you're in contact with the seller, your first step after spotting a potential encroachment might be to call and ask for more information, as well as whether an official survey has been done in the past. And if the neighbors have been friendly so far, you might simply ask, "Can you help me figure out where the lines between our property are?"

If the truth remains muddy, however, you can hire a licensed land surveyor to create and record an official map. The surveyor will also place permanent markers on the property lines, for all to see. (Don't worry, the markers are ordinarily unobtrusive—metal pipes hammered into the ground with a labeled brass or plastic plug on top.) Local professional organizations, such as the California Land Surveyor's Association (www.californiasurveyors.org), can provide information on how to choose and work with a land surveyor. Expect to pay from $500 to $1,000 or more.

Dealing with boundary issues

What if your research confirms a problem—for example, your fence is a few feet over the neighbors' property line and you'd intended to build a pool there, or their tree is growing onto your side? Don't act rashly. You should be able to sort out such situations in a cooperative fashion. First, read the rest of this chapter for advice on your basic rights and dispute resolution tactics.

Getting or granting permission to use land

One of the easiest—and from a legal standpoint, most mutually protective—ways to deal with an encroachment is to make it official, with a written document granting permission. For example, your neighbor may be willing to grant you the right to use a little slice of his or her land to grow vegetables, especially if you've both been treating it as yours, anyway. You may need to pay something in return—after all, your use of part of the property will reduce the current owner's ability to use it, and thus diminish its value.

There are two reasons to get this in writing: The first is for the sake of subsequent owners, who'll want to know how much land they're actually paying and responsible for. The second is because such documents can create an end run around a troublesome area of neighbor law called "adverse possession." Adverse possession basically means that if someone trespasses on your property long enough—for example, builds a fence or garage over it—and fulfills other requirements (which depend on state law), that person can become the legal owner of the bit of property they're using. Usually, the encroacher's possession will have to be out in the open, over several years, without you or anyone else having used the property. But drafting a written permission agreement can help avoid adverse possession claims.

The document you draft should identify who owns the property in question and how the other neighbor is allowed to use it. Then both you and the neighbors (all owners) should sign it in front of a notary public. You should also file a notarized copy of the agreement with the recorder's office in the county where your property is located. See the sample below.

Agreement Granting Permission to Use Property

I, Haley Harding, owner of the property located at 354 Hill Drive, Detroit, Michigan, give my permission to Barry and Eloise Lafferty to plant and tend a garden located on a five-foot strip of my property bordering the west side of the property line. I reserve the right to revoke this permission at any time.

Haley Harding	April 7, 20xx
Haley Harding	Date
Barry Lafferty	April 7, 20xx
Barry Lafferty	Date
Eloise Lafferty	April 7, 20xx
Eloise Lafferty	Date

TIP

Concerned someone may have an adverse possession claim to your land? If a neighbor is using your property and refuses to quit, make sure to voice your objections with "No Trespassing" signs, a locked gate, and a firm letter. If that doesn't solve matters, see a lawyer.

When neighbors can temporarily access your property

Even with clear boundary lines, your neighbors—and others—may have limited rights to walk across, dig under, or otherwise access your property for a limited purpose. This right is called an "easement." Your title insurer should have mentioned any and all easements on your property. Some easements are held by utility companies, so that they can fix utility lines and the like. But it's possible for neighbors to have a private easement, most commonly when they need to use a path or piece of road to access their own property (this is commonly known as a "right of way").

If easement-related issues come up with your neighbors—for example, because you want to fence off an area of your property that would block the neighbor's access to his or her detached garage—check your title insurance to see whether your neighbor has an established right of use.

If that doesn't clarify matters but your neighbor has been using the property long enough, your neighbor may have a "prescriptive easement," allowing him or her to keep doing the same thing. The good news is, someone with a prescriptive easement isn't allowed to expand use of the property without your agreement, for example by paving over or widening the path being used. But it probably means you won't be able to alter the property in a way that interferes with the neighbor's use, either.

Which celebrity would you most like as a neighbor?

A 2007 survey by ERA Real Estate found that people would most prefer to live next door to Tiger Woods (24%), Regis Philbin (15%), or Teri Hatcher (8%).

However, if there's nothing official, you'll want to discuss alternate options with the neighbor. And if you can't reach agreement, you may need the help of a lawyer to establish your boundary rights, negotiate a new easement, or find a reasonable alternative.

Other Basic Property Rights: Nuisances, Fences, Trees, Noise, and Pets

Although being a good neighbor means a lot more than obeying the law, various state and local ordinances do affect your responsibilities to be a good neighbor (and your rights to expect others to do the same). If you both understand good etiquette and these basic legal concepts, you should be able to head off major problems.

Laws against nuisance

If one landowner's unreasonable action interferes with a neighbor's enjoyment of his or her property, the landowner has created what's called a "private nuisance." This might include, for example, a neighbor who starts every day by practicing the drums, one who throws the dog's tennis ball into your yard regularly, or children who make a game of ringing your doorbell. Even having to inhale secondhand smoke may constitute a nuisance if you're in a condominium or living particularly close to your neighbor.

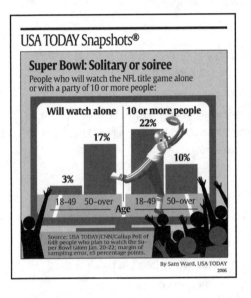

USA TODAY Snapshots®

Super Bowl: Solitary or soiree
People who will watch the NFL title game alone or with a party of 10 or more people:

Will watch alone
17% — 50-over
3% — 18-49

10 or more people
22% — 18-49
10% — 50-over

Age

Source: USA TODAY/CNN/Gallup Poll of 648 people who plan to watch the Super Bowl taken Jan. 20-22; margin of sampling error, ±5 percentage points.

By Sam Ward, USA TODAY
2006

One-time incidents don't qualify, nor do problems you haven't tried to resolve yourself first. The idea is that the person affected has asked the offender to stop the unreasonable behavior and was refused or ignored. To get rid of a nuisance, the offended party can sue and request that the behavior stop, or that the offender pay damages.

If you have any habits that could disturb your neighbors—loud music, frequent parties, or a particularly vocal pet—you can take a few steps to avoid being considered an official, legal nuisance. Start by making sure your behavior doesn't violate any laws, ordinances, or community association rules. If it doesn't, notify your neighbors ahead of time, whenever possible, that you'll be engaging in the behavior. For example, if you and your band need to practice in the garage once a week, talk to nearby neighbors and try to set up a convenient time. Thursday night may seem perfectly reasonable to you, but next door they may be pulling their hair out trying to get the baby to sleep.

Finally, if a neighbor complains to you, take the complaint seriously. Keep in mind that the same laws that protect you from a neighborhood nuisance apply to your neighbor, and be considerate.

What About Those Garage Sales?

USA TODAY's Haya El Nasser reports that some cities are so fed up with makeshift signs on utility poles and traffic clogging residential neighborhoods that they're cracking down on one of America's favorite warm-weather rituals: yard sales.

Many towns require permits and restrict signs along public roads, but the laws are not always enforced. Others have no regulations.

Concern is mounting because yard sales are proliferating, a byproduct of the popularity of websites such as eBay and increased interest in collecting everything from baseball cards to old toasters.

Some yard sales might as well be full-time businesses, says Bill Clark, a city councilman in Nitro, West Virginia, who's miffed at residents who have yard sales almost year-round.

"It creates, in general, an eyesore," he says.

 "As yard sales proliferate, so do traffic and clutter complaints," by Haya El Nasser, July 24, 2006.

Laws against excessive noise

No one is entitled to complete quiet at all times, but there are limits. In addition to private nuisance laws, almost every community has a noise ordinance prohibiting excessive, unreasonable, and unnecessary noise. These typically designate certain hours—for example, 10 p.m. to 8 a.m. weekdays and 11 p.m. to 10 a.m. weekends—as quiet times, when no one should

USA TODAY Snapshots

Americans snooze on the weekends

Number of hours adult Americans say they sleep on weekdays compared to the weekend:

Weekdays ■ Weekends

Less than 6	6-6.9	7-7.9	8 or more
16% / 10%	24% / 15%	31% / 24%	26% / 49%

Hours

Source: Poll of 1,506 adults conducted for the National Sleep Foundation

By Sam Ward, USA TODAY
2005

be making enough noise to wake others. Some towns also set decibel limits, and will measure noise levels if asked. And your state may have laws against disturbing the peace, or other more general but helpful restrictions. Some local ordinances also prohibit "rude, obscene, or insulting remarks" that could create a breach of the peace.

Laws regarding fences

Perhaps your property already has a fence, in which case you don't have to think about this section for a while. But if you're planning to build a fence, or if your fence is in disrepair, do some research before you build. City and local fence ordinances are often both strict and detailed. They're likely to cover, for example, where you can put your fence; how high it can be; what you build it with; whether it has to be set back from the street, sidewalk, or corner; and its overall appearance.

USA TODAY Snapshots

The roar of nature

When they emerge this spring, male cicadas will sing to attract females. Cicada chorusing compared with other noises when heard from nearby:

City traffic **80 decibels**   Cicadas **90 decibels**

Firecrackers **120 decibels**

Source: Oregon Hearing Research Center and USA TODAY research

By Charlotte E. Tucker and Bob Laird, USA TODAY 2004

Local laws may also forbid dangerous or dilapidated fences—for example, those with protruding rusty nails or likely to fall over. And many local laws forbid "spite fences," which serve no purpose except to annoy or inconvenience a neighbor.

If a fence will go right down your property line, you've got to talk to your neighbor about it. Unless you two agree otherwise, a fence on a boundary line is owned by both owners when both are using it. That makes a certain amount of sense, given that the alternative would be to build back-to-back fences. On the other hand, state's laws vary on what it means to "use" the fence—attach another fence to it so that it helps enclose the property? Plant crops right up to it? If you and your neighbor can't agree, you'll have to look up your state's fence law to find out.

If it will be a jointly owned and used boundary fence, most states' laws require both owners to pitch in on the building as well as maintenance costs. But that doesn't mean you can choose an elaborate fence out of the most expensive wood and demand 50% payment—see your state's law about that, too.

You've heard of a spite fence, but how about a spite house?

They exist. Examples include a seven-foot wide house in Alexandria Virginia's Old Town, built in 1830 to keep horse-drawn wagons and loiterers out of the alley next to a house; the Skinny House on Hull Street in Boston (ten feet wide, reportedly built to block a view); and a since-demolished five-foot-wide house on Lexington Avenue, New York, built in 1882 to block the light in a neighboring building due to a grudge against its owner.

> ! CAUTION
> **Be careful if building a fence that leaves some of your land on the neighbor's side.** The neighbor could eventually lay claim to the land. Create a written agreement setting out your intentions.

Laws regarding trees

Trees aren't concerned with whose property is whose. They will grow, drop leaves, and fall over according to the laws of nature, not property ownership. But plenty of laws and local ordinances have been written about trees. Here are the basic rules:

- **If a tree trunk is entirely on your land, the tree is yours.** If the trunk is straddling a property line, the tree's ownership is shared. If the trunk starts on one side of the line and grows across, who owns the tree depends on your state's laws.

- **If you own a tree (or other plant, such as shrubs, flowers, or crops), and someone damages it, they're liable.** That means, for example, that a neighbor who chops down your tree, stomps on your flowerbed, sprays chemicals that leach over and burn your plants, or prunes a tree or shrub in a way that seriously injures it, can be made to pay you money damages. One important exception would be if you've been neglecting to deal with a tree or shrub that presents a danger to others, so that your neighbor had no choice but to prune it or cut it down.

- **If your tree or other plant extends into the neighbors' yard, they have certain rights, too.** They can trim the branches or roots right back to the property line, so long as they don't injure the tree's health. Or they can ask you to do the trimming.

- **Trees may also be covered by broader land-use ordinances.** For example, those used as fences may have to comply with fence height restrictions, and those blocking neighbors' views may have to meet view requirements.

- **If you co-own a tree, you must cooperate.** For example, you'll need to share any costs of hiring someone to trim or maintain the whole tree, unless you both agree to trim your side up to the property line. You'll also be jointly responsible if the tree causes damage or injury. And neither of you can cut down or otherwise damage the tree without the other's permission.

- **The tree's owner also owns any fruit, nuts, or flowers it produces.** Even if your apple tree's branches hang over the neighbor's fence, the apples hanging from it are yours. But you might have to trespass to pick them, which means you'd best discuss the matter with your neighbor in advance—and perhaps come to a compromise in which you share the overhanging fruit. Once the apples have fallen on the ground, it's anyone's guess who owns them—the law on this matter is silent. All the more reason to rely on human interaction rather than dry legal principles.

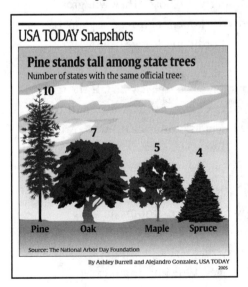

USA TODAY Snapshots

Pine stands tall among state trees
Number of states with the same official tree:

10 Pine
7 Oak
5 Maple
4 Spruce

Source: The National Arbor Day Foundation

By Ashley Burrell and Alejandro Gonzalez, USA TODAY
2005

When Holiday Lights Get Too Bright

As USA TODAY's Alan Gomez reports, even festive holiday lighting can give rise to disagreements among neighbors:

A Cincinnati-area man had to shut down his 25,000-light, computer-synchronized spectacle last December after traffic became so heavy that emergency responders couldn't reach the neighborhood. A week before Christmas, a Pittsburgh-area man took his lawyer to the Ross Township commission in a failed attempt to shut down an 80,000-watt display on his cul-de-sac.

Boston-area homeowner Dominic Luberto, who put up nearly 200,000 Christmas lights, says his first electricity bill was nearly ten times what he normally pays. The lights automatically go on at 3:30 p.m. each day and stay on until 1:30 a.m. They'll stay on 24 hours on Christmas Day.

"It's all for the kids," says Luberto, who has eight children, 16 grandchildren, and two great-grandchildren. "There's not one car with a kid in it that doesn't stop to look when they pass by. They love it."

USA TODAY "All is bright at Boston-area home," by Alan Gomez, November 27, 2006.

Laws regarding views

If your house is on a hillside or your condo on an upper floor, you may have paid a little extra to gain a beautiful view. But what happens if your neighbors across the street begin building upward, or their tree grows faster than you thought possible? You may rightly worry that your property value will decrease.

Unfortunately, it's rare for local laws to protect your right to a view. In most areas, you'll need to either find another applicable law that will block the construction, or if you live in a planned community, check the CC&Rs for applicable restrictions.

For example, in the absence of a view ordinance, you might claim that the neighbor's trees (particularly if they're planted in a row) constitute a fence, and violate fence-height laws. Other laws may regulate tree height and location in relation to an intersection or electric wires. Any new construction will be subject to zoning regulations, which tend to be complex. But you can call or visit the city's planning or zoning department to ask about guidelines for your neighborhood. It's even possible that your neighbor is trying to build without the appropriate permits.

And if it's your trees blocking the neighbors' view, consider it from their perspective. Especially if the height of the trees doesn't offer you anything more (like significant shade, or reduced noise pollution), it's probably not worth the neighbor's ire to refuse to trim them.

If you plan to do some major remodeling that will affect the neighbor's view, expect some (understandable) resistance. Even if the neighbor doesn't have a right to the view, he or she may fight to prevent the project on other grounds. For more information, see "Getting Neighbor Buy-In on Your Remodel Plans," later in this chapter.

Laws against blighted or trash-covered property

If property falls into such disrepair that it creates a danger to others or reduces the value of surrounding property, it may violate local ordinances. Some of these ordinances list items not allowed on the property, such as old cars, broken windows, and cracked driveways. Similarly, most towns prohibit high or noxious weeds, rubbish, and garbage on property. As we'll discuss below, many community associations also have limits and requirements for making a property presentable. Of course, you don't want be the neighbor who gets turned in for that kind of violation, so make sure your property doesn't turn into the neighborhood eyesore.

Laws regarding animals

If a dog barks a lot, runs around off leash, or poops on others' lawns, chances are there's a local ordinance that prohibits it. Other local laws may limit the number of certain animals allowed per household or prohibit particular animals (such as roosters and farm animals). Do your research before you bring new pets into your home.

Your rights in a planned community

If you live in a condominium, planned community, or other development subject to a community association, all the above rules apply to you and your neighbors—and more. Hopefully you carefully read the governing documents (often called "Covenants, Conditions, and Restrictions," or CC&Rs), when you bought your home. Read them again now. Though some may strike you as silly—for example, restrictions on paint color or the size of your pet—many homeowners' associations are mercilessly strict about enforcing them. Repainting your house would be absurdly expensive and giving up your new puppy heartbreaking, so it's best to plan ahead.

Approximately 39% percent of U.S. households own at least one dog, and 36% own at least one cat.

If your neighbor violates the CC&Rs in a way that impacts you negatively, and you're not able to resolve things informally, you can report it to your homeowners' association. Try not to get a reputation as a complainer early in your stay, however.

> **TIP**
>
> **Consider getting involved in your homeowners' association.** It's easy to complain about association decisions, but remember that they're largely being made by fellow homeowners who either join the board or attend open meetings. By joining in, you can directly affect issues that impact your life, like how your dues are spent or how the green space and common-use areas are maintained. Plus, you'll get to know your neighbors even better.

Typical CC&R Restrictions

If you live in a community governed by a homeowners' association, don't be surprised if you must follow community rules regarding the following (not an exhaustive list):

- shingles and exterior paint
- fences and hedges
- trees, lawns, and weeds
- pools
- swingsets and basketball hoops
- garages and sheds
- mailboxes
- clotheslines and garbage cans
- outdoor lights and TV antennas
- window coverings and wreaths
- home businesses
- pets (size or even acceptability), and
- noises and obstructions of views.

Getting Neighbor Buy-In on Your Remodel Plans

If you're considering a remodel that in any way affects your neighbors—blocks a view, removes a tree, makes noise, or anything else—better dust off your diplomacy hat. Secrecy is impossible, and angry neighbors have been known to try to delay construction or even have it torn down or moved after it's completed, regardless of whether the homeowner got all the appropriate permits.

Of course, the first issue is whether you will be getting all appropriate permits. A building permit is normally required whenever you're doing structural work, expanding or changing the basic living area of your home, or dealing with plumbing, electric, or heating. If you aren't sure whether you need a permit, call your city planning office—requirements vary significantly. While there's no denying that going through local bureaucracies to get these permits can be difficult, the fees can be high, and their decisions about what you can and can't do may seem arbitrary, having a permit makes it much easier to ward off challenges by the neighbors. We'll explain more about the permitting process in Chapter 10.

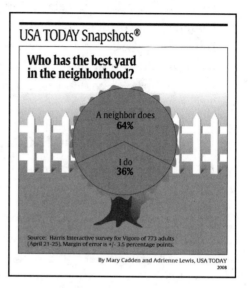

USA TODAY Snapshots®

Who has the best yard in the neighborhood?

A neighbor does
64%

I do
36%

Source: Harris Interactive survey for Vigoro of 773 adults (April 21-25). Margin of error is +/- 3.5 percentage points.

By Mary Cadden and Adrienne Lewis, USA TODAY
2008

Even assuming you have the appropriate permits, neighbors may still call city officials and complain about anything that they feel will negatively impact them. And the people in the permitting office may have a fair amount of discretion over your plans, for example in deciding whether the style you propose is consistent with the neighborhood, or in granting you a waiver or variance from the rules. At worst, they can block your plans—but more commonly, they'll just significantly delay the process. That's why it's best to open communications with your neighbors directly, before they call the city and make a fuss.

USA TODAY's Carol Jouzaitis describes how one house-owning couple avoided neighbor animosity: "Dana and Kent Petersen invited neighbors over for a cocktail party and showed them their architect's blueprints for a renovation that almost doubled to 5,600 square feet the size of the rambler they'd lived in for 11 years. When one neighbor objected to the idea of a curbside Porta potti for construction workers, the Petersens agreed to let crews use one of their bathrooms. 'Their house is bigger,' neighbor Ellen Myerberg says. 'But I'm glad they've stayed instead of moving. As our lives become so busy, there are things that are special, like watching your neighbors' kids grow up.'"

Many homeowners report that a face-to-face meeting with neighbors, plans in hand, is a good way to start the process. If the neighbors have concerns, you can work them out privately. And as explained below, community mediation services may be available to help you reach a compromise. Once the neighbors are comfortable with your plans, you might ask them to sign a short letter of agreement or support for your project, which you could include with your permit application.

Creating Peaceable Solutions to Neighbor Issues

Unfortunately, you don't usually get to pick your neighbors, which means there is little you can do to control one who acts unreasonably. Understanding the rules we've already explained will probably help you avoid a fair number of disputes, but you may still find that one neighbor insists there's no good time for you to run the lawn mower, or contends, right as the fruit ripens, that the peach tree that's clearly yours is really on the property line.

For most brewing disputes, here are the appropriate steps to take until a solution is reached (don't do them all at once!):

- **Research your rights.** Use this chapter and the resources mentioned here to find out homeowners' rights and local rules. State and local laws can often be found in local libraries and on the Internet, for example via www.statelocalgov.net or www.nolo.com (state laws only). Calling city planning or other staff can also yield helpful information.

- **Talk to fellow community members.** Others in the neighborhood may be affected by your neighbor's behavior. Find out the history and whether others might be willing to join in your efforts at change.

- **Keep a log.** If you're concerned with an ongoing activity, don't rely on your memory. Write down the date and a description of every relevant occurrence. This will help later if the neighbor denies your account of things, and in talking to the authorities or going to court.

Woo the Neighbors With These Chocolate-Filled Cookies:

The recipe below for Grandma Sylvia's Salt Butter Cookies was contributed by Sue Grapel, of Chappaqua, New York, to *America's Best Lost Recipes: 121 Kitchen-Tested Heirloom Recipes Too Good to Forget.* Like many recipes in the book, there's a story behind it: "When I was growing up, every time I saw my grandmother, she made these cookies for me. You knew when you walked into her house you were going to get something special."

Cookies

2 large egg yolks
1 teaspoon whiskey
2¼ cups all-purpose flour

1 teaspoon vanilla extract
⅔ cup granulated sugar
16 T (2 sticks) salted butter, softened

1. Adjust an oven rack to the middle position and heat the oven to 350 degrees. Line a baking sheet with parchment paper. Whisk the yolks, vanilla, and whiskey together in a measuring cup.

2. With an electric mixer at medium-high speed, beat butter and granulated sugar until fluffy, about 2 minutes. Reduce speed to medium, add yolk mixture and beat until combined. Add flour and beat until incorporated. Shape dough into ¾" balls and space balls 1" apart on baking sheet. Bake until lightly browned around the edges, 10 to 12 minutes. Cool on the baking sheet for 2 minutes, then transfer to a wire rack.

Filling

1 ounce unsweetened chocolate, chopped ¼ cup water
2 cups confectioners' sugar

1. Combine chocolate and water in a small saucepan and stir over low heat until smooth, about 5 minutes. Off the heat, whisk in confectioners' sugar until smooth.

2. Turn half of the cookies flat-side up, spread with about 1 tsp of filling. Top with another cookie. Let filling set until hardened, about 20 minutes. (Store in an airtight container up to 3 days.)

 "Old recipes bind families; And with this new cookbook, the proof is in the pudding," by Nanci Hellmich, October 10, 2007.

- **Approach your neighbor.** In a nonconfrontational way, of course. Allow for the very real possibility that your neighbors have no idea that the parrot squawks nonstop while no one's at home, or that the fence is leaning in your direction. Approaching matters as a joint concern (as in, "Can we talk about how best to keep your tree healthy without the branches draping over my garage?") is often most effective. Offering a compromise or to share in an expense may also defuse potentially angry reactions.

- **Write the neighbor a letter.** If talking isn't working—or you just don't feel you can comfortably start the conversation—a diplomatically worded letter can be very effective. It also becomes important evidence to show the authorities or a judge later. Explain the problem, enclose a copy of any relevant law or ordinance, and suggest a solution. If relations are already close to rock bottom, you might mention that if the matter isn't cured with a certain time, you will contact the authorities. Send the letter by certified mail with a return receipt requested so you can later prove it got there, and keep a copy for yourself.

- **Have an attorney write the neighbor a letter.** Whether you're defending your actions or asking for action from your neighbor, it's amazing what legal letterhead and independent verification of the applicable laws will do. This also shows you're serious about addressing the problem.

- **Contact the appropriate authorities.** Depending on the problem, the right place to call may be the local police (for example, if the neighbors are dealing drugs out of their house), zoning board, health department, or another entity. They probably get a lot of angry cranks calling them, so being ready with a copy of your log and complaint letter will help. In some cases (for example, cleaning up trash), the city will fix the problem and send a bill to your neighbor. In other cases, the authorities may simply order the neighbor to comply with the law or impose criminal penalties.

- **Suggest mediation.** This means asking the neighbor to sit down with you and a trained, neutral third party. Sometimes just a chance to be heard will help achieve a spirit of compromise.

The realization that this is the last step before going to court doesn't hurt, either. Many communities have free neighborhood mediation centers, which your local small claims court or police can direct you toward.

- **For damage that's already been committed, contact your home-owners' insurance company.** It may be willing to compensate you for your damaged property (for example, up to $500 for a tree your neighbor cut down) and turn around and sue your neighbor.

- **Sue your neighbor in small claims court.** The procedures are relatively easy, the cases are heard quickly, and you don't need a lawyer. The catch is that you must, in most cases, be seeking money damages (as opposed to an order to move the fence or trim the tree), and the damages cannot exceed a certain limit set by your state, usually between $2,000 and $10,000. For a chart of state-by-state limits, see the online Nolopedia at www.nolo.com (search for the article called "How Much Can I Sue for in Small Claims Court?"). For complete procedures, read *Everybody's Guide to Small Claims Court*, by Ralph Warner (Nolo).

- **Hire a lawyer and sue in state court.** Yes, it's time-consuming and expensive, but your peace of mind and the value of your property may be at stake. The court can order the neighbor to stop committing a nuisance or other illegal behavior, and award you money for any actual damages you've suffered plus your inconvenience.

> CAUTION
>
> **Don't take matters into your own hands.** Many frustrated neighbors have topped trees they thought were over the height limit, removed fences they thought were over the property line, or taken other self-help remedies they've lived to regret. If the court finds you were wrong, you could end up paying actual and punitive damages and facing jail time.

Keeping Up With Your Mortgage

It All Looks Like Fine Print! What's in Your Mortgage_____116

   Types of mortgages_____116

   Reviewing your mortgage_____119

Keeping Your Mortgage Costs Down_____123

   Make partial prepayments_____123

   Get rid of PMI_____126

   Stop paying taxes and insurance from an impound

     account_____127

Troubled Times: What to Do If You Can't Pay_____128

   Cut your expenses_____129

   Contact your lender_____130

   Make alternative payment arrangements_____134

   Sell the property yourself_____136

   Give the house to the lender_____137

   File for bankruptcy_____138

   Don't fall for a scam_____138

Getting a mortgage on your home was a big step, and probably a gigantic relief. But are the headlines about foreclosures making you nervous? Even if you're thinking, "That won't happen to me," it's worth taking another look at your mortgage documents, to avoid unwelcome surprises.

This chapter will help you:

- understand the mortgage you signed up for
- manage your mortgage, including deciding whether to prepay it, and
- take action if you have trouble making your payments.

It may be that, after reading this chapter, you decide the loan you originally chose isn't the best one for you after all. If so, the next chapter will explain how to refinance to a more appropriate loan.

It All Looks Like Fine Print! What's in Your Mortgage

No doubt you have a stack of loan documents stuffed away—that is, carefully filed—somewhere. Time to pull those out. Though they may have been a blur at the time, you'll want to read them carefully now, to fully understand the details.

Types of mortgages

You probably know whether you have a fixed or adjustable-rate mortgage, and what that means. But if you don't, don't be embarrassed. You had plenty of other things to think about when you bought your home. You likely have one of the following:

- **Fixed-rate mortgage.** If your interest rate was set when you got your loan and will never change, it's a fixed-rate mortgage. A 30-year term is normal, though you might instead have signed up for a 15- or 20-year term or even a 40-year term (which keeps your monthly payment low, but means you'll pay more interest over the years).

- **Adjustable-rate mortgage (ARM).** If your interest rate can fluctuate either now or in the future, you've got an ARM. Most ARMs start with low initial rates, but adjust monthly or yearly.

Homeowners Struggle to Keep Up With Adjustable Rates

For 45 years, Robert and Lorraine Brown have lived in their ranch-style home in Florissant, Missouri. One of their four children was even born there. But for the past eight months, the couple have been locked in a sleep-wrecking race to keep up with their rising mortgage bills. They've switched to cheaper phone service, cut back on groceries, and sometimes put off ordering medicine.

When they refinanced their home two years ago to pay off some bills, Robert was working as a deliveryman. But his employer went out of business last April. Now he and Lorraine, a retired nurse, are both seeking work. The rate on their mortgage has jumped from 7% to 10.5%.

"We were having a hard time meeting bills at the time we refinanced. It seems once you get behind, you do desperate things to catch up, and you never do," says Lorraine, trying to hold back tears.

They feel alone, but they're not. America's five-year real estate boom was fueled partly by a tempting array of cut-rate mortgages that helped millions of Americans qualify for home or refinance loans. To afford soaring home prices, many turned to adjustable-rate and other, riskier loans with low initial payments.

Now, the real estate market is cooling, interest rates are rising, and tens of thousands more Americans are starting to have trouble paying their mortgages.

 "Some homeowners struggle to keep up with adjustable rates," by Noelle Knox, April 3, 2006.

- **Balloon loan.** With a balloon loan, your interest rate probably started below the market rate on a 30-year fixed-rate mortgage and your monthly payments are calculated as if you will pay off the loan over 30 years. (The technical way to say this is that the loan is amortized over a 30-year period.) While this keeps payments low, you won't actually have 30 years to make payments. After a set period of time, usually between three and ten years, your entire loan balance will become due and you'll have to either pay off the loan, refinance, or sell.

- **Interest-only loan.** This is probably an ARM, set up so that you initially pay only interest and have low monthly payments. But you don't build equity by reducing principal until a set date (years later), when your payments increase to include principal.

- **Option loan.** Also a type of ARM, an option loan lets you decide what amount to pay monthly. Your choices are an accelerated payment that will help you pay off the loan early, a regularly amortized payment of principal plus interest (adjusted monthly), an interest-only payment, or a minimum payment that would cover the initial interest payment if the interest rate were fixed. If the interest rate has adjusted upward, that last option may not cover the interest that accrues in that month. The unpaid interest is added to the loan principal, and you end up further in the hole than when you started (called "negative amortization"). If you've got an option loan, avoid trouble by paying the accelerated or principal-plus-interest payment.

- **Hybrid loan.** This combines features of fixed-rate and adjustable-rate mortgages. For a set period of time (probably three, five, seven, or ten years), you pay interest at a fixed rate, most likely below the rate on a fixed-rate mortgage. After that, the rate becomes adjustable and changes every six months or one year. If you're planning on moving within the fixed-rate period, your hybrid ARM will give you stability without the relatively high interest that you'd pay for a regular 30-year fixed-rate mortgage. However, if you stay in your home after the expiration of the fixed term, your interest rate may go up significantly, and you may have to refinance.

- **Two-step loan.** This is essentially a hybrid loan with only one adjustment. For a while—most likely either five or seven years—the loan has a fixed rate, probably starting below that of a fixed-rate mortgage. Then the rate adjusts to a newer fixed rate, based on the index at the time of the adjustment plus a margin. You're betting that if the rate goes up, you'll be able to afford the correspondingly higher monthly payments or can refinance.

Reviewing your mortgage

Now that you know what type of mortgage you have, take a closer look at the details. This will help you think strategically. For example, to get the most from your mortgage, you may want to send in regular prepayments (to lower the total interest owed, as discussed in the next section), refinance (as discussed in Chapter 7), or simply stick to the original payment plan. Here's what to figure out before you make such decisions.

- **Interest rate.** Your interest rate is probably the most important piece of information—it tells you how you're paying the bank for the privilege of borrowing.
- **Prepayment penalties.** Check whether there's any penalty for paying your loan off early. If so, figure out how much it is. It might make the cost of making any prepayment prohibitive, thus locking you in.
- **Loan payoff.** Make sure you know when you'll pay off the loan completely, and whether you'll face any big changes in the amount you pay—for example, because you'll have to make a balloon payment, or your interest rate will adjust—before that happens.
- **Impound account.** Your lender may have required you to set up and make monthly payments to this account, to cover property taxes and insurance. Further below, we'll discuss whether you can and should get rid of the impound account.

Mortgages at a Glance	
Type of Mortgage	Description
Fixed rate	You repay at an unchanging interest rate, with identical monthly payments for the full term, usually 30 years.
Adjustable rate (ARM)	Monthly payments go up and down depending on certain market indexes, the lender's profit margin, and any built-in caps.
Balloon loan	Starts out at a fixed rate for a limited time period, after which you owe the entire loan balance.
Interest-only loan	You start out paying back only what you owe in interest, usually at an adjustable rate, for a fixed time; after that, you begin repaying principal as well, either as a lump sum or spread out.
Option loan	An ARM that gives you several choices of how much to pay each month, the lowest being a partial-interest payment.
Hybrid loan	Starts out at a fixed rate, then switches to an adjustable rate after a certain number of years.
Two-step loan	Starts at one fixed rate, then after a certain number of years, switches to another, market-determined fixed rate.

- PMI. If you didn't put 20% down, you probably pay private mortgage insurance, or PMI, to protect your lender if you don't make your loan payments. (Or you may have avoided it by financing two mortgages, perhaps a primary mortgage for 80% and a second, very likely a home equity loan, for up to 20%.) As we'll explain below, when you have more equity, you can eliminate this insurance.

Pros	Cons
Predictability, ability to lock in a low rate (if you get in at the right time).	Interest rate usually starts out higher than an ARM's, and won't go down if market rates do.
Rates start out relatively low. If market rates remain low, so does yours.	Unpredictability. Caps still allow for significant rises in interest rate and monthly payments.
Predictability; starting rate usually very low.	Problems if you can't pay off that remaining chunk of the loan balance when the time comes.
Initial monthly payments very low.	Later monthly payments very high! And even the initial payments can vary, if it's an ARM. Also, during the interest-only period, you haven't reduced what you owe at all.
Flexibility and very low monthly payment choices, especially useful if your income varies.	Paying the lowest amount can lead to deeper debt as you start paying interest on the unpaid interest.
Starting rate lower than regular fixed-rate mortgages. Useful if you know you'll sell the home before the loan converts.	Unpredictability after the loan turns into an ARM.
Starting rate lower than regular fixed-rate mortgages. Useful for people who know they'll sell their home before the new rate kicks in.	Unpredictability of second fixed rate.

- **Payment due date.** Make sure you know when and where to make your mortgage payment. And read correspondence from your lender closely—often, lenders sell loans on the secondary mortgage market, sometimes almost immediately after the house is sold. That could mean you send your payment to a different address.

- **Late fees.** Pay close attention to any late fees you'll owe if you don't make your mortgage payments on time. These usually kick in 15 days after the mortgage payment is due.

Got an adjustable-rate mortgage? Your monthly mortgage payment could change quickly and dramatically, and you need to know by how much. Pay attention to these additional terms:

- **Index.** This is a market-sensitive interest rate that the lender uses to adjust your rate. Hopefully, your ARM is based on one of the more stable indexes, like the 11th Federal Home Loan Bank District Cost of Funds (COFI), U.S. Treasury Bills, or Certificates of Deposit (CDs), rather than a volatile index like the London Interbank Offered Rate (LIBOR).

- **Margin.** The margin is the amount of additional interest the lender charges you over the index to make a profit. The margin should be 2%–3%.

- **Adjustment period.** This is how often your interest rate can adjust, such as monthly, every six months, or yearly. A less-frequent adjustment period provides a more stable payment.

- **Life-of-the-loan cap.** This is the absolute maximum interest rate you'll pay, regardless of how high the index rises. It shouldn't be more than 6% higher than your starting rate.

- **Periodic cap.** This is the maximum amount your interest rate can change at any adjustment period. Ideally, this will be low—2% is common.

> **CAUTION**
>
> **How high could it go?** You should now be able to figure out the maximum payment you'd make if your loan adjusted to the maximum interest rate, using an online calculator like the one called "How much will my adjustable rate mortgage payments be?" at www.nolo.com/calculators. If you can't afford that payment when it could come due, consider refinancing to a more predictable mortgage, as discussed in Chapter 7.

Keeping Your Mortgage Costs Down

If you've discovered some unpleasant truths about your mortgage, don't rush out and refinance just yet. The costs might not be worth it, especially if you'd owe prepayment penalties. First, consider these other ways to reduce the flow of cash to your mortgage lender.

Make partial prepayments

If you have extra cash—maybe because you're making more money than when you first bought your house—paying more of the principal you owe can shave thousands off the interest you'll pay in the long term. This is particularly true if you prepay in the early years, when your scheduled payments are probably made up of far more interest than principal.

For example, if you have a $300,000 mortgage at 5.5% on a 30-year, fixed-rate mortgage, and you make the minimum payment, you'll pay about $313,000 in interest over the life of the loan. But by paying just $100 extra each month, you'll pay the loan off almost four years earlier and spend only about $267,000 on interest. To run these numbers for your own mortgage, go to www.nolo.com/calculator and click "How much will I save by increasing my mortgage payment?"

USA TODAY Snapshots®

Staying on track

Which is more challenging to stick to?

55%

A diet

45%

A budget

Source: Kelton Research for Medifast. Jan. 25-29 survey of 1,000 adults ages 18 and over; margin of error is ±3 percentage points.

By Cindy Clark and Julie Snider, USA TODAY 2006

Prepaying your mortgage also gives you future freedom. With a shorter mortgage term, you'll know that you can remain in your home for the ensuing years with no threat of losing it to a bank. And we're sure you have plenty of ideas for spending the money that will no longer be going toward mortgage payments!

So what's the downside? Money spent prepaying your mortgage can't be invested or spent on other things now. For example, if you know you want to remodel your kitchen in a few years, and would have to borrow money and pay interest to do so, it might make more sense to save and invest the money you'd otherwise spend on prepayments.

Also, you'll need to balance your retirement goals against prepaying your mortgage. First off, if your employer matches contributions to a 401(k), you don't want to turn away that free money. Also, take into account what you might earn by investing the money. The earlier you start saving, the more your money will grow by the time you're retired, thanks in part to the power of compound interest: As you earn money on your investment, that cash is reinvested, earning interest on interest.

For example, if you start saving $500 per month at age 30 and earn about 8% on your investments, then retire at 62, you'll have almost $840,000. On the other hand, if you don't start saving that amount until age 40, you'll have only about $347,000 by retirement. Talk to a financial adviser for a complete analysis.

TIP

Who's the best candidate to prepay a mortgage? As Greg McBride, financial analyst for Bankrate.com, told USA TODAY's Sandra Block, people who don't deduct mortgage interest from their taxes (perhaps because the amount is too low to exceed the standard deduction) and those who can avoid PMI by paying down their mortgages early will benefit the most.

Financial Priorities Before Paying Off Your Mortgage Early

There are other ways to invest your extra cash that will provide even more security than a paid-off mortgage, says Keith Gumbinger, vice president of mortgage tracker HSH Associates. Some examples:

- **Your retirement.** Before you put extra money toward your mortgage, make sure you've taken full advantage of tax-advantaged retirement savings plans, such as your 401(k) and an individual retirement account. Owning your own home won't provide much retirement security if you can't afford to buy groceries.

- **Insurance.** If you have dependents, you need life insurance. Make sure your policy provides enough money to cover your family's mortgage, living expenses, and education costs. Disability insurance, while more expensive, is also a good idea. Your family will be protected if you're unable to work for a long period of time.

- **An emergency fund.** Most financial advisers believe you should have enough in savings to cover your expenses for six months to a year.

And you shouldn't even think about prepaying your mortgage if you have other high-cost debts. Credit card interest rates are more than twice that of most home mortgages. Extra cash should go toward paying off the balance.

 "Who should pay off their mortgage early—and how to do it," by Sandra Block, February 26, 2002.

If you have two mortgages, you'll probably want to prepay the one with the higher interest rate. For most people, that's the second mortgage. (The higher interest compensates the second mortgagor for the fact that, if you default, it may get shortchanged, since it will get paid only what's left after the first mortgagor collects.)

Get rid of PMI

If you're paying monthly private mortgage insurance (PMI) premiums as part of your mortgage payment, you've got good reason to want this obligation to go away: PMI doesn't benefit you directly. Its purpose is to pay the lender if you default on your mortgage payments at a time when your house isn't worth enough to entirely repay the lender through a foreclosure sale.

The real question now is whether the lender still needs PMI protection. If the equity in your house has already gone up to 20% or more because you've paid down the mortgage, or the market value of the house has gone up, or some of both, the lender really doesn't need PMI anymore. As soon as you suspect you have that 20% equity, try to get your PMI cancelled.

Under the federal "Homeowners' Protection Act," you can ask that your PMI be canceled when you've paid down your mortgage to 80%, and the lender must automatically cancel your PMI when you've hit 78%.

It's possible, however, you'll hit that 20% in part because your property has appreciated. Such value-based rises in equity can be hard to prove to your lender, and some lenders require you to wait a minimum time (around two years) before they will approve cancellation of PMI on this basis. Others may require you to have the home appraised, which can cost around $300–$400.

The exact procedures for canceling PMI are largely in the hands of your lender—or, more accurately, in the hands of the company from whom your lender buys the insurance (though you'll never deal with that company directly). Start by writing a letter to your lender formally requesting guidelines. The response will probably advise you to:

- **Get your home appraised by a professional.** Your lender may require an appraisal even if you're asking for a cancellation based on your many payments, as reassurance that the home hasn't declined in value. Although you'll normally pay the appraiser's bill, it's best to use one whom your lender recommends and whose findings the lender will therefore respect. (Note: Your tax assessment may show an entirely different value from the appraiser's—don't be concerned, tax assessments often lag behind, and the tax assessor won't see the appraiser's report, thank goodness.)

- **Calculate your "loan to value" (LTV) ratio using the results of the appraisal.** This is a simple calculation—just divide your loan amount by your home's value, to get a figure that should be in decimal points. If, for example, your loan is $200,000 and your home is appraised at $250,000, your LTV ratio is 0.8, or 80%, and your equity is 20%.

- **Compare your "loan to value" (LTV) ratio to that required by the lender.** Most lenders require that your LTV ratio be 80% or lower before they will cancel your PMI. If the loan to value ratio is at the percentage required by your lender, follow the lender's stated procedures for requesting a PMI cancellation.

USA TODAY Snapshots®

The check's in the mail

The order in which Americans pay bills when they are late:

Mortgage/rent **79%**
Car payment **41%**
Auto insurance **39%**
Credit card/cellphone **38%**
Cable/satellite television **32%**

Source: Survey of 1,000 consumers for AmeriCredit for Market Facts

By Darryl Haralson and Frank Pompa, USA TODAY 2004

If your lender refuses, or is slow to act on your PMI cancellation request, write polite but firm letters requesting action. Such letters are important not only to prod the lender, but to serve as evidence if you're later forced to take the lender to court. Small claims court can be a good avenue, and you won't need a lawyer to accompany you. For more information, including how to write polite but forceful demand letters, see *Everybody's Guide to Small Claims Court*, by Ralph Warner (Nolo).

Stop paying taxes and insurance from an impound account

If you purchased your house with less than 20% down, your lender probably requires you to add a little extra to your monthly payment, which it will save up and use to pay your tax and insurance bills. These bills are typically large lump sums due near the beginning of the new year—and the lender doesn't want to risk you coming up short. It stores the cash in what's called an escrow impound account.

Until the tax and insurance bills come due, your money is in the lender's hands to invest. Unless you're in a state that requires lenders to pay interest on impound accounts—such as California—you'll never see a penny of the return. If that's making you feel righteously indignant, you could call your lender and try to renegotiate. But first:

- **Check your loan documents.** Most lenders won't allow you to cancel the impound-account arrangement. The ones that do tend to charge a hefty fee, usually several hundred dollars.

- **Consider whether you can offset any fee by investing the money.** If you know that you'd just spend the money throughout the year, then scramble to make a last-minute payment, there's no point in paying the extra now. The same is true if you know you plan to sell or refinance soon. (If you refinance and have sufficient equity, you can elect not to set up an impound account, but may have to pay a small, one-time fee, such as ¼ of a point, to get out of it.) On the other hand, if you plan to keep your current mortgage for awhile, and are disciplined enough to prudently invest the cash throughout the year, you may want to pay the fee and take control of your money.

Troubled Times: What to Do If You Can't Pay

No one wants to think about the prospect of being unable to make a mortgage payment. Unfortunately, the unexpected—the loss of a job, or an unforeseen illness—can make this a reality. Rather than closing your eyes and letting your bank lead you down the path to foreclosure, realize that there are steps you can take, even after missing a payment, to prevent this. Here's what to do if trouble hits.

Is Foreclosure Starting to Sound Good?

After a long fight to stay afloat, foreclosure can start to look like a welcome relief. No longer would you be saddled with a heavy debt or a depreciating asset. And with recent troubles in the mortgage market, foreclosure is losing its moral stigma.

But here are some reasons to keep up your payment efforts. If you allow the lender to foreclose:

- You won't recover any of the money you may have put into the property.
- The lender may be able to go after you for the difference between what you owe and what the foreclosure sale brings in (and charge you for foreclosure expenses). As a practical matter, the lender may decide to give up on getting any more cash out of you, but the risk is still there.
- Your credit rating will suffer. As David Jones, president of the Association of Independent Consumer Credit Counseling Agencies told USA TODAY's Sandra Block, foreclosure will wreck your credit report for years, making it impossible—or at least extremely expensive—to buy another home.
- By the time your credit rating recovers from the foreclosure, home values may have risen again. You could have trouble reentering the market, and won't have the benefit of the equity from the property you lost.

Cut your expenses

Take stock of where your cash is going, and eliminate all nonnecessary expenses. Most people, no matter how stretched, can either cut back on or put off some of their usual expenditures. Perhaps you can live a few months without a haircut, housekeeping, cable television, or your gym membership.

Then, think about what you absolutely need: food and utilities, and possibly a car to get to work or expenses for child care while you're there. You may be able to reduce spending in these areas—for example, by limiting your food purchases to strictly necessary items, carpooling, or finding cheaper car insurance. Of course, you won't be able to eliminate these necessities altogether. Figure out the absolute minimum you can get by on, and compare that to how much cash you have available.

USA TODAY Snapshots®

Spending habits women find hardest to break

Eating out or getting takeout — 49%
Shopping for clothes — 28%
Daily coffee fix — 17%
Personal beauty products — 14%

Note: Respondents could select multiple answers.
Source: Harris Interactive QuickQuery of 1,202 women, Nov. 21-23. Margin of error ±4 percentage points.
By Mary Cadden and Julie Snider, USA TODAY 2006

If you're still coming up short, you may need to put off paying other obligations like credit card or car payments. Though you'll eventually have to face the consequences, they won't be as harsh as not paying your mortgage. Your house is probably your biggest asset and the one most likely to appreciate in the future, so don't risk losing it.

If you're still spending more than you have coming in, you may need to seek help from your lender, as described below.

Contact your lender

If you've got no choice but to miss a mortgage payment, contact your lender, preferably before the due date. (As a practical matter, you may have to contact the servicer—the company that handles your payments and issues your statements.) Your purpose is to explain why you can't make your payments and to talk about what relief the lender may be able to offer. We'll talk about the most likely forms of relief in the next subsection.

It's best to make your first contact by phone, for the sake of speed. If you're 15 days late on your payment, you'll probably be charged a late fee. Once you're 30 days late, the lender may report it to the credit bureaus, thus lowering your credit score. By the time you've missed two mortgage payments, your credit will likely be so severely damaged that you wouldn't qualify for another loan if you tried. In fact, your own lender may not accept any further payment until you make up all the ones you've missed.

Within just three to four months, the lender can file a Notice of Default (legal notice in the public record that says you've defaulted on the loan) and begin foreclosure proceedings. In the meantime, you'll be accruing more debt in the form of late and penalty fees, and if you get to foreclosure proceedings, you could be stuck with fees for those, too.

Despite their apparent heavy-handedness, lenders don't like to foreclose. It's a time-consuming process that often leaves them with a property they don't want that requires paying lawyers and other professionals to handle. It's particularly unappealing if the homeowner doesn't have a lot of equity, because then the foreclosure sale may bring in less than the amount of the outstanding loan. The upshot is that your lender should be highly motivated to work out a payment arrangement with you.

> **TIP**
>
> **See whether your lender offers a "freeze."** Under a 2008 initiative called "Project Lifeline," six major lenders (Bank of America, JPMorgan Chase, Citigroup, Countrywide, Washington Mutual, and Wells Fargo) will postpone foreclosure for 30 days if a borrower is late on mortgage payments by 90 days. That creates time to work out a repayment plan.

That said, there is no guarantee that the people you'll deal with will be courteous or pleasant. They may barrage you with personal questions about your financial situation and ask why you aren't able to make your payments. They'll need to know whether you're working and how much you're making, what other loans you have against the property, and how you spend your money. You may have to provide documentation, like pay stubs, to back up your assertions.

They may also expect you to raid every possible source of income before coming to them for help. If you want to protect other assets —like your child's college savings account or your retirement accounts —expect a fight, and anticipate that the lender will at the very least require you to stop making contributions to these accounts before agreeing to help you.

Get the name of the person or people you speak with, and if you agree to anything, follow up with a confirming letter. The letter will also show that you're proactively trying to manage the problem. It probably goes without saying that you should respond to your lender whenever you're contacted, too.

If you aren't comfortable talking to your lender, get in touch—quickly—with a housing counselor approved by the Department of Housing and Urban Development (HUD). Such counselors usually charge little or nothing and can help you review your financial situation and contact the lender, plus give you more information on financial, legal, or other services and programs. To find a list of HUD-approved counseling agencies, visit the HUD website at www.hud.gov or call them at 800-569-4287.

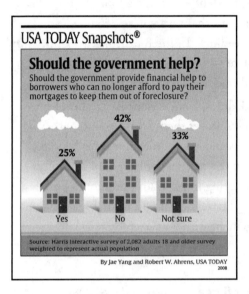

USA TODAY Snapshots®

Should the government help?

Should the government provide financial help to borrowers who can no longer afford to pay their mortgages to keep them out of foreclosure?

42% Yes 25% No 33% Not sure

Source: Harris Interactive survey of 2,082 adults 18 and older survey weighted to represent actual population

By Jae Yang and Robert W. Ahrens, USA TODAY 2008

Help for Mortgage Holders in Trouble

With foreclosures reaching record highs, the federal government has implemented several programs to assist struggling homeowners. These include:

Help for those with adjustable-rate mortgages. Many borrowers with adjustable-rate mortgages are subject to a rude awakening when their interest rates reset, often increasing payments by hundreds or even thousands of dollars. To help those borrowers who may not qualify for a traditional refinance mortgage, the federal government has developed a government-backed refinance loan called FHASecure. If you have an adjustable-rate mortgage that resets between June 2005 and December 2009 and at least 3% cash or equity in your home, you may be eligible for FHASecure.

Borrowers must have a history of good credit and on-time payments prior to the interest rate reset. Cash-out refinances aren't permitted, but homeowners can roll up to six months' delinquent mortgage payments into the overall loan amount, as well as back taxes and insurance. For more information on FHASecure loans, visit the website for the Department of Housing and Urban Development (HUD) at www.hud.gov (search for "FHASecure").

Help for borrowers who can't afford their mortgages. Borrowers who took out loans on or before January 1, 2008 who spend at least 31% of their gross monthly income on mortgage debt may be eligible for the FHA's "Hope for Homeowners" program. The program allows them to refinance their current mortgages to FHA-backed mortgages, but comes with serious restrictions—the lender must agree to writing down the loan to 90% of the home's current value, and the homeowner must share any future equity with the FHA. For more information, visit the FHA's website at www.fha.gov.

When More Debt Might Be the Solution

Here's a thought that may have already occurred to you: Take out a second mortgage or home equity line of credit (as discussed in the next chapter), use the funds to make your mortgage payments in the short term, and then pay off the new loan when your income stabilizes. It's actually not a bad strategy if you have significant equity and know you'll have a source of cash with which to start making payments soon. Perhaps you were recently laid off, but are confident you'll find work in the next few months.

But don't try this otherwise. You could end up reducing your home equity and having to sell your home anyway.

If you're sure this strategy can work for you, act now—even if your lender tells you not to do anything until you've missed two mortgage payments. By then, your credit score will have dropped so significantly that you're unlikely to get another loan. That's just what your primary lender wants—to avoid competing for your cash at a time when you have very little.

Make alternative payment arrangements

When you call your lender, be prepared to ask what your "workout" options are—your alternatives to foreclosure. Here are a few of the most common ones:

- **Repayment plan.** This means continuing to make your monthly payments, but adding a little extra to make up for what you've already missed. The advantage is that you don't have to make all your back payments right away. You'll usually be given 12 to 24 months to bring the loan current.

- **Forbearance.** The lender can agree to let you reduce or even suspend your payments for a period of time, usually less than 18 months. At the end of that time, you must start your payments again, plus make up the payments that you missed, either all at once or over an agreed-upon time period. If everything goes as planned, the lender won't suffer any loss and you'll keep your house. Of course, the lender will agree to forbearance only if it believes you'll be back on your feet again soon, so you'll need to come up with a persuasive argument.

- **Partial claim.** If you have an FHA-guaranteed loan, you may be able to get a one-time, interest-free loan from HUD to bring your account current. Your loan must be between four and 12 months delinquent, and you must be able to begin making full mortgage payments immediately. For more information, see the HUD website at www.hud.gov and type "Partial Claim" into the search box.

- **Loan modification.** If these temporary forms of relief won't solve your problem—perhaps because you're in a hybrid adjustable-rate mortgage and expected to refinance when the rate adjusted, but didn't qualify—your lender may agree to modify your loan. For example, the lender may agree to add your missed payments to your loan balance, to stretch out your loan over a longer term (lowering your payments but resulting in more interest over the life of the loan), or convert an adjustable-rate to a fixed-rate mortgage. A lender will be willing to do this only if it costs less than foreclosing—so ironically, you're more likely to get a loan modified if you have very little equity in the property. Still, lenders are reluctant to do loan modifications, for fear that everyone will want one. You'll have to be persistent.

As you discuss potential workout arrangements with the lender, ask key questions like:

- **What's my timeline?** Find out how long it will take the lender to make a final decision on the workout option you want to pursue, and when it will go into effect. Knowing this will help you plan your finances and help ensure the lender is working on the solution and staying in contact with you. But don't wait for the phone to ring: Lenders are notoriously unresponsive to borrowers seeking workout options. You'll have stay on top of the timeline and call when you haven't heard back.

- **Will you put a stop to foreclosure proceedings?** If you're working with a loan servicer, make sure that the lender will postpone foreclosure until the servicer reviews and approves your workout options.

- **What will my obligations be?** Make sure you understand, and get in writing, your exact responsibilities under the workout arrangement, including due dates and amounts due.

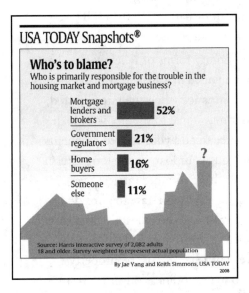

USA TODAY Snapshots®

Who's to blame?
Who is primarily responsible for the trouble in the housing market and mortgage business?

Mortgage lenders and brokers — **52%**

Government regulators — **21%**

Home buyers — **16%**

Someone else — **11%**

Source: Harris Interactive survey of 2,082 adults 18 and older. Survey weighted to represent actual population

By Jae Yang and Keith Simmons, USA TODAY 2008

Sell the property yourself

If you're in over your head, none of the above-mentioned arrangements may work for you. But it's still your house, and you can sell it if you want to. It's better to do this as soon as you know you won't be able to salvage the deal. Once the lender files a Notice of Default, you'll be responsible for additional fees and expenses, which can reduce your equity significantly. And the further behind you get on your payments, the more desperate you seem to buyers, who may be tempted to submit lowball offers (that you'll be equally tempted to accept). Finally, with notice of your troubles in the public record, you'll be easy prey for scammers, discussed below.

Depending on the market where you live, you may not be able to sell the house for as much as you paid for it. But if you can at least sell it for enough to cover your loan, you'll have dodged the foreclosure bullet.

Of course, some homeowners find that property values have dropped below the amount of their loan. In that case, ask your lender to agree to a short sale, in which it accepts all the sale proceeds and cancels the loan even if those proceeds don't cover what you owe. (Be prepared to convince the lender that there isn't another alternative, and that you're not just going to sell the house cheap to a friend or relative.)

If you're able to find a buyer to buy your house for what you owe on it and assume your current mortgage, the lender may agree to this, even if the terms of your original loan were not assumable. This is called a workout assumption. Again, you won't walk away with any of the cash you put in, but it will free you of the house. If a qualified buyer thinks your house is worth more than the value of the loan, he or she may be eager to assume the debt.

Give the house to the lender

As a last resort, you can simply give your lender title to the house. Called a "deed in lieu of foreclosure," this saves both you and the lender expense and hassle. The lender then sells your house (as with an actual foreclosure) but doesn't report it as a foreclosure to the credit rating agencies—in fact, you can negotiate with the lender about how it can help you preserve your credit rating.

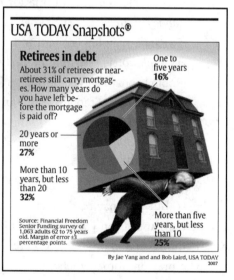

USA TODAY Snapshots®

Retirees in debt

About 31% of retirees or near-retirees still carry mortgages. How many years do you have left before the mortgage is paid off?

One to five years **16%**

20 years or more **27%**

More than 10 years, but less than 20 **32%**

More than five years, but less than 10 **25%**

Source: Financial Freedom Senior Funding survey of 1,063 adults 62 to 75 years old. Margin of error ±3 percentage points.

By Jae Yang and and Bob Laird, USA TODAY 2007

What if the lender doesn't want to accept the property? You can prepare a quitclaim deed that unilaterally transfers your property rights even without the lender's consent.

File for bankruptcy

If your financial situation is particularly dire, you may be considering bankruptcy. With a Chapter 13 or "reorganization" bankruptcy, you set up a court-approved plan to repay your debts. Your lender must allow you to make up missed payments according to the plan, over a period of as long as five years. However, you'll also have to continue to make your mortgage payments going forward.

Less available, and less desirable if you want to keep your home, is a Chapter 7 bankruptcy, in which your debts are actually discharged. If you qualify for Chapter 7 bankruptcy, you'll no longer have the mortgage to worry about—but you probably won't have a house, either. And you'll lose a lot of your other assets too, which will be sold to pay your creditors.

RESOURCE

Need more information on bankruptcy? Check out *Solve Your Money Troubles: Get Debt Collectors off Your Back & Regain Financial Freedom*, by Robin Leonard and Attorney John Lamb (Nolo); *Chapter 13 Bankruptcy: Keep Your Property & Repay Debts Over Time*, by Robin Leonard and Stephen Elias (Nolo); and *How to File for Chapter 7 Bankruptcy*, by Stephen Elias, Albin Renauer, and Robin Leonard (Nolo).

Don't fall for a scam

We've told you about the legitimate ways to get out of a foreclosure mess. But you may be contacted by seemingly helpful people, who perhaps appear on your doorstep or telephone line, peddling other methods. Watch out: Chances are they're among the many scammers who prey on homeowners desperate to save their homes. According to USA TODAY's Noelle Knox, "The Better Business Bureau has received complaints from every state and has issued an alert to warn consumers to be cautious about foreclosure-rescue companies."

Here are a few of the most common scams to steer clear of:

- **Equity skimming.** A buyer approaches you and offers to repay your mortgage and sell your house if you sign over the deed and move out. Signing the deed will indeed take the house off your hands—but not the mortgage. You get stuck with the bill, but the scammer gets your property. In another nasty trick, the scammer may actually pay off the original loan, but then take out another one for more money—and pocket the difference.

- **Phantom rescue.** Some companies will charge exorbitant up-front fees for counseling services you can get for free or to do things you take care of yourself. The worst ones fail to provide the requested services, then abandon you when the foreclosure gets underway.

- **Bailout.** Similar to equity skimming, with a bailout, the scammer will have you sign over your house deed. But you won't move out—you'll stay and pay rent, ostensibly to buy back the property. The scammer may tell you that signing over the deed is necessary so that someone with better credit can get favorable financing. But then the terms of your buyback will be so onerous you won't be able to afford it, and the scammer will keep the house. Alternatively, the scammer may take your money but not pay the mortgage, leaving you in foreclosure and stuck with the loan.

- **Bait and switch.** Some scammers trick homeowners, for example by having them sign documents that are supposedly to secure a new loan when they actually transfer title. At very worst, a scammer may forge your signature.

Con Artists Circle Over Homeowners on the Edge

A family that's more than two months behind on a mortgage will often come home to a mailbox stuffed with brightly colored envelopes and postcards from companies promising to help them save their homes.

One such postcard that Steve and Dawn Reyes received after Steve lost his job as a carpenter was from Mortgage Assistance Solutions, a Florida-based company that's known by its customers as Fresh Start.

"YOU WILL LOSE YOUR HOUSE IF YOU DON'T CALL US NOW!!!" the postcard said.

When Dawn called, the company promised to refund its $1,200 up-front fee if it couldn't help them. A month after they signed up, the Reyeses received a summons stating that their house was scheduled for auction on December 12, 2006.

The Reyeses had signed a document in November 2006 giving Mortgage Assistance Solutions permission to negotiate with the family's lender. But the Illinois Attorney General's office, which filed a lawsuit against Mortgage Assistance Solutions, told Dawn that their lender didn't receive that document by fax until December 14—two days after Dawn received the summons, and called them.

Angry, Dawn demanded her family's money back. Mortgage Assistance Solutions sent her $700 and said it was entitled to the remaining $500 because of the time it spent on her case.

Yet soon after Dawn canceled the services, she says, she received another green-and-white envelope in the mail from Fresh Start. It read: "FORECLOSURE COMPLAINT NOTICE. Your House Is Scheduled To Be Sold At Auction. National Bank."

When USA TODAY told Michael Stoller, a Los Angeles attorney and owner of Mortgage Assistance Solutions, that a nonprofit counselor was able to help the Reyeses obtain a new fixed-rate loan with a much lower interest rate in June, he suggested that

Con Artists Circle Over Homeowners on the Edge, continued

lenders are more willing to modify delinquent loans to help an owner stay in a home than they were before.

Mortgage Assistance Solutions, Stoller says, has handled more than 6,000 cases in 2007 and refunded $1.1 million to homeowners it couldn't help. "That's not a company that takes money from customers and runs away," he says. "Our goal was always to help homeowners."

Still, Stoller says his company is winding down its operations and will stop doing business, because of increased regulation and competition.

 "Con artists circle over homeowners on the edge: 'Foreclosure rescue' scams can rob victims of house and hope," by Noelle Knox, November 9, 2007.

To avoid falling victim to a scam, avoid anyone who:

- **Approaches you.** A great deal of information about you, your mortgage, and your property is easily accessible, online and off—like the Notice of Default, which is a matter of public record. Predators often choose their victims, focusing on those in the most dire circumstances. Avoid any person or company that calls itself a "mortgage consultant," "foreclosure consultant," or "foreclosure service."

- **Makes promises that sound too good to be true.** They probably are. Flyers or mailings that promise to "save your credit," or buy your house and rent it back to you until you're back on your feet are red flags.

- **Advises you not to contact your lender, lawyer, or other real estate professional.** Hmm, why wouldn't they want you to get in touch with people who might recognize that you're being taken advantage of? By the time you realize your mistake, it may be too late to undo.

- **Asks you to send your mortgage payment to them or pay a big up-front fee.** That lets the scammer take your cash then walk away. You'll be deeper in the hole than when you started, with fewer options for getting out.

- **Asks you to sign anything you don't understand.** Some home-buyers have been presented with a stack of papers—not unlike the stack you got when you first closed on your house—and signed without reading. Unfortunately, these papers sometimes include deeds transferring the property away. Read everything you sign. Don't sign anything with blanks, which can be filled in later.

- **Tells you to sign over your home.** Once you sign over your home, there's little you can do to get it back.

- **Tells you to rely on a promise or verbal agreement.** A legitimate buyer will want everything in writing. ●

Is It Time to Refinance?

Why Refinance?_____144

Calculating the Costs and Benefits of Refinancing_____148

    Examine your up front costs_____148

    Find your "break-even" point and difference in total
       interest owed_____150

Choosing the Right Loan_____154

    Where and how to find the best loan_____154

    Working with a mortgage broker_____156

    Working with a lending institution_____157

Qualifying for Your New Loan_____158

    Your debt-to-income ratio_____158

    Your credit score_____159

    How much home equity you've built up_____160

    The refinancing application process_____161

Alternatives to Refinancing_____162

    Home equity loan_____163

    Home equity line of credit_____164

You're just settling in. You're getting used to the monthly mortgage, tax, and insurance payments. And now it may be time to refinance your mortgage and get a new loan. Why?

If your financial picture is different than when you bought, you've built up some equity and could use it to finance home improvements, or if the mortgage market has changed—for example, interest rates have gone down—refinancing can be worthwhile. But it's not something you want to do every day, so let this chapter show you how and when to refinance. It covers:

- when the time is right to refinance
- calculating the cost of refinancing
- choosing the right loan
- qualifying for the loan you want, and
- alternatives to refinancing.

Why Refinance?

Refinancing makes sense for one main reason: You can save money, usually by finding a mortgage at a lower interest rate or with better terms. Unfortunately, you can also lose money if you don't refinance wisely. For instance, it wouldn't be financially prudent to choose a new mortgage that lowers your monthly payments without also taking into account the type of mortgage you're getting, the fees you'll pay to refinance, or the increase in total interest you may pay by starting your loan term over.

But let's not get ahead of ourselves. When the time comes, you'll obviously need to run some numbers to figure out whether refinancing makes sense for you. First, let's look at some situations when refinancing is usually worth considering:

- **Interest rates have gone down.** If interest rates have dropped since you got your original loan, you may pay significantly less by refinancing at a lower rate. Even a change of 0.5% can make a big difference.

- **You want to remodel or renovate.** If you have some significant equity in the property, but don't have ready cash, you may be able to do a "cash-out" refinance. Your new loan would be for more than the existing amount of your original loan, and you'd pocket the difference. In the best-case scenario, the money you'd put into the remodel or renovations would raise the value of your home, further justifying this financial maneuver.

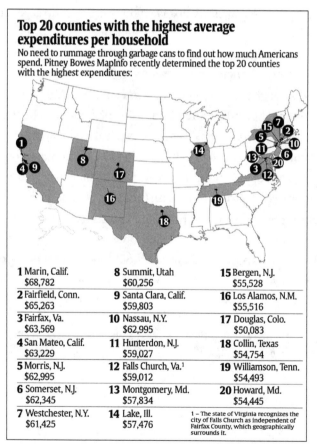

Top 20 counties with the highest average expenditures per household

No need to rummage through garbage cans to find out how much Americans spend. Pitney Bowes MapInfo recently determined the top 20 counties with the highest expenditures:

1 Marin, Calif. $68,782	**8** Summit, Utah $60,256	**15** Bergen, N.J. $55,528
2 Fairfield, Conn. $65,263	**9** Santa Clara, Calif. $59,803	**16** Los Alamos, N.M. $55,516
3 Fairfax, Va. $63,569	**10** Nassau, N.Y. $62,995	**17** Douglas, Colo. $50,083
4 San Mateo, Calif. $63,229	**11** Hunterdon, N.J. $59,027	**18** Collin, Texas $54,754
5 Morris, N.J. $62,995	**12** Falls Church, Va.[1] $59,012	**19** Williamson, Tenn. $54,493
6 Somerset, N.J. $62,345	**13** Montgomery, Md. $57,834	**20** Howard, Md. $54,445
7 Westchester, N.Y. $61,425	**14** Lake, Ill. $57,476	1 – The state of Virginia recognizes the city of Falls Church as independent of Fairfax County, which geographically surrounds it.

By Adrienne Lewis, USA TODAY
2007

Flush With Home Equity? Careful How You Spend It

Your front porch sags, you need a new roof, and there's shag carpeting in the family room, but because you live in a desirable neighborhood, the value of your house has soared. Should you turn some of that equity into cash?

A cash-out is not free money. You're replacing your mortgage with a new loan, and rolling the amount you took out into the balance. That means you could end up paying more in interest over time than you would with a home equity line that you repay in a couple of years. What to consider:

- Whether refinancing will lower your existing mortgage rate or improve the terms of your loan. Refinancing usually involves closing costs. If you lower your rate, the savings on your monthly payments may offset those costs.

- How much money you need. If you want $10,000 to pay off your credit cards, a home equity line of credit may be the better option, especially if you can pay it off in a year or two.

- Whether the cash-out will add value to your home. If you take cash out of your home to renovate your kitchen or add another room, you'll probably increase the value of your home.

Which brings up another point. Some folks feel like their home equity is burning a hole in their floorboards and can't wait to spend it. But equity is not something you should squander. If home prices decline in your region, it will provide you with a valuable cushion, especially if you have to move before prices recover.

 "Flush with huge home equity? Careful how you spend it," by Sandra Block, August 16, 2005.

- **Your credit score went up.** If your credit score wasn't stellar when you bought your house—maybe because you simply didn't have enough credit to beef it up—you probably didn't get the best rate available. By now, you may qualify for a better rate.

- **You make more money.** If your income has gone up since you bought your home, you may qualify for better loan terms. For example, if you have an adjustable rate mortgage because that's all you qualified for, you may now be able to get a fixed-rate mortgage.

- **You want to change mortgage types.** Maybe you've decided you want a different mortgage type—for example, you originally got a 5/1 hybrid loan, thinking you'd move on before the fixed period ended, but now plan to stay put for at least seven or eight years. You might want to find a loan with a longer fixed-rate period.

On the flip side, there are situations in which refinancing doesn't make much sense or may not be possible:

- **Interest rates have gone up.** The only reason you'd consider refinancing to a higher interest rate is if you want out of your current mortgage ASAP—perhaps your rate isn't fixed, and might soon climb much higher than current fixed rates, or your mortgage has other undesirable or risky terms.

- **You make less money.** If your income has gone down, you might not qualify to borrow as much, so you may find it difficult to get a loan on favorable terms.

- **You have a lower credit score.** You're now considered a riskier borrower—and riskier borrowers pay higher interest rates.

- **You don't have much equity.** While lenders used to allow borrowers to finance 100% of the value of a property, they're more cautious now, fearing they might not recover everything they're owed if you don't pay your mortgage. If you owe more than 95% of the property's value, you probably won't qualify for a refinance.

Calculating the Costs and Benefits of Refinancing

Now let's assume that refinancing looks like a good idea for you. Your next step is to factor in two things:

- your up-front costs for a new loan, and
- whether you'll save money over the long term.

> **!** CAUTION
> **There's no magic about a 2% drop in interest rates.** You might have heard an old rule of thumb that, for fixed-rate mortgages, it's time to refinance when interest rates have dropped by two percentage points since you got the loan (for example, from 7% to 5%). But that theory dates from a time when closing costs were consistently high enough to undo the benefits of refinancing. So run the numbers, as described below, to find out whether it's really worth it.

Examine your up-front costs

To refinance, you may have to pay title insurance and escrow fees, lender fees, points (optional), appraisal fees, credit reporting fees, and any amounts needed to bring your insurance and tax obligations up to date. These probably sound familiar, from when you first took out your current loan. So why do you have to pay them all over again? Because this is a whole new loan and your new lender wants to hear for itself that you're a responsible borrower, that no other owners are lurking in the wings, and that the house can be sold for enough to cover your loan balance if necessary.

> **!** CAUTION
> **Watch out for prepayment penalties on your current mortgage.** Technically, when you refinance, you pay off your existing mortgage—meaning you'll also have to fork over any prepayment penalty fees.

The best way to estimate your true costs is to ask for a Good Faith Estimate (GFE), a summary of the fees you're likely to pay. Brokers are required to give you a GFE within three days of submitting a loan application, but you can ask for one before that. As we'll explain more below, you can help control your costs by getting the GFE early and negotiating away unnecessary costs.

When looking at your GFE, you may notice some fees with vague, administrative-sounding names like application fees, processing fees, or administrative fees. These may be junk fees—a little padding for the lender's profits. To avoid paying them, tell your lender or mortgage broker that you want to keep costs down, ask for an explanation of each fee you're charged, and challenge any that sound superfluous. Many lenders will waive some fees if asked.

You might also be able to lower the title insurance fees by using the same title company you did when you first bought the house. And some lenders skip the appraisal if you bought the house fairly recently or you have so much equity in it that they're all but guaranteed to get their money back in a foreclosure.

After all these warnings about up-front costs, your ears may perk up when you hear advertisements for "no-cost" mortgages, promising zero closing costs. It's true that you may get away without writing a check at closing—but that doesn't mean you're not paying these costs somehow. As USA TODAY's Sandra Block found, "Some no-cost loans carry a higher interest rate," while "in other cases, the costs are rolled into the loan, which means you would end up financing them for the next 30 years."

Still, a no-cost mortgage isn't always a bad idea. The best time to go for one is if you plan to stay in your house for only a short while, say a few years. Refinancing will still be worthwhile if it lowers your interest rate below your current rate. And while you won't have time to save much on interest, you will have saved a lot on the closing costs. But, adds Block, "make sure you're dealing with a reputable lender and… scrutinize all offers."

Loyalty to Your Lender Can Pay Off

The big industry players who write rules on who gets a mortgage and under what terms cut a lot of slack to lenders who want to retain customers by quickly swapping one mortgage for another at better terms. The Federal Housing Administration, the Veterans Administration, Fannie Mae, and Freddie Mac all have rules that streamline procedures for a lender dealing with an existing borrower.

For the borrower, it can mean a cheaper, quicker refinancing than would be the case if the customer went to a new lender to refinance. Originating a mortgage under streamlined refinance rules can be thousands of dollars cheaper for the lender. Just how much of the savings get passed along to the borrower varies by lender.

One certain benefit to the borrower is less hassle. Among normal requirements that may be eliminated or minimized: documentation of income and assets, a credit check, and a formal property appraisal. Such deals still carry title-related expenses and require a formal closing. To qualify, a customer needs a good record of payments on the old mortgage. Closing costs may be rolled into the new mortgage balance, but a streamlined refinance can't be used to generate cash from home equity.

 "Take the trick out of refinancing; Do your homework first to avoid mumbo jumbo," Thomas A. Fogarty, March 21, 2003.

Find your "break-even" point and difference in total interest owed

Next, you need to figure out whether and at what point the refinancing will pay for itself in the reduced interest rate you're going to pay. Online calculators make this task fairly easy, but you need to understand a few things about the results you'll see first.

The best calculators ask for complete data on your existing loan balance and terms, how long you have left to pay off your mortgage, any up-front costs and points to refinance, and the new interest rate. They then tell you three important things:

- **Your new monthly payment amount.** Hopefully this will be lower—but lower monthly payments aren't everything, as the next two sets of results will show.

- **Your break-even point.** This means the number of months or years it will take you to work off your initial closing costs by saving on interest each month. If you think you'll stay in your home for less time than it takes to reach your break-even point, the refinance definitely isn't worth it.

- **The difference in total interest you'll owe.** Starting over with a new mortgage term (most likely 30 years) means adding several months or years to your payment schedule (depending on how long you've already been in the house). And the more time you take to pay, the more interest you'll owe in total. The upshot is that even if you work off your closing costs (reach your break-even point) before you sell your house, you could end up paying so much more in total interest that you lose money through the refinance—unless you create a repayment schedule that sticks with your old end date.

To illustrate, imagine that you bought your house five years ago and still owe $200,000 on your 30-year fixed-rate mortgage at 8%, which you'd thought would be paid off in another 25 years. Your current monthly payment is $1,544. But interest rates on 30-year loans have dropped to 7%; and if you're willing to pay two points, you can get a loan at 6.5%.

The table below shows how these two refinance options might play out, including a comparison of paying over the full, new 30-year term with sticking to your original, 25-year loan payoff date (by adding to your monthly payments). As you'll see, going for the first, 7% option gives you a break-even point of only ten months, but you'd end up paying $15,000 more in interest if you kept the loan for the full 30-year term.

Loan Comparison: 30-Year Fixed Rate Loans for $200,000				
	Refinance loan 1		Refinance loan 2		Lessons learned
Interest rate	7%		6.5%		
Points	0		1		Paying points and higher costs can lower the interest rate.
Closing costs	$2,000		$2,500		
Monthly payment	Spread out over new, 30-year loan term: $1,331 ($213 reduction)	Sticking to original loan term: $1,414 ($130 reduction)	Spread out over new, 30-year loan term: $1,264 ($280 reduction)	Sticking to original loan term: $1,350 (a $194 reduction)	A lower interest rate will always lower your monthly payments.
Break-even point	10 months	16 months	18 months	26 months	Calculating your break-even point by sticking to your original loan term is a more accurate comparison, because you haven't added months of additional payments.
Total interest difference over the life of the loan	You'll pay $15,928 MORE in interest.	You'll save $39,022 in interest.	You'll save $8,001 in interest.	You'll save $57,966 in interest.	If you keep the loan for the full term, you'll pay a lot more interest.

Of course, refinancing to a lower interest rate can always lower your monthly payment. If that's your ultimate goal—perhaps because your current ARM payments have skyrocketed and you're struggling to keep your home—a refinance may make sense even if you don't stick to your original loan term. But whether it will really save you money in the long term depends on how long you keep the loan.

USA TODAY Snapshots®

Cities with costliest homes
City, cost of the median three-bedroom and two-bath home:

$816,022
$670,959
$624,466
$527,908
$486,556

| Santa Barbara, Santa Maria, Lompoc, Calif. | San Francisco, Oakland, San Jose, Calif. | Honolulu | Los Angeles, Riverside, Orange County, Calif. | San Diego |

Source: Zillow.com

By Jae Yang and Karl Gelles, USA TODAY
2008

The example also shows that you probably won't want to pay points on a refinance unless your new interest rate is rock bottom and you plan to stay put. That's because it will take you a significant amount of time to "pay off" the value of the points with the lowered interest rate. And while you can deduct points on a refinance mortgage, you must prorate the deduction over the life of the loan. In that way, it's different from a purchase loan, when you can deduct all points in the year they're paid.

Now, for the calculators: To compare fixed-rate mortgages, the best one we've found is at http://realestate.yahoo.com (Under the "Finance & Mortgage" tab, click "Home Loans," then "Should I refinance my home mortgage?"). Unlike many calculators, this one runs the numbers as in the illustration above, automatically comparing the impact of starting over with a new 30-year mortgage with the option of sticking to your old mortgage term.

To calculate whether to switch from an ARM to a fixed-rate mortgage, go to www.mtgprofessor.com, click "Calculators," and scroll down and click "Mortgage Refinance Calculator: Refinancing an ARM into a FRM."

Choosing the Right Loan

Once you've decided on a loan type and figured out the costs, it's time to shop around for the best deal.

Where and how to find the best loan

The easiest place to start is on the Internet. In addition to sites operated by individual lenders, various sites aggregate lender information and allow you to compare different loan options. At Bankrate.com, for example, you can compare rates based on your geographic location, the amount you want to borrow, and the terms you're seeking. Then you can contact the prospective lenders directly to get more information.

While you're online, get yourself a "Mortgage Shopping Worksheet," available at the Federal Trade Commission website (www.ftc.gov; search for it by name). This will help you compare different mortgage features like interest rates, fees, and other terms or requirements. Or, you can create such a worksheet yourself. The important thing is to organize your findings early on, before they become a tangle of numbers. No need to fill out your worksheet for every mortgage, just the few you're seriously considering.

At the comparison stage, be careful about any websites that require you to enter personal information like your name, Social Security number, or address. In the worst case, you can actually agree to purchase a mortgage online—not the smartest impulse buy. More likely, you'll be contacted by potential lenders, or they'll check your credit history (a risk, since multiple inquiries can affect your credit score, though all checks within a 14-day window are treated as one).

The next place to look is in the real estate sections of local newspapers. Lenders often list the different loan products they offer, with their base interest rate, APR, any points, and sometimes fees charged. To translate these, see "Basic Mortgage Lingo," below.

Keep in mind that the rates you see online or in a newspaper are just ballpark figures. Mortgage rates change daily, and these advertised rates don't take into account your particular situation. To get a better idea of what a loan will cost you, you'll have to go straight to a mortgage broker or lender.

Basic Mortgage Lingo

Here are some of the key terms you'll need to understand when mortgage shopping (refer back to Chapter 6 for other important terms with adjustable rate mortgages):

- **Base rate.** The base rate is the actual rate used to calculate your payment.
- **Annual percentage rate (APR).** The APR is the total cost of taking out the loan, expressed as an annual percentage of the loan amount. It takes into account not only the interest you owe, but any fees you pay, like appraisal and credit report fees. Lenders provide the APR because they're legally required to. The APR should be a good indicator of what a loan really costs, except that it factors the costs over the life of the loan—and the chances of keeping the same mortgage that long are pretty low. However, the APR can be informative—like when a loan is advertised at a very low interest rate, but a slew of additional fees increase its overall cost dramatically.
- **Points.** A point is a loan fee equal to 1% of the principal on the loan (so one point on a $100,000 mortgage is $1,000). Points are added to the cost of some mortgages in exchange for a lower interest rate. You probably won't be offered more than two or three points on a loan, because the lender would have to significantly reduce your interest rate to make it financially beneficial to you.

Working with a mortgage broker

To make the most of your search, you might want to work with a mortgage broker. The broker's job is to "shop lenders" to find you the best possible loan terms, given your financial situation and goals. A good broker will:

- Talk with you about your financial situation and goals.
- Find and explain financing options available to you.
- Help you complete and assemble the documentation the lender needs. This might include your loan application, confirmation of employment and wages, financial information, and credit report.
- Once approved, review loan documents before you sign them. If the lender refuses to approve your new loan, your mortgage broker should explain what went wrong, and help look into alternative mortgage options.
- Coordinate the property appraisal.
- Continue to act as a liaison between you and the lender.

If you liked the mortgage broker you worked with when you bought your house, you might want to work together again. Otherwise, you can get recommendations from friends, coworkers, and other homeowners. The real estate agent you worked with is another good resource.

Although you'll ultimately choose just one broker, you may get a better deal by talking to several brokers first. If you know what type of loan you're looking for, have your credit score available, and have assembled all your financial documents, you can ask each broker for a Good Faith Estimate (GFE). As mentioned, the broker is required to give you a GFE within three days after you apply for a loan, but you can ask for one earlier. Instead of having each broker check your credit score, provide it yourself (as described under "Your credit score," below) and agree that the estimate is based on that score.

Ideally, get three GFEs from three different sources. Compare the rates and fees of each, then decide which broker and loan to go with (or use the information from one broker to negotiate with another). Because mortgage rates can change daily, try to get GFEs on the same day.

The GFE can help you puzzle out how you'll be paying your mortgage broker (it won't be a direct payment). Mortgage brokers make most of their money by marking up the costs on the loan the wholesale lender is offering. Look for "Origination Points," "Mortgage Broker Fee," and the "Yield Spread Premium" (or YSP), any of which may represent the mortgage broker's markup. Origination points and the broker fee will appear as "add-ons," but the YSP is part of the interest rate you'll pay (though there is a separate space on the form to break it out). If, for example, the YSP is 1% and the overall interest rate is 6.5%, the lender pays the broker a 1% commission on the loan. When you refinance and don't pay closing costs, the broker's commission is usually in the YSP.

> **CAUTION**
> **Not all brokers disclose the YSP.** If you get a GFE without one, ask the broker to provide it.

Of course, a good mortgage broker should be able to save you the equivalent of his or her earnings and then some, by finding you a more affordable mortgage than you could locate on your own. Nonetheless, it's to your advantage to limit these fees as much as you can, and you're best poised to do that if you understand what fees there are. Finish any negotiations before you sign the GFE, and ask the broker to commit to keeping final non-third-party closing costs (meaning the broker's fees) to within 10% of what was estimated on the GFE. This will help prevent any rude surprises when the loan closes—for example, a $500 processing fee the broker agreed to waive, which suddenly reappears when you're ready to sign the paperwork.

Working with a lending institution

Another option is to go right to a lender, rather than dealing with a mortgage broker. You may take this option if you find a loan you want online, even if you never walk into the bank branch.

If you decide to work with a lender, you'll probably still be dealing primarily with a person within the institution, called a "mortgage banker" or "loan officer." This person performs the same duties (more or less) as a mortgage broker, except that instead of scouring several wholesale lender portfolios, the loan officer will help you identify which of the bank's own loan products suits your needs. In other words, you'll be limited to the loan packages offered by that institution.

The loan officer should help you fill out your application and handle necessary paperwork like obtaining your credit report and getting an appraisal. However, once you've chosen a bank, you won't be able to choose your loan officer as you would a broker—or your available choices will be limited.

How much personal contact you have with a specific loan officer depends on the lender. Lenders come in all shapes and sizes, from the behemoth bank to the local credit union. Some operate almost entirely online, even having you apply online. These lenders may be keeping their overhead low by cutting out the operating costs of the local office, passing the savings on to you. If you work with online lenders, you'll have to rely more heavily on technology (email, fax machines, and scanners) to transmit documents. You may also have to accept that you'll never meet the loan officer face to face, or that you'll be dealing with several different people during the transaction.

Qualifying for Your New Loan

After deciding you'd like to refinance, your next question may be whether you'll qualify for the loan you want, and what hoops you'll have to jump through to get it. Remember the first time around, when the lender ran your credit report, verified your salary information, and asked for a few other things that flashed by in the flurry of home buying? You'll be going through almost the same process again. Here's a refresher course on what will happen.

Your debt-to-income ratio

The first thing the lender will look at is your debt-to-income ratio: how much money comes in each month, compared to how much goes out. That means adding up your household's gross monthly income (the amount you earn before taxes and other monthly withdrawals, plus income from all other sources, like royalties, alimony, or investments), then making sure that your combined minimum debt payments—for your PITI (principal, interest, taxes, and insurance), credit card, car, student loan, and others—don't eat up more than a certain percentage of that amount. The idea is to make sure you have enough cash left over for your mortgage payment.

Traditionally, lenders have said that your PITI payment shouldn't exceed 28% of your gross monthly income, and your overall debt shouldn't exceed 36%. If you've taken on a lot of new debt since you bought your house, you may not fall within these ratios. To qualify, you'd probably either need to pay off some of the debt or find a way to increase your income.

USA TODAY Snapshots®

Paying off the plastic

Fifty-eight percent of adults have monthly credit card bills. Monthly bill-paying habits:

✔ Have regular credit card bills	**58%**
Pay credit card bill in full	**24%**
Make a credit card payment	**31%**
It depends	**3%**
✔ Do not have regular credit card expense	**41%**
✔ Don't know	**1%**

Source: Pew Research telephone survey of 2,000 adults, Oct. 18–Nov. 9, 2006. Margin of error, ±2.5 percentage points.

By Mary Cadden and Adrienne Lewis, USA TODAY 2007

Your credit score

Aside from your available income, your lender's main preoccupation will be with your credit history and score. Most lenders want to know who they'll be competing with to get your monthly dollars, how much you're borrowing from those various sources, and how good you've been about paying money back.

Credit reporting bureaus exist to keep track of your borrowing habits. The three major companies are Equifax (www.equifax.com), Experian (www.experian.com) and TransUnion (www.transunion.com). They use a formula compiled by the Fair Isaac Corporation to calculate your "FICO" score (which we'll call your "credit score"; but beware when you see this term other places, because anyone can compile a number and call it a "credit" score).

The best way to know what information your prospective lenders will be looking at is to look at it yourself first. Federal law requires the three major consumer reporting companies (named above) to provide you with a free copy of your credit report (but not your actual score) once every 12 months. You can get yours at www.annualcreditreport .com. It's a good idea to ask all three agencies for your credit report. They sometimes have different information, and your lender may be looking at all three reports. You can do this simultaneously, but it means that you won't be able to get another free report from any of them for another full year.

You'll probably have to pay extra to get your credit score. You can get it either from the individual consumer reporting company websites or by going to www.myfico.com.

Your credit score will be a number somewhere between 300 and 850—the higher the better. If your score is in the 700s, it's considered pretty strong. A higher number tells the lender you pay your debts on time, have limited sources of revolving credit, and have an established record of using credit prudently, making you a good credit risk. A lower number means you look more risky, and decreases the chances of you getting the loan you want on favorable terms.

RESOURCE
Need to raise your credit score? See the "Credit Education" section of www.myfico.com.

How much home equity you've built up

A final factor that affects whether a lender will lend you money is the amount of equity you have in the property. If you put a significant amount of money down when you bought your house—say the traditional 20%—and the value of your home has held steady, a lender will more comfortably assume that if you were to default on the loan and the house went into foreclosure, it would be able to recover all of what it's owed. The same is true if you put a small amount down but have seen the value of the property rise significantly. (To figure out whether the property's value has changed, the lender will probably conduct an appraisal.)

On the other hand, if the value of your property has dropped, or even if it hasn't changed much but you didn't put a lot down, the lender might think twice before letting you borrow. As of the printing of this book, lenders have begun to tighten their lending practices, and get especially nervous about funding loans when borrowers have less than 10% equity. They rarely lend to anyone with less than 5% equity—at least on terms that would make refinancing worthwhile.

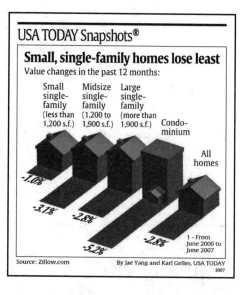

USA TODAY Snapshots®

Small, single-family homes lose least

Value changes in the past 12 months:

Small single-family (less than 1,200 s.f.) — -1.0%
Midsize single-family (1,200 to 1,900 s.f.) — -3.1%
Large single-family (more than 1,900 s.f.) — -2.8%
Condominium — -5.2%
All homes — -2.8%

1 – From June 2006 to June 2007

Source: Zillow.com

By Jae Yang and Karl Gelles, USA TODAY 2007

The refinancing application process

Before your lender will approve and fund your loan, you'll need to:

- **Assemble paperwork.** Your new lender will want to see things like your pay stubs for the last 30 days, two years' tax returns and W-2s (or business tax returns if you're self-employed), proof of other income or assets, three months of bank records for every account you have, information about your employers for the last two years, and information about your current debts.

- **Fill out an application.** Many lenders use a standard mortgage application form called the Uniform Residential Loan Application (sometimes called "Form 1003"). You can take a peek at the form before it's given to you, at www.efanniemae.com. Although the form is quite long, a lot of the information is stuff you already know. The rest, the loan officer or mortgage broker should be able to help you with—he or she may even fill it out for you.

- **Get an appraisal.** Most likely, you'll literally stand back while the lender chooses the appraiser and tells you what day to meet him or her at your house. You also pay the appraiser's fee, around $300–$400. The appraiser's job is to determine the value of the house, and thus make sure you're not borrowing more than it's worth.

- **Sign paperwork.** Once the lender is ready to fund the loan, you'll be presented with a slew of documents, including a promissory note (guaranteeing to repay what you owe), the mortgage or deed of trust (promising your house as collateral), a Truth-in-Lending Disclosure Statement (confirming your interest rate, APR, and the total cost of the loan over its life), a Settlement Statement (usually on a HUD-1 form, itemizing the terms of your loan and the different fees you're paying), and a monthly payment letter (telling you how much you'll pay monthly in principal and interest). As with your house, you'll need to attend a "closing" meeting at which you sign the documents (bring photo ID).

USA TODAY Snapshots®

Fraud in mortgage applications increases

Property valuation fraud has fallen ...

70%
64%
43% 41%
29% 33% 36% 39%

... while identity mortgage fraud has risen

2004 2005 2006 2007¹ 2004 2005 2006 2007¹

1 – 1st quarter

Source: Interthinx

By Jae Yang and Bob Laird, USA TODAY 2007

Alternatives to Refinancing

If one of your goals is to borrow cash from the equity in your home—perhaps to pay for some remodeling—you may be considering a cash-out refinance, described above. But a home equity loan or home equity line of credit may be a cheaper and easier alternative.

Home equity loan

A home equity loan is sometimes called a "second mortgage," because it's an additional loan secured by your property. To compensate the lender for being second in line to your primary mortgage holder if you default, the interest rate is usually a little bit higher. If you use the home equity loan to purchase or improve your home, the interest you pay is tax deductible up to $1 million. If you use it for any other purpose, it's deductible up to $100,000 (with the caveat that you can't deduct debt that exceeds the house's fair market value).

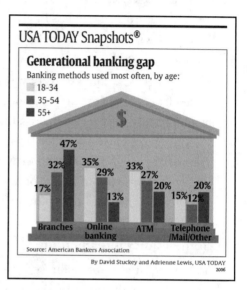

USA TODAY Snapshots®

Generational banking gap

Banking methods used most often, by age:
- 18-34
- 35-54
- 55+

Branches 47% 32% 17%
Online banking 35% 29% 13%
ATM 33% 27% 20%
Telephone/Mail/Other 20% 15% 12%

Source: American Bankers Association

By David Stuckey and Adrienne Lewis, USA TODAY 2006

With a home equity loan, you'll be able to borrow against the equity in your home—the difference between the value of the home and what you owe on it. It goes without saying that if you still owe all of or close to the total amount of your purchase, and the value of your property hasn't changed much, you probably won't be able to get a home equity loan. In that case, it will probably be difficult to get cash out at all. One alternative, if you're planning on spending the cash on your home, is to use a construction loan, discussed in Chapter 10.

To shop for a home equity loan, approach it like you would a refinance—by getting estimates from several brokers and lenders. You'll be able to choose either a fixed rate or adjustable rate. Likewise, you'll incur the same sort of fees on a home equity loan as you'd pay for a refinance, but they're usually much lower (in part because the loan amount itself is probably lower, and some of these fees are percentage-based). You can also find no-fee home equity loans, though (no surprise here), the costs are rolled into the loan itself, usually into the interest rate.

If you need a limited amount of cash, perhaps to remodel your kitchen, and you have a good interest rate on your current mortgage, a home equity loan is probably preferable to a cash-out refinance. You'll likely save money, because home equity loans usually have shorter terms than mortgages, such as ten to 15 years. In addition to lower closing costs, that means paying less interest overall—even if the interest rate is a little higher.

While some homeowners use home equity loans to finance non-house-related purchases, doing so is risky. If you later can't make the payments, the lender can foreclose on your house. And even if you sell it first to avoid foreclosure, you face the risk that, after you pay transaction costs like your real estate broker's fee (usually 5%–6% of the sale price), you won't have enough money left to cover what you owe. If you've used the money to improve your home, on the other hand, at least some portion of it should come back to you in the increased sale price.

Home equity line of credit

A home equity line of credit, or HELOC, is comparable to using your house like a credit card. That's because a HELOC is a form of revolving credit. Instead of getting a check in hand, you get an open account, with a certain amount of time to use it (called a draw period). When you decide you want to begin using your credit line, you'll be able to use checks or a credit card specially designated for that purpose. This is a useful feature for those who have ongoing expenses, such as small remodeling projects.

During the draw period (usually between five and ten years), you usually pay only interest on the money you borrow. At the end of the term, you begin to pay off principal, usually over a ten- to 20-year term.

The interest you pay on a HELOC is tax-deductible up to $1 million if the money is used to improve your home and $100,000 when used for any other purpose (as long as the mortgage debt doesn't exceed the house's fair market value, in which case you can deduct the debt up to that value).

> **CAUTION**
> **Watch out if you're subject to the Alternative Minimum Tax (AMT).** If so, your HELOC or home equity loan may be deductible only if it is used to purchase or improve the home.

The amount of money you can borrow with a HELOC is based on the amount of equity you have in your home. Often, the maximum credit limit will be based on some percentage of the home's appraised value (such as 75%), reduced by the existing mortgage. For example, if your house is worth $350,000 and you owe $200,000 on the mortgage, you might qualify for a credit limit of $62,500 ($350,000 × 0.75 = $262,500 – $ 200,000 = $62,500).

Unlike home equity loans, the interest rate on a HELOC is usually variable, so it could start out low but climb much higher. In fact, HELOCs often have a very high maximum interest rate, often much higher than the life-of-the-loan cap on an ARM. HELOC interest rates are usually tied to the prime rate, reported in *The Wall Street Journal,* rather than to one of the other indexes.

> **CAUTION**
> **Don't rely on the APR.** The APR on a HELOC takes into account only the periodic interest rate, not other charges. It would be a mistake to compare the APR on a HELOC to the APR on a home equity loan—it's apples and oranges.

You may be able to get a HELOC from your bank. Alternatively, you can shop around just as you would with a refinance or home equity line of credit. Here are the things you'll want to find out:

- **The maximum rate.** Most HELOCs have high maximum rates, around 18%.

- **The margin.** Though most lenders will set the interest rate based on the prime rate, their margins may vary. Look for a margin around 2%.

- **Minimum draw or loan balance.** Some lenders require you to take out a minimum amount on your HELOC—otherwise, they won't make any money from it. Find out what the amount is before agreeing.
- **Closing costs.** Although you'll be paying many of the same fees as you did to get your original mortgage, most lenders don't charge points on HELOCs, and the third-party fees tend to be small (and often paid by the lender).
- **Annual fee.** Some lenders require an annual fee, in the $25–$75 range. The lender may waive this in the first year.
- **Cancellation fee.** A lender may charge a cancellation fee of around $350–$500. Again, in some cases—if you keep the HELOC for three years, for example—this may be waivable.

Even though a HELOC is like a credit card, we don't recommend you treat it like one. As explained above, it's best to use home equity to increase the value of your home, rather than to fund other purchases. Many homeowners get HELOCs for emergencies, but don't draw on them otherwise.

Tax Breaks for Homeownership

Are You a First-Time Itemizer?_____169

Tax Deductions for Homeowners_____172

   Mortgage interest deduction, including points_____172

   Prepayment and late payment penalties_____173

   Private mortgage insurance (PMI)_____173

   State and local property taxes_____174

   Interest on a home improvement loan_____174

   Interest on home equity debt_____175

   Home office expenses_____175

   Moving costs_____176

Tax Credits for Homeowners_____177

In Case You Sell: Plan Ahead to Avoid Capital Gains Taxes___180

Your Property Tax Bill: Keeping It Low_____183

   How property taxes are calculated_____183

   How to protest a rise in your property tax assessment___184

Y ou've probably heard about the tax benefits of owning a home, and now it's time to cash in. Fortunately, even if you hate numbers, some of the tax rules are pretty easy to understand.

If they're so easy, why not just wait until April to read this chapter? One reason is that if you understand what you're going to owe, you can change your current tax withholdings. That puts cash into your pocket now, rather than waiting to receive a refund. (Refunds are fun, but you could probably put that money to use, rather than giving the IRS the benefit of investing it, right?) The ideal is to calculate your withholding so that you break even—you neither owe nor receive money at the end of the tax year.

RESOURCE
Need help estimating how much money to have withheld from your paycheck? See the IRS's withholding calculator, at www.irs .gov (click "More Online Tools," then "IRS Withholding Calculator").

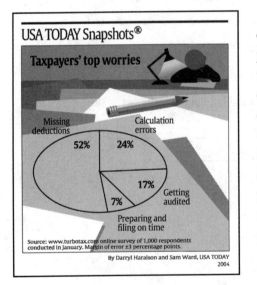

USA TODAY Snapshots®

Taxpayers' top worries

Missing deductions 52%

Calculation errors 24%

17% Getting audited

7% Preparing and filing on time

Source: www.turbotax.com online survey of 1,000 respondents conducted in January. Margin of error ±3 percentage points.

By Darryl Haralson and Sam Ward, USA TODAY
2004

More importantly, you can't claim what you can't prove. Many people get a smaller refund than they're entitled to because they either fail to keep good records or don't know that tax deductions or credits are available to them. So, create files for the categories covered in this chapter, and you'll be ready to file a lower tax return—and back it up if the IRS asks questions.

This chapter will cover:

- what it means to itemize deductions, and why you probably should
- home-related tax deductions you'll benefit from
- tax credits for homeownership
- ways to minimize your capital gains tax when you sell, and
- how to monitor and potentially appeal reassessments of your property tax bill.

Are You a First-Time Itemizer?

When you file your federal taxes, you're guaranteed one of two choices to reduce your overall tax liability: You can take the "standard deduction" or you can "itemize" your deductions. The standard deduction is a set amount you subtract from your taxable income—for 2008, $5,450 for a single person, $8,000 if head of household, and $10,900 if married filing jointly. For example, if you're single and make $50,000 in 2008, and you take the standard deduction, you will be taxed on only $44,550 ($50,000 − $5,450) when you file your 2009 return.

USA TODAY Snapshots®

Who prepares your tax return?

I do my own 59%

I hire a professional 41%

Source: TD Ameritrade survey of 1,000 investors with assets of $100,000 or more. Margin of error ±5 percentage points.

By Jae Yang and Dave Merrill, USA TODAY 2007

Your other option is to "itemize" your deductions. That means that you subtract certain qualifying expenses from your income, including mortgage interest and property tax, instead of taking the standard deduction. If the amount of those qualifying expenses is higher than the standard deduction, you're better off itemizing (that is, separately listing and claiming them).

Choosing the Best Tax Preparer

USA TODAY's Sandra Block has reported extensively on tax preparers at major franchises who've faced criminal penalties for filing tax returns claiming fraudulent refunds. Many of these tax preparers were inadequately educated and poorly trained, and their compensation was directly tied to the number of returns they prepared.

As Block notes, however, you are responsible for the information on your tax return, even if the guy who did your taxes is carted off to jail.

In response to such past problems, Congress passed a law in 2007 under which, Block explains, "Tax preparers are subject to tougher standards for positions taken on taxpayers' returns." And Francis Degen, an enrolled preparer in Setauket, New York, told Block, "Don't be surprised if your tax preparer requests more documents to support your deductions."

Nevertheless, before hiring a tax preparer, Block suggests you:

- **Check the preparer's credentials.** An enrolled agent is a tax professional who has at least five years' work experience at the IRS or has passed an IRS-administered two-day exam. A certified public accountant has a college degree and has passed a certification exam. Both are authorized to represent you in an IRS audit.

- **Find out if the preparer has taken continuing education courses.** Ask about the types of returns he's prepared and how long he's been in business, says Roger Harris, chairman of the government relations committee for the National Association of Enrolled Agents.

- **Ask for an estimate of the cost.** Many preparers base their fees on the complexity of your return, so the preparer might not be able to give you an exact price, Harris says. But a reputable preparer should be able to provide a range of costs.

Choosing the Best Tax Preparer, continued

If the preparer bases the fee on a percentage of your refund, head for the door. Those preparers have a vested interest in illegally inflating your refund.

- **Make sure the preparer will be around after April 17.** Some tax preparers close their doors once the tax season is over. That could be a problem if the IRS raises questions about your return.

Finally, a reputable preparer won't be afraid to tell you that you're not eligible for a particular tax deduction or credit that would reduce your tax bill. When you ask a tax preparer a question, Harris says, "You want an honest answer. Sometimes, that answer is no."

 "Don't just go to any old tax preparer: Do some checking around first," by Sandra Block, April 10, 2007; "Bone up before you tackle those taxes," by Sandra Block; February 15, 2008.

If you're like many new homeowners, you've never itemized your tax deductions before. But homeownership will probably change that picture. Itemizing involves a step up from the good old 1040EZ, but it's not all that complicated.

EXAMPLE: Josh bought his home using a $200,000, 30-year, fixed-rate mortgage at 6% interest. He'll pay around $12,000 the first year in interest alone. (That doesn't count property taxes, points on the mortgage, or any other tax-deductible expenses.)

The standard deduction is $5,450. But if Josh itemizes his deductions, he can deduct the $12,000 in interest payments instead. By itemizing even this one deduction, almost $7,000 less of Josh's income will be taxed.

TIP

Keep good records of all deductible expenses. You'll want to set up separate files of receipts for common non-household deductions such as unreimbursed business expenses (office equipment and travel), educational expenses (tuition and books), charitable contributions, and unreimbursed medical expenses. Consider getting help from a tax professional—even your meeting might be tax deductible!

Tax Deductions for Homeowners

Below is a rundown of the tax deductions you may be eligible for. Fortunately, you won't have to meticulously keep track of each expense. That's because your lender (for mortgage or home equity loans) will send you a statement at the end of each year, summarizing how much you spent on qualifying deductible interest. If you pay your property taxes from an escrow account, that will also be included on the statement.

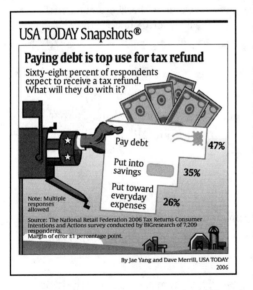

USA TODAY Snapshots®

Paying debt is top use for tax refund

Sixty-eight percent of respondents expect to receive a tax refund. What will they do with it?

Pay debt 47%

Put into savings 35%

Put toward everyday expenses 26%

Note: Multiple responses allowed

Source: The National Retail Federation 2006 Tax Returns Consumer Intentions and Actions survey conducted by BIGresearch of 7,209 respondents. Margin of error ±1 percentage point.

By Jae Yang and Dave Merrill, USA TODAY 2006

Mortgage interest deduction, including points

One of your biggest deductions will be the interest you pay on your home mortgage, until you hit the limit of either $1 million for individuals and married couples filing jointly or $500,000 for marrieds filing separately. This deduction is particularly helpful during the early years of a fixed-rate mortgage, when most of your payment goes toward paying off the interest you owe. If you have an interest-only loan, your entire mortgage payment will be deductible for several years.

If you bought your house within the last tax year, and you paid points, you get to deduct those, too. (Points are additional and usually optional fees paid when you first took out your mortgage, in exchange for a reduced interest rate—which is why they're regarded by the IRS as prepaid interest.) Points are tax-deductible in the year you paid them to buy your main home, assuming they meet certain IRS criteria (including that they were computed as a percentage of the loan, that they not be excessive for your area, and that they're really points as opposed to service fees, as shown on your settlement statement).

If you later refinance, you can also deduct points on the new loan, but not all at once—you must instead prorate (spread) them over the life of the loan.

RESOURCE
For more information: See IRS Publication 936, *Home Mortgage Interest Deduction*, available at www.irs.gov.

Prepayment and late payment penalties

We're hoping you didn't get a mortgage with a prepayment penalty, but if you did, and then prepay it, your penalty payment will be tax deductible. (Your prepayments might be in the form of advance payments of principal, a refinance, or the sale of your home.)

Similarly, if you make a late payment on your mortgage and are charged an interest-based penalty (as opposed to a flat fee), it's also deductible. (If you're prone to paying late, think about setting up an automatic bill pay arrangement at your bank.)

These penalties should be listed on Form 1098, the tax document you get each year from your mortgage lender.

Private mortgage insurance (PMI)

If your mortgage was for more than 80% of your home's purchase price, the lender probably required you to buy PMI. This insurance reimburses the lender if you default on the loan and the foreclosure sale price is less than the amount you owed (the mortgage plus the costs of the sale). (Notice that you pay the premiums, but the lender gets the protection.)

USA TODAY Snapshots®

Two lengthy codes
Number of pages in:

King James Bible **1,472**

U.S. tax code **20,000**

Sources: Amazon.com and Internal Revenue Service

By David Stuckey and Adrienne Lewis, USA TODAY
2005

PMI is tax-deductible for mortgages taken out in 2007 through 2010. However, the amount of the deduction depends on your income—once it goes over $100,000 per year, the deduction starts to phase out. Check in with your tax adviser for details.

State and local property taxes

Most people pay around 1% to 4% of their home's value each year in state and local property taxes, though the amount varies between localities. These taxes are deductible from your federal tax. Check your records from the closing. You may have paid a chunk of the year's taxes at that time.

Interest on a home improvement loan

If you take out a loan to make improvements that increase your home's value, prolong its life, or adapt its use (such as for older or disabled people), you can deduct the interest on that loan, with no limit. These improvements might, for example, include adding a deck, replacing the roof, or installing a shower accessible for a person with disabilities. You can't, however, deduct the interest on loans used for normal maintenance and repairs, such as repainting the kitchen or fixing a window.

Interest on home equity debt

You can deduct interest you pay on a home equity loan. That means any home equity loan, even if you don't use the money to buy, build, or improve your home. You can, for example, use such a loan for a child's college tuition or family medical bills. However, certain dollar limits apply. The maximum you can deduct is whichever of the below two is less:

- **If you're an individual or a married couple filing jointly,** the interest on a $100,000 loan; or the interest on a $50,000 loan if you're married but filing separately, or

- **The amount by which your total home equity and mortgage debt exceeds the fair market value of your home**—for example, if your home is worth $200,000 and you already owe $175,000 on a mortgage, you can't deduct interest on more than $25,000 of home equity debt.

While this deductibility makes it tempting to take out a home equity loan to finance other purchases, there is reason to be cautious, as discussed in Chapter 7.

Home office expenses

If you use part of your home regularly and exclusively for a home-based business, you may be able to deduct a portion of the related expenses— including your mortgage, utility bills, and home maintenance and repair costs. And you can deduct the full amount of any expenses that are solely and directly for your home office (or workshop or studio), such as painting the room and adding a rug or lamp.

However, the home office deduction can be more trouble than it's worth. For starters, the exclusive-use requirement prevents many people from using the deduction, because they can't give up space to solely business use. For example, you may need the same desk area for your business as for your online shopping and personal emailing. (If you can at least section off a portion of a room for exclusive use, you may be able to get around this—but the smaller the amount of space devoted to your home office, the less the deduction will be worth to you.)

Another issue is that if you sell, you'll have to pay capital gains tax on the profit you earn from the portion of your home used as a home office within the last two years. You won't be able to shield it under the capital gains tax exclusion of $500,000 for married couples filing joint returns and $250,000 for singles.

> **RESOURCE**
> **Need more information on the home office deduction?**
> See *Working for Yourself: Law & Taxes for Independent Contractors, Freelancers & Consultants,* by Stephen Fishman (Nolo).

Moving costs

If you move because of a new job that's more than 50 miles farther from your current residence than your previous job, you may be able to deduct certain moving expenses—for example, the cost of packing and moving your household goods to your new home and transporting yourself and your family. But, as USA TODAY's Sandra Block explains, "That's about it. You can't deduct house-hunting trips or temporary living expenses. If you stay overnight in a hotel while traveling to the new home, that's deductible, but restaurant meals aren't."

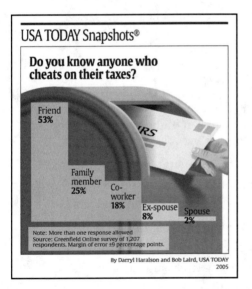

USA TODAY Snapshots®

Do you know anyone who cheats on their taxes?

Friend **53%**

Family member **25%**

Co-worker **18%**

Ex-spouse **8%**

Spouse **2%**

Note: More than one response allowed
Source: Greenfield Online survey of 1,207 respondents. Margin of error ±9 percentage points.

By Darryl Haralson and Bob Laird, USA TODAY 2005

Perhaps your new employer has offered to reimburse you for some or all of your moving costs. That's all very well, but Block warns that it "can create big tax headaches later on. Any employer-provided reimbursement that isn't a deductible moving expense—basically the cost of moving your stuff and yourself—is considered taxable income by the IRS. So if your company pays for house-hunting trips, closing costs, or temporary living expenses, the cost of those services will show up on your W-2 as taxable income.

"That could result in a big tax bill at the end of the year. By increasing your taxable income, the reimbursements could also make you ineligible for some tax credits and benefits that phase out at specific income levels."

If you're still at the negotiation stage, you can ask your employer for what's known as a "gross-up"—meaning that money for the tax bill is included in your relocation package.

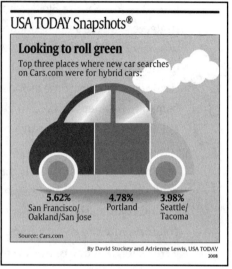

USA TODAY Snapshots®

Looking to roll green

Top three places where new car searches on Cars.com were for hybrid cars:

| 5.62% | 4.78% | 3.98% |
| San Francisco/ Oakland/San Jose | Portland | Seattle/ Tacoma |

Source: Cars.com

By David Stuckey and Adrienne Lewis, USA TODAY
2008

RESOURCE

For more information on the various tax deductions: See IRS Publication 530, *Tax Information for First-Time Homeowners*, available at www.irs.gov.

Tax Credits for Homeowners

Occasionally, the government will come up with a tax credit that benefits homeowners. It's usually based on something you bought, like an energy-efficient water heater. Unlike tax deductions, tax credits are actually a dollar-for-dollar reduction in your tax liability. A tax deduction merely lets you subtract an amount from your gross income before calculating how much of that income will be taxed. For example, if your gross income is $80,000 and you have a $2,000 tax deduction, your taxable income is $78,000. Your tax will be reduced, but you won't get to knock $2,000 off what you owe.

Missed a Deduction? How to File an Amended Return

USA TODAY's Sandra Block compares the feeling of realizing you neglected to take a tax deduction to "that dreadful feeling you get when you've locked your car, only to realize the keys are still in the ignition." But, she adds, you can claim any credit or deduction you overlooked the first time around, by filing an amended return. And filing one is easier than you might think, says Bob Scharin, senior tax analyst for RIA-Thomson Tax & Accounting.

You need your original tax return and Form 1040X, available at www.irs.gov. Form 1040X has three columns. In the first column, copy the figures you reported on your original tax return. In the second column, show any changes on your return. In the third column, write the correct amount.

Form 1040X is one of the few forms that can't be filed electronically with the IRS. Some tax software programs include a program for filing an amended return, but you'll still have to print out the form and mail it. A tax preparer can file an amended return, but the preparer's fees may exceed the amount of the refund.

The IRS recommends waiting at least three weeks after you e-file your original return, or eight weeks after you file a paper return, before submitting an amended return. "You want to make sure the IRS processes them in appropriate order," Scharin says.

Don't file an amended return if you discover you made a math error on your original return, or failed to attach some documents. Many of these errors are caught by the IRS when it processes returns. In that case, the IRS will automatically adjust your refund to reflect the correct amount. If documents are missing, the IRS will contact you.

 "Missed a deduction? File an amended tax return to get your money," by Sandra Block, April 24, 2007.

You may be able to take advantage of some of the tax credits for homebuyers or homeowners, including:

- **Hybrid car tax credit.** Purchase a brand-new hybrid vehicle before 2010, and you may qualify for a tax credit (the maximum amount for most cars is around $3,000). The catch is that the total number of credits available per vehicle model is limited, so popular models like the Toyota Prius have already reached their maximum allowance and don't qualify. The exact amount of the credit varies by the size of the car. For more information, visit the IRS website at www.irs.gov (search for "hybrid cars and alternative fuel vehicles").

- **Solar tax credit.** If you install a solar water-heating or electric power system by December 31, 2008, you may qualify for a tax credit of up to $2,000 per year. More information is available on the IRS website.

- **First-time homeowner tax credit.** This came from the housing bailout legislation passed in July 2008. As USA TODAY's Sandra Block explains, "First-time homebuyers who purchase a primary residence between April 9, 2008 and July 1, 2009 will be eligible for a tax credit of $7,500 or 10% of the purchase price, whichever is less. On the surface this looks like a pretty good deal. And this tax credit is refundable, which means you'll qualify even if your federal tax bill is less than $7,500, says Bob Scharin, senior tax analyst for Thomson Reuters. For example, a first-time home buyer who owes the IRS $2,000 would receive a refund of $5,500. But this provision includes a lot of caveats, including:

  - **You'll have to pay it back.** While this break has been labeled a tax credit, it's really an interest-free loan. Homebuyers who claim the credit will be required to pay it back in equal installments over 15 years, starting in the second year after the home is purchased. If you buy a house in 2008 and claim a $7,500 credit on your 2008 tax return, you'll have to pay an additional $500 a year in taxes for 15 years, starting in 2010.

- **If you sell your house before the 15 years has elapsed,** you'll have to repay the entire balance, unless you sell at a loss.
- **If your income exceeds certain thresholds,** you're ineligible for the credit. The tax credit phases out for single taxpayers with adjusted gross income of $75,000 to $95,000. For married couples who file jointly, the phaseout is $150,000 to $170,000."

Keep your eyes on the news and on the updates to this book at www.nolo.com for new or renewed tax credits. And to find out whether there are energy-saving incentives available where you live, check the website for the Database of State Incentives for Renewable Energy at www.dsireusa.org.

In Case You Sell:
Plan Ahead to Avoid Capital Gains Taxes

While it may be too soon for you to imagine selling your first home, an important benefit is available if and when you do. Thanks to the Taxpayer Relief Act of 1997, you won't have to pay capital gains tax (normally 15%) on the first $250,000 you make on the place. Double that to $500,000 if you're married and filing jointly, or to $250,000 per person if you co-owned your home.

To qualify, you usually must have lived in the home (as your principal residence) for two out of the previous five years before selling. You may, however, qualify for a partial exclusion if you sold your house because the location of your job changed; for health reasons; or due to other unforeseen circumstances such a natural disaster, death, act of terrorism, pregnancy resulting in multiple births, or divorce.

If you're recently married and file jointly, you can qualify for the full $500,000 deduction as long as one meets the ownership requirement and both have lived there two of the last five years (as long as neither of you have excluded gain from the sale of another home in the last two years).

If you're in a starter home and plan to move, keep a close eye on the calendar—if the home appreciates significantly, you don't want to sell before the two years are up.

TIP

Won't owe any capital gains tax on your home sale? No need to report this to the IRS. But, as USA TODAY's Sandra Block explains, "If you've lived in the home for less than two years, you should keep good records in case you're audited. Useful documents include notice of a job transfer, a letter from your doctor, or birth certificates for the quadruplets."

Chances are you won't earn profits over the $250,000/$500,000 exclusion, in which case you won't have to worry about capital gains tax at all. Still, big profits can happen. If home values appreciate crazily in your area, or you simply stay in your home long enough to enjoy the overall rises in value that seem to characterize U.S. real estate, you could be looking at major gains—and thousands of dollars in tax liability.

Let's say, for example, that you bought a house for $200,000 when you were single. Three years later, you married and your spouse moved in (but the title is still in your name alone). The next year, you sell the house for $475,000 and buy a bigger one to fit your growing family. It looks like your taxable profit will be $25,000 after subtracting out the $250,000 exclusion. Will you have to pay tax on that entire amount? (A 15% bite out of $25,000 would be $3,750.)

Fortunately, there's more to the analysis. Yes, your profit is the amount that you gained over and above the amount you paid for the house—but the true amount that you paid for the house (in tax lingo, your "basis") may be more than just its purchase price. It also includes amounts you laid out to:

- **bring about the house purchase** (such as closing costs, including recording fees, title insurance, transfer taxes, utility installation fees, and more; but not including the costs of getting your mortgage)
- **later bring about the house sale** (such as advertising costs, commissions to the real estate agents—averaging 5% of the sales price legal fees, and loan charges you agreed to pay), and
- **make improvements to the house** (like adding a new room or deck or installing a new heating system, but not performing maintenance or repairs; see the IRS's list of examples of acceptable improvements below).

You can add all of these investments to your basis to reduce your taxable profit. It's only fair to you—if, for example, you spent $100,000 converting your garage to a cottage, why should the IRS benefit from your house's resulting rise in value? But you can't claim costs that you can't remember, so make copies of all your receipts and records of improvements and keep them in a separate file.

IRS List of Examples of Home Improvements

Additions

Bedroom

Bathroom

Deck

Garage

Porch

Patio

Heating & Air Conditioning

Heating system

Central air conditioning

Furnace

Duct work

Central humidifier

Filtration system

Plumbing

Septic system

Water heater

Soft water system

Filtration system

Lawn & Grounds

Landscaping

Driveway

Walkway

Fence

Retaining wall

Sprinkler system

Swimming pool

Interior Improvements

Built-in appliances

Kitchen modernization

Flooring

Wall-to-wall carpeting

Insulation

Attic

Walls

Floors

Pipes and duct work

Miscellaneous

Storm windows, doors

New roof

Central vacuum

Wiring upgrades

Satellite dish

Security system

> **RESOURCE**
>
> **Looking for more details on capital gains taxes?** There's more to know—for example, what happens if one spouse dies, or how to factor in accumulated depreciation if you take the home office deduction. See IRS Publication 523, *Selling Your Home*, available at www.irs.gov.

Your Property Tax Bill: Keeping It Low

Owning a house makes you sort of a sitting duck for tax collectors. Although the United States has no federal property tax, your state, local, and municipal governments may all be eager to extract property taxes from you.

How property taxes are calculated

How much you'll have to pay in property tax each year usually depends on the value of your house. And many governments levy taxes on only a percentage of your house's market value, such as 80% of market value. (So if your house was worth $100,000 and the tax rate was 2%, you'd have to pay 2% of $80,000, or $1,600.) The exact percentages or formula depends on where you live.

You have no doubt already experienced your first bit of sticker shock, when you had to pay a portion of the year's taxes at the house closing. And if you're not already paying your upcoming taxes as part of your monthly mortgage payment, you'll most likely receive a hefty bill once or twice a year from now on.

USA TODAY Snapshots®

Top five states with highest median property tax
(In percentage of income)

New Jersey	6.2%
Vermont	5.5%
North Dakota	5.2%
Rhode Island	5.2%
Illinois	5.0%

Source: Zillow.com

By Jae Yang and Sam Ward, USA TODAY 2008

But the sticker shock could get worse. Depending on your state's laws, your property taxes may rise regularly. These rises could be based either on a recent reassessment of your house's value or, in states that limit how much your taxes can rise all at once, on a schedule that has your taxes ultimately catching up with your property's true value year by year. Some states reassess property values on a schedule (every three years in Ohio or five years in Utah, for example); others (like California) wait until you sell the house or construct something new on the property before taking another look.

Find out the basic assessment rules where you live by going to the tax assessor's page on your local government's website (www.netronline.com is a useful portal for individual counties) or by viewing summaries on websites like www.retirementliving.com.

You'll be especially interested in your state's rules if and when your property gets reassessed. Mistakes happen. (In fact, many mistakes took place when physical records were converted into computer data.) Depending on how busy your local assessor's office is, they may not even send someone to look at your property—or may hire nonprofessionals to do mass assessments. Sometimes the mistakes are as basic as the assessor saying you have two bathrooms rather than one or overestimating your lot size or square footage. Other mistakes are less obvious, for example if the assessor has an inflated view of your property's current market value.

You may also qualify for special exemptions, such as for senior citizens or veterans. For more information, contact your local assessor's office.

How to protest a rise in your property tax assessment

Whatever you do, don't just open your property tax bill, groan, and assume you're stuck. Your state should have a procedure for filing an appeal. And if you can show that the assessor did make a mistake, or overvalued your property, an appeal could save you thousands of dollars.

But you'll need a legitimate argument. This isn't like a traffic ticket, where a sympathetic judge might cut you a break just for showing up. Nor will arguing that your kids need braces and you'll have trouble paying the new tax bill carry any weight. The more you can do to back up your appeal with independent documentation, the greater your odds of success.

Why Property Taxes May Go Up Even When Home Values Drop

Reporting in 2007, USA TODAY's Dennis Cauchon found that property taxes were rising nearly everywhere for homeowners even as house prices were falling in many parts of the country.

A key reason: Despite the downturn, the market value of millions of homes still exceeds their assessed value used for tax purposes.

"Some people are irritated to learn the news," says Jim Todora, a property tax assessor in Sarasota County, Florida. "Their home's value may have gone down, but their property tax is still going up."

Property tax limits were passed to prevent big increases during times of soaring home values. Those laws let assessments rise, slowly but steadily, until they reach market value.

Property taxes from homeowners and businesses go mostly to local governments, paying for schools, roads, police, and other services. Collections rose 7% in 2006 to a record $377 billion, although the median home price climbed just 1% nationwide and fell in many places. The disconnect is likely to continue.

All but five states limit how quickly property taxes can rise. After a decade of soaring housing prices, it can take years for a home's tax value to catch up to its market value, even with the current dip.

In the long run, property tax limits save homeowners money. Clark County, Nevada, Treasurer Laura Fitzpatrick would owe $4,781 in taxes on her Las Vegas house if it were assessed at market value. Instead, she'll pay $3,036. "Those are big savings, even if this year my taxes went up more than the value of my house," she says.

Other reasons few tax bills will shrink:

- **Higher tax rates.** Many local governments where home values have softened—including the Washington, DC, suburbs of Northern Virginia—are increasing tax rates to offset lower assessments. The city of Fairfax, Virginia, for example, plans to raise its tax rate by 4.5% to offset a 3% decline in house values.

Why Property Taxes May Go Up Even When Home Values Drop, continued

- **Delayed assessments.** Property taxes often are based on market values that are several years old. New Hampshire revalues property once every five years, most recently in 2006 when prices peaked.

"People read about how the market has crashed," says Polk County Assessor Jim Maloney in Des Moines. "But that change doesn't show up for a long time."

 "Property taxes up as house prices fall; Most values higher than assessments," by Dennis Cauchon, April 25, 2007.

For example, if the assessor thinks your property is worth more than it is, you can search the local tax records and make copies to show that comparable properties (ideally around five to ten of them) have been assessed for less. A comparable property is one within about six blocks, of a similar size and number of rooms, with similar features and upgrades. Gathering actual sales information on comparable properties—sold during the same tax year, not more recently—will also help. (See free websites such as www.zillow.com and www.domania.com, and print out the result pages.) You may also want to take photos of neighboring properties to show their condition relative to your house's.

CAUTION
Learn your appeal rights. Many states impose a time limit, often 30 days. Sit around too long, and you've essentially agreed to pay your new, higher tax bill. One more thing to consider: In some states, you can file an appeal only every few years; so don't waste your chance on an appeal that you can be fairly certain will go nowhere.

Depending on the local rules, the first step toward your appeal may simply be to attend an informal meeting with the assessor. If that doesn't resolve matters, you'll probably be asked to prepare a written argument and attend a hearing, usually with a board composed of people from the assessor's office. If their decision doesn't go your way, you can normally appeal again, often to an independent board of review first and then up through the state court system.

Who pays the highest property taxes?

It's doesn't always correlate with home values. Here's a look at the top payers in each U.S. region:

Where you live	County with highest taxes	Median property taxes	Median home value
Northeast	Hunterdon, New Jersey	$7,999	$475,300
Midwest	Lake, Illinois	$5,508	$281,900
West	Marin, California	$4,973	$901,900
South	Loudoun, Virginia	$4,467	$558,800

Source: *The Tax Foundation, www.taxfoundation.org.*

Of course, the appeal process will involve paying various filing fees, and if you end up in court, you'll probably want a lawyer's help. Also, the assessor's office has the same appeal rights as you do. That means that even if you win, your tax bill will not be lowered until all the appeals are done. And you'll need to weigh the hike in your tax bill against the legal and court costs.

TIP

Make your best case from the start. Once you're presenting a case in state court, you can't, except in rare situations, submit new information. The court just checks to see whether the lower reviewing body made a legal mistake applying the rules to your situation. The court won't hear your whole case over again, so get all the relevant documents and sources of support in from the beginning.

Sweat Equity:
Home Renovation Projects
That Pay Off

How Renovations Can Increase Resale Value_____190

    Factors that affect resale value_____191

    Projects that increase resale value_____193

What You Can Do ... And What to Leave to the Pros_____195

    Definitely DIY material_____195

    Iffy territory for DIY-ers_____196

    Hands off: Hire a pro_____197

Before You Leap: Learning More About the Project_____197

    Deciding what you want_____198

    Finding how-to information_____199

    Creating a project budget_____201

    Saving on equipment and materials_____202

Scheduling Your Project_____204

Hiring Extra Hands_____206

    Who should you hire?_____206

    Who pays if a worker gets injured?_____206

    How much should you pay for services?_____209

C hances are, your home wasn't "just right" the day you moved in. The former owner doubtless left some personality behind in the paint colors, tile choices, and more. And you've probably discovered other little quirks and imperfections, like a showerhead with abysmal water pressure or a tacky old light fixture that doesn't match your modern furniture. Perhaps you have bigger ambitions, like taking out a wall to expand the kitchen area.

But how do you know when it's realistic—not to mention cost-effective—to forge ahead? The key is proper planning. In this chapter, we'll cover:

- deciding which projects will pay off in resale value
- figuring out which projects you can do yourself
- researching a renovation project to make sure it's doable
- budgeting the project and making your dollar stretch
- planning the project, and
- hiring unskilled workers.

The next chapter will pick up with how to hire and work with skilled professionals on major home-improvement projects.

How Renovations Can Increase Resale Value

Home improvements cost money, whether you do them yourself or hire others. But you may be able to recoup some of your investment when it's time to sell. (Who wouldn't pay more for that expanded kitchen?) The catch is that not all projects have such a positive financial impact.

In fact, even the projects that offer the highest investment return don't always raise your house price enough to recoup their full cost. So, before we launch into a full discussion of resale values, let's remember: This is your house, and your primary goal should

How long will you be staying?

U.S. homeowners stay in a home an average of six years.

be to make it a place you'll love living in. If that means adding a double vanity in the bathroom, replacing the carpet in the living room with eco-friendly cork, or turning a tiny extra bedroom into a super-sized closet, so be it—as long as your budget can handle it. The longer you plan to live in the home, the longer you'll get to enjoy the improvements yourself.

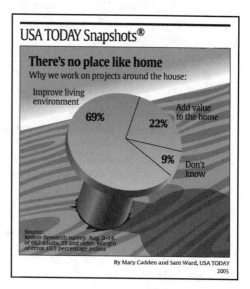

USA TODAY Snapshots®

There's no place like home
Why we work on projects around the house:

Improve living environment
69%

Add value to the home
22%

9% Don't know

Source: Kelton Research survey, Aug. 9-14, of 662 adults, 25 and older. Margin of error ±3.5 percentage points

By Mary Cadden and Sam Ward, USA TODAY
2005

Also keep in mind that even if you don't recover the full cost of a renovation, you may be able to save money if the improvements allow you to stay put longer. For example, though you probably won't recoup every cent when adding a bedroom, it may be cheaper than buying a bigger house (and paying transaction and moving costs). And if you like your home's location, that's another good reason to renovate.

Factors that affect resale value

Whether your project increases your home's resale value will depend on many factors, such as:

- **Market conditions.** When the local real estate market is hot and favors sellers, you're more likely to see a return on your investment, because the competition among buyers will drive up the selling price.

- **Neighborhood.** Your home will retain its value best if it fits the neighborhood, because potential buyers will look to the neighborhood for a particular kind of home. For example, if you're in a neighborhood of three-bedroom, two-bath homes, and you add on to create a five-bedroom, four-bath home, you may find it difficult to sell later, because people who can afford that size home will be looking in different neighborhoods. Then again, if lots of people in the neighborhood are renovating, doing the same will help you compete—as long as your project remains consistent with the types of changes others are making.

- **Quality of upgrades.** Generally speaking, you'll get more out of midpriced upgrades than expensive, high-quality ones. If you're renovating a kitchen, for example, custom cabinets will cost you significantly more than off-the-shelf ones or semicustom ones, but you're not likely to see that return in your bottom line.

- **General appeal.** The more your house inspires "oohs" and "ahs" from a broad spectrum of potential buyers, the more likely you are to get good value from a renovation—and vice versa. For example, if you replace an existing bathtub and shower combo in your master bath with a deluxe steam shower, you may not get as much return, because the lack of bathtub will be a turnoff for many buyers.

- **Age of your home.** If your home is relatively new, it's less likely to seem dated or in need of renovation by the time you sell. That means you're less likely to increase its value significantly by remodeling. On the other hand, if your beautiful older home in a nice neighborhood badly needs a kitchen update, you stand to do well when you sell.

- **The rest of your home.** While it may be important to you to make one particular room or feature shine, doing it at the expense of the rest of the house can be a drawback for buyers. For example, if you put in a pool and landscape the backyard to create a tropical oasis, yet leave the 70s décor inside, the yard will stick out like a sore thumb instead of a shining star.

- **Price range.** As a practical matter, you're more likely to recoup your investment in a home at the higher end of the price spectrum. If comparable homes go for $250,000, you probably won't come out ahead if you spend $35,000 adding a deluxe master bathroom. The same isn't necessarily true in a $800,000 home, however—there, you're more likely to find a buyer willing to pay extra for the luxury.

💡 TIP

Don't forget the maintenance. As USA TODAY's Thomas A. Fogarty explains, "A home improvement changes the look or character of your house. Major maintenance is usually invisible. It's what needs to be done to assure your home remains standing for the next generation or two—a new roof, foundation repair, modernizing plumbing and wiring. Experts say homeowners should view major maintenance not in terms of boosting future sales prices, but in terms of protecting the investment they've already made."

Projects that increase resale value

With these general factors in mind, past homeowner experience has shown that certain projects are more likely to increase value than others. These include:

- **Kitchens.** Although remodeling kitchens is comparatively expensive, it can yield one of the highest returns on investment.

- **Bathrooms.** Purchasers are drawn to newer and expanded bathrooms, especially in older homes where the original facilities tend to be modest by today's standards.

- **Front-yard facelifts.** First impressions count—and even small changes like a flower border can have a big impact.

- **Siding.** Buyers may size up your home exterior before they even get out of their car. Vinyl siding lasts 20 years or more; more expensive fiber-cement siding even longer. Buyers will appreciate and pay more for these low-maintenance improvements.

USA TODAY Snapshots®

Clicking on home improvement

Online retail spending on home improvement products: (in billions)

2001 — $1.8

2006 — $13.6

Source: Jupiter Research

By David Stuckey and Robert W. Ahrens, USA TODAY
2008

- **Roofs and windows.** Unfortunately, roofs and windows in good repair are something that buyers expect. If yours are in poor condition, the value of your home will go down, because buyers will realize they'll have to come up with extra cash soon. Thus while replacing roofs and windows won't necessarily increase the value of your home, not replacing them could decrease it.

Small Improvements Can Bring the Biggest Return

Thomas A. Fogarty of USA TODAY spoke with Bradley Inman, founder of Internet realty company HomeGain, about the value of dealing with minor home issues—even if the house has some major shortcomings.

As Inman says, a common mistake by those preparing a house for sale is excessive spending on improvements.

Sellers are better advised to deal with major shortcomings of a house in negotiations rather than to fix them.

A HomeGain survey of 2,000 realty agents found that small upgrades can have a big payback at sale time.

For example, a $470 yard clean-up and landscaping job can be expected to add about four times that sum to the eventual sales price, the survey says. Painting, floor repairs, and carpet replacement in preparation for a sale also carry big returns.

USA TODAY usatoday.com "Upgrades can raise home's value; Some improvements have a bit more price-boosting potential than others," by Thomas A. Fogarty, April 26, 2002.

What You Can Do ...
And What to Leave to the Pros

You may be itching to tackle these various home renovation or improvement projects yourself, even if you've never so much as looked at a hammer. There's nothing like the satisfaction of knowing you did it on your own—plus the thrill of saving the cash you would have spent paying a pro.

Indeed, many house projects can be done yourself, or "DIY," with no special expertise or equipment. But not all of them. For the more challenging projects, factor in the time you'd spend, the frustration you might feel, and in the worst case, the extra money you might eventually pay to bring in a pro to not only do the work, but to clean up your mess.

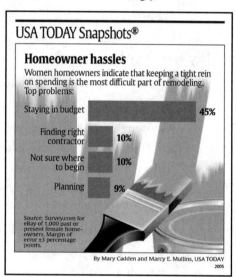

USA TODAY Snapshots®

Homeowner hassles

Women homeowners indicate that keeping a tight rein on spending is the most difficult part of remodeling. Top problems:

Staying in budget — 45%
Finding right contractor — 10%
Not sure where to begin — 10%
Planning — 9%

Source: Survey.com for eBay of 1,000 past or present female home-owners. Margin of error ±3 percentage points.

By Mary Cadden and Marcy E. Mullins, USA TODAY
2005

Definitely DIY material

Even if you don't aspire to DIY superstardom, almost anyone can handle the basics. It's reasonable to expect to take care of:

- **Regular maintenance.** Most people can learn to do simple but mundane tasks like mow the lawn, clean the gutters, or vacuum the coils on the refrigerator. (For a complete list of regular maintenance tasks and when to do to them, see Chapter 3.)

- **Basic fix-its.** These might include tasks like replacing a cracked tile, installing new locks, or repairing a broken fence. If the instructions you find online or in your local hardware store seem clear, go for it.

- **Simple upgrades.** If you're motivated, you can probably learn to do simple upgrades like putting in a dimmer switch, replacing the bathroom fixtures, or installing new baseboard trim.

- **Cosmetic changes.** Even simple changes, like repainting a room, replacing old hardware, and planting a tree can have a big impact. Motivated DIY-ers find it isn't too hard to make these changes themselves.

Iffy territory for DIY-ers

If you're going to do any of the following, you should at least look into hiring a professional:

- **A major kitchen or bath overhaul.** Ripping apart what you've got and starting over can take a lot of time—particularly inconvenient when dealing with such essential rooms—and require you to learn a variety of new skills, from plumbing to building cabinetry to installing lighting.

- **Repairing or replacing major appliances.** Don't take apart anything you're not sure you can put back together. And while it may be relatively easy to replace some of your appliances, you may want help with some of the more complicated ones, like installing a new range or dishwasher.

- **Building new outdoor features, like a deck or patio.** It may be possible to do this on your own, but it will probably take a significant amount of time and skill.

- **Replacing doors, windows, or the roof.** Water coming in where it shouldn't can cause major problems. Don't do these yourself unless you're positive you can get it right.

- **Installing insulation.** Though installing insulation doesn't necessarily require much skill, it may be more trouble than it's worth. That's because professionals today use spray guns to blow it in—making it a relatively quick and inexpensive task.

Hands off: Hire a pro

There's no way around it: Getting the following jobs done without the help of a professional (or a whole crew) won't be practical or in some cases possible:

- **Moving walls or changing the roofline.** If you're making major structural changes, you'll probably have no choice—your local city planning department will likely require that a structural engineer confirm that the planned project meets building codes and is structurally sound.

- **Adding on.** If you're going to be adding square footage, you'll probably be required to work with at least an engineer (and maybe a land surveyor) to get it done. You'll also likely need someone to lay the foundation, plus install the electrical, plumbing, and heating and air conditioning.

- **Moving gas lines, wiring, or plumbing.** Don't risk your health and safety to save a few dollars. Unless you have relevant experience, you're better off hiring experienced professionals to deal with any of these changes.

Of course, these lists don't cover every possible home project or renovation. (You don't need us to tell you not to try installing your own swimming pool.) And we haven't begun to discuss your many options when it comes to working with professionals. You may hire a general contractor to manage an entire kitchen remodel, or you may just want to hire an electrician to install lighting and grounded outlets after you do everything else yourself. We'll talk about how to hire professionals in Chapter 10.

Before You Leap: Learning More About the Project

Unlike many other new tasks—would you go skydiving without learning how to use a parachute first?—it's tempting to jump into improvement or renovation projects before you've really figured out what's involved. But there are many good reasons to resist that temptation.

First, a little research will allow you to see what skills and materials your project will take. If you don't have the skills, you'll either have to learn them or hire someone else to pitch in. Likewise, your range of tools and supplies may not include those you need to get the job done, so you'll have to figure out whether to borrow, purchase, or rent them, and what it will cost.

Next, your research will allow you to accurately estimate the time and expense it will take to complete the project. True, estimates aren't always accurate, but you'll at least get a ballpark figure and be able to decide whether the project is realistic given your budget and other commitments.

CROSS REFERENCE

Not sure what to do first? Look back at Chapter 2, where you first set your priorities.

Deciding what you want

You may already have a sense of what changes you want to make in your home. But to fill in the details and get more inspiration, check out home improvement television shows and magazines. Also visit home improvement stores and showrooms to see how a finished room or product looks.

RESOURCE

Want a green remodel? Now's a great time to make your house more energy efficient, bring in more natural lighting, reduce your exposure to toxic chemicals, and minimize waste. See Chapter 4 for more information. And for a handy series of guides from one of the greenest U.S. cities, go to www.seattle.gov/dclu and click "Green Building," then (under "Green Building Tools"), "Green Remodel Guides." Also see www.greenhomeguide.com.

Start clipping pictures or even taking photos of designs and products that appeal to you. (And without getting too obsessive, keep track of the price tags where possible.) Before the clippings turn into a mountain, get organized. Find an accordion file or designate a space in a filing cabinet.

Remodeling activity amounts to about 2% of the total U.S. economy. (Source: Harvard's Joint Center for Housing Studies.)

You next step is to create a list of all the features that you want in your renovation—no doubt based, at least in part, on what your current, unrenovated house lacks. Think of this as a dream list, which you'll probably refine and narrow as you gather more information. For example, you may later find that the changes would over-improve the home, you can't afford to do everything you'd hoped, or your home's structure won't support the renovation. But if you end up working with a design professional or architect (discussed in Chapter 10), your clipped pictures and list will give that person a good starting place.

Finding how-to information

Once you know what you want, you'll want to know what it takes to make it happen. Thanks to the trend in DIY, you shouldn't have to look far to get basic information on any home renovation project. Your best sources will include:

Websites. For both instructions and costs, the easiest place to look first is online. Try the websites for home improvement television networks (www.hgtv.com, www

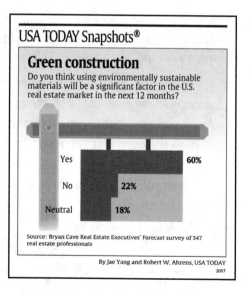

USA TODAY Snapshots®

Green construction

Do you think using environmentally sustainable materials will be a significant factor in the U.S. real estate market in the next 12 months?

Yes — 60%
No — 22%
Neutral — 18%

Source: Bryan Cave Real Estate Executives' Forecast survey of 347 real estate professionals

By Jae Yang and Robert W. Ahrens, USA TODAY
2007

.diynetwork.com), magazines (www.thisoldhouse.com, www.finehomebuilding.com), or stores (www.lowes.com, www.homedepot.com). Also check out forums or blogs where other DIY-ers discuss their trials and tribulations.

Books. Save some money: Many local libraries offer a wide selection of home improvement manuals. We also know someone who sat down in a comfy chair in a bookstore, pulled a few relevant titles off the shelf, read for a few hours, and retiled a bathroom the next day. Look for books dealing with your specific project, and buy a general how-to guide (such as *Reader's Digest's Complete Do-It-Yourself Manual*). But don't rely too heavily on cost estimates in books, which may be out of date and won't account for regional and other price differences.

USA TODAY Snapshots®

A place to store stuff
What Americans value most in their dream homes:

Built-in storage **63%**
Bathroom connected to every bedroom **24%**
High-tech features[1] **12%**
Luxury appointments[2] **2%**

1 – includes security video monitors, surround sound, Internet connections
2 – includes gold-plated faucets, crystal chandeliers, marble floors.
Note: Total does not add up to 100 due to rounding.
Source: Beazer Homes survey of 548 adults with a minimum annual household income of $40,000, conducted by MarketTools.
Margin of error: ± 3 percentage points.

By Michelle Healy and Sam Ward USA TODAY
2008

Instructional videos. These can be great for walking you through a particular home improvement project, step by step and visually. Of course, the videotaped version will go more smoothly and quickly than you should anticipate. Again, check your library as well as your DVD or video subscription club like Netflix.

Classes. These will give you some hands-on training and help you accurately estimate all the materials you'll need and their total cost. Home improvement stores sometimes offer these classes at no or low cost, in the hope that you'll purchase materials from their store.

Speak with professionals. You can always contact professionals to ask them about the work they do and the costs it entails. This is a particularly good idea if you're trying to weigh whether to hire a professional to do the job. For more information on how to find professionals in your area, see Chapter 10.

Also, home improvement stores, suppliers, and wholesalers often have knowledgeable professionals on staff. They're usually ready to dispense advice, especially if it helps them get your business.

Creating a project budget

Use a budget worksheet like the one below to help you estimate what a project will cost. Be sure to account for every cost. (If you're planning a large project, your worksheet will probably be much longer than the one here.) For example, if you're redoing your kitchen, will it be out of commission for several weeks? If so, are you going to eat out every meal? Even if you're not doing a kitchen remodel, you may end up spending more money eating out, because you're just too busy or tired to cook.

CROSS REFERENCE

Short on cash? See Chapter 7 for information on ways to borrow money for home improvements, using the equity in your home.

This worksheet doesn't include the cost of your time, which can be hard to calculate. That sweat equity is among your most powerful ways to save actual cash, because as we'll discuss in Chapter 10, adding in professional labor will significantly increase your costs. Of course, if you have to take time off work or hire a babysitter, you'll have a concrete dollar figure. Add that to your calculations.

Finally, we recommend adding a 10% cushion, for unanticipated expenses like multiple daily trips to the local hardware store, an extra coat of paint when the underlying color bleeds through, or materials to patch a damaged floorboard that was hidden by the previous owner's furniture.

TIP

Check out more money-saving tips. You may be able to shave some costs from this budget after reading the section below called "Saving on equipment and materials."

Worksheet: Project Costs	
Project Description:	
Expense	Cost to rent or purchase
Materials	$
	$
	$
Tools	$
	$
	$
Training	$
	$
	$
Outside labor (handyman, electrician, babysitter, etc.)	$
	$
Permits	$
Subtotal of costs	**$**
+ 10% cushion	$
Total cost	$

If the work turns out to cost more than you can handle now, figure out whether parts of the project can be done first while others are put off. For instance, if you haven't moved into your home yet, it may make sense to remodel both the bathrooms and the kitchen now, when you don't need to use them. On the other hand, if you and your family are already in the house and plan to be there for some time, it may be less hassle to spread the work out over a few years.

Saving on equipment and materials

Does the budget look unmanageable? Here are some other options that may help stretch your hard-earned dollars.

- **Negotiate.** Particularly if you're buying materials from a local supplier, you may be able to get a lower price simply by asking for it. You'll have the most leverage if you're making a large order—for all new kitchen appliances, for example.

- **Buy from wholesalers.** Wholesalers primarily sell goods in large quantities to retailers for resale. If you deal with a wholesaler directly, you can avoid the retailer's markup. Find wholesalers through the phone book, then call and ask if they sell to the public—not all do.

- **Buy discontinued items.** If you buy last year's model refrigerator or a cabinet the manufacturer won't be making the next year, you may be able to get a discount. Just make sure you buy enough of whatever it is you need, plus replacement parts.

- **Borrow or rent tools.** Renting tools you need only occasionally can be a lot cheaper than buying them. Your city may also have a tool-lending library, or you can ask neighbors or friends to lend you tools or go in on a joint purchase.

- **Use free labor.** Friends, family, and neighbors may all be willing to help you out in exchange for a free meal and some good company. Keep this to simple tasks that are hard to mess up—you won't save cash if you have to redo it all.

- **Plan ahead.** You don't want to rent an expensive piece of equipment or pay someone to do some labor on a specific day, only to find you're not ready because you didn't finish a prerequisite task. Plan well in advance and give yourself a cushion—you won't be able to do things as quickly as a pro.

- **Calculate the value of rebates and tax credits.** Check with your electric company to see whether it provides rebates for energy-saving appliances or materials, like insulation. If any relevant tax credits are available (Congress changes these year by year), you'll find details at www.irs.gov.

- **Shop around.** Use all the resources available: the Internet, local and chain retailers, and salvage yards.

Staying Put in a Small Space

USA TODAY spoke with Libby Langdon, design expert with HGTV's *Small Space, Big Style*, about how to make the most of a space-challenged house.

"A lot of people live in smaller spaces by choice," says the designer, citing her own 450-square-foot New York apartment. "A home is not defined by dimensions." As an alternative to costly improvements that may never pay off, Langdon offers "five no-fail tips" for homes that have started to feel too small:

De-clutter. "Nobody wants to hear this. But a big, elegant home feels big and elegant because it's open and uncluttered. A small space that's organized can feel the same way."

Paint. One of the cheapest ways to open up a space. And don't be afraid to go bold. "White walls don't look bigger. They just look white."

Lighting. Dark corners make your room feel small. "Buy three-way bulbs. And no dinky lamps—get tall ones."

Extend to the ceiling. Draperies, closet doors, anything that draws your eye up creates the illusion of more height. "You will be amazed how your room expands."

Mirrors. "Do a big honking huge mirror and position it on a wall opposite a window or door to reflect the light. It's like cutting a hole in your room."

 "Instead of moving on up, some stay and upgrade; Modest homes become dreams," by Linda Bixby, January 6, 2006.

Scheduling Your Project

It's difficult to stick to a home improvement schedule—but if you're not hiring a contractor to oversee the project, you'll have to put on a coordinator's hat. For example, if you're renting equipment or hiring a professional for a particular task, you'll want to make sure everything's ready to go when they are. And of course, no one wants to live in a construction zone forever, so setting a schedule will help ensure that you actually finish the project.

Start by writing down all the tasks the project will involve, in order. Include any down time—for example, waiting for paint or caulking to dry, or for sod to set. Make sure you know what materials you'll need for each step, as well as what permits the local building department will require. For more information on permits, see Chapter 10.

Also, take a look at your own schedule of work and other obligations, and be realistic. You'll probably find it difficult to paint your kitchen one evening after work, but you might be able to do it over a few nights, for example. Again, allow extra time to deal with emergencies or unexpected surprises, either in the project or in your "regular" life. Don't plan to finish remodeling a guest bathroom the same day you expect your first houseguest to arrive.

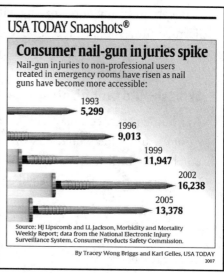

USA TODAY Snapshots®

Consumer nail-gun injuries spike

Nail-gun injuries to non-professional users treated in emergency rooms have risen as nail guns have become more accessible:

1993
5,299

1996
9,013

1999
11,947

2002
16,238

2005
13,378

Source: HJ Lipscomb and LL Jackson, Morbidity and Mortality Weekly Report; data from the National Electronic Injury Surveillance System, Consumer Products Safety Commission.

By Tracey Wong Briggs and Karl Gelles, USA TODAY
2007

Once you have a schedule, order your materials well in advance, to make sure everything you need will be available as you need it. Also figure out a place to store the materials while the project is underway—to avoid having boxes of new kitchen cabinets crowding your current kitchen or sitting in the rain in the backyard. When materials arrive, confirm that they're what you ordered and in good condition. If possible, do this before accepting the goods. It will make it easier to get your money back or get the materials replaced.

Hiring Extra Hands

Whether or not you're undertaking some of the work on your own, it can be good to have an extra body to help lift heavy or awkward items or just get a simple project done faster. In Chapter 10, we'll talk in detail about hiring and working with general contractors and other licensed professionals. Here, we're going to cover everyone else—from your weekly gardener to the occasional one-time helper.

Who should you hire?

As a homeowner, you may have already discovered that landscapers, painters, and other would-be workers are leaving flyers on your front porch. But you'll want to be careful when it comes to getting extra help. Get referrals from friends, neighbors, your real estate agent, or colleagues in the area. Find out what relevant experience the person has doing the kind of work you need help with. Ask for, and call, references.

You're so ... handy!

According to a poll by Angie's List, a consumer organization that helps homeowners find professionals in a variety of services, 67% of homeowners planned to hire a "handyman" in the next 30 days.

For the sake of both your project and your financial risk, make sure the person you hire has complied with any state rules and licensing requirements. In some states, for example, it's illegal for homeowners to hire unlicensed contractors for certain kinds of work. And federal law makes it illegal to hire undocumented workers. Although many people do so anyway, you're also risking personal liability if a worker is injured, as discussed next.

Who pays if a worker gets injured?

Experienced workers can climb on roofs and deal with electricity without much risk of injury—but just in case, you'll need to find out who will cover the costs if a worker is injured in your home. It may not be your homeowner's insurance policy. Many policies exclude workers who should be separately covered by workers' compensation insurance, which covers work-related injuries suffered by employees. (The exclusion will be in your written policy; call your carrier if you have any doubt.) When you hire a single worker, like a handyperson, that person won't have recourse through the workers' comp system (it's only for employees), but should have an insurance policy of his or her own.

If your homeowners' insurance will not cover certain workers while they're at your home, it's especially important that anyone you hire, or the company they work for, have either individual insurance or coverage under a workers' comp policy. If not, you could be personally liable for their injuries—that's right, out of pocket. Ask for proof of insurance, then call the insurer to make sure the policy is current.

Of course, hiring workers or employers who've bought their own insurance will cost you, because you'll end up paying extra, in the form of an increased job bid, to cover their insurance premiums. But you take on less risk as a result. Many service providers (like general fix-it, lawn care, or pool service companies) carry both liability insurance (covering damage to your property) and workers' compensation insurance. If the worker is your employee (see "Don't Become an Accidental Employer," below) and you are covered by workers' compensation laws (many states exempt small employers), you may be able to purchase a worker's compensation endorsement to your homeowner's policy. That will probably be more expensive than hiring an independent contractor who carries his or her own insurance.

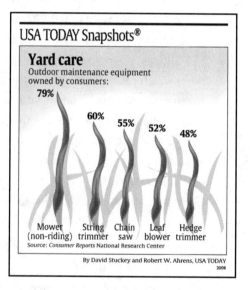

USA TODAY Snapshots®

Yard care
Outdoor maintenance equipment owned by consumers:

79% Mower (non-riding)
60% String trimmer
55% Chain saw
52% Leaf blower
48% Hedge trimmer

Source: *Consumer Reports* National Research Center

By David Stuckey and Robert W. Ahrens, USA TODAY
2008

Don't Become an Accidental Employer

When you hire someone to stain your deck, mow your lawn, or retile your bathroom, you probably don't think of that person as your "employee." But the IRS or other governmental agencies may feel differently. And if you are an employer, you may be legally required to secure proof of the worker's authorization to work in the United States, and to withhold and pay Social Security and Medicare taxes. You may also need to pay workers' compensation insurance and state unemployment taxes.

Unfortunately, there's no hard and fast rule about whether a worker is an employee rather than an independent contractor (in which case you don't have the same obligations). For IRS purposes, the more control you exercise over the tasks a worker does and how he or she does them, the more likely the person will be considered an employee. Your state tax, unemployment, or worker's compensation agencies may have different ways of making this determination—you'll have to contact them to find out. But workers are more likely independent contractors if they:

- can earn a profit or suffer a loss from the work
- furnish the tools and materials needed to do the work
- are paid by the job, not by the hour
- work for more than one place at a time
- invest in equipment and facilities
- pay their own business and traveling expenses
- hire and pay any assistants, and
- set their own working hours.

For example, if you hire a lawn care service, pay for every visit, and the company offers this service to the general public, provides its own tools, and hires its own workers, the IRS won't view you as the employer. But, if you hire a worker to help you remodel the kitchen, expect him to work certain hours each day, pay him hourly, and direct his work, the IRS may consider you the worker's employer.

RESOURCE

For more information, see IRS Publication 15-A, *Employer's Supplemental Tax Guide*; IRS Publication 926, *Household Employer's Tax Guide*; and *Working With Independent Contractors*, by Stephen Fishman (Nolo).

How much should you pay for services?

For the sake of your budget, you're probably hoping for cheap labor—and yet using a highly skilled worker, who charges much more but does better work in less time, can also be cost-effective. Just another reason not to hire the guy with the flyer until you've done some shopping around!

How much you'll end up paying for the worker you choose depends on several factors, including where you live, how skilled the worker is, and whether you hire an individual directly or through a company. You can always negotiate the pay if you think it's higher than the standard wage for that type of work. For questions to ask, see Chapter 10.

For regular services like gardening and pool cleaning, most professional companies will work for a flat rate, such as $50 every week. As long as the work is done, you'll make the payment, even if it takes the worker two hours one week and four hours the next. Other times, you may agree to an hourly rate. Be sure to take skill—and likely work speed—into account when determining a fair hourly rate.

Remodeling Your Home With a Contractor's Help

Blueprints and Rock Piles: Planning Your Remodel_____212

  Drafting plans_____213

  Hiring an engineer_____215

  Hiring a contractor_____216

  Getting permits_____216

  Demolishing the old stuff_____218

  Buying construction materials_____219

  Doing the actual construction_____220

  Finish work_____220

Who's Going to Help? Hiring Contractors_____221

  Getting names of the best general contractors_____222

  Interviewing prospective general contractors_____223

  Getting bids_____225

Negotiating a Written Contract_____227

  Payment terms_____228

  Other terms_____228

  Making midproject changes_____233

Figuring Out Where the Money Will Come From_____234

  Paying with cash_____235

  Using home equity_____235

  Construction loans_____235

  Other payment options_____237

Living Through a Remodel_____238

With no landlord to stop you, your mind may be swimming with creative visions of a major overhaul, perhaps adding a room, refacing the cabinets, or building a patio. Remodeling is a great way to add or improve space without having to move, especially if your family is expanding. As Gopal Ahluwalia of the National Association of Home Builders told USA TODAY's Maria Puente, "The most important reason for (remodeling) is that people do not want to move from their neighborhoods."

But you may need some professional construction help—and lining that up can be a project unto itself. In this chapter, we'll cover planning a major remodeling project, including how to:

- design the project
- choose the best contractor
- draft a contract for services
- finance the remodel, and
- stay sane while it's all happening.

USA TODAY Snapshots®

Just like new

Number of households that had work done to their homes in prior 12 months (by remodeling project):

Remodel bathroom **15.5 million**

Roof **11.6 million**

Carpet **10.8 million**

Remodel kitchen **10.7 million**

Remodel bedroom **8.1 million**

Source: Census Bureau   By David Stuckey and Bob Laird, USA TODAY 2006

Blueprints and Rock Piles: Planning Your Remodel

Here's a picture of how to turn your initial dream into final construction. The major steps, as discussed below, will probably include:

- drafting plans
- hiring skilled professionals
- getting permits
- demolishing what's there

- buying materials
- doing the actual construction (at last!), and
- doing the finish work.

CROSS REFERENCE
For more information on how to decide what you want, come up with ideas, research costs, and estimate resale value, see Chapter 9.

Drafting plans

When you do a remodel with the help of a professional, you'll need a set of plans that lays out exactly what you want done, complete with measurements, engineering and structural details, and visual representations. In some cases, such designs are also necessary for getting a permit from the local planning department—for example, if you'll be moving a wall or a gas line.

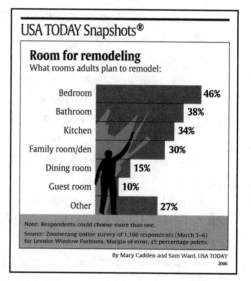

USA TODAY Snapshots®

Room for remodeling
What rooms adults plan to remodel:

Room	Percentage
Bedroom	46%
Bathroom	38%
Kitchen	34%
Family room/den	30%
Dining room	15%
Guest room	10%
Other	27%

Note: Respondents could choose more than one.
Source: Zoomerang online survey of 1,166 respondents (March 3–6) for Levolor Window Fashions. Margin of error, ±5 percentage points.

By Mary Cadden and Sam Ward, USA TODAY
2006

Who will draw up your plans? That depends. For simpler projects, or if you're a particularly skilled or patient draftsperson, you may be able to do them yourself. In the midrange, a contractor or a draftsperson can put plans together for you. But if your project is large and complex, or involves moving walls or adding square footage, you'll probably want to hire an architect, engineer, or both.

TIP

Check your inspection report. For a reminder regarding the current state of your home, review the report your home inspector prepared for you. It will give you a basic idea of what you're starting with and what condition it's in.

Drafting plans yourself. If you're drafting plans yourself, start by measuring the existing space and the position of doors, windows, electrical outlets, and the rest. If you're fortunate enough to already have these plans—perhaps the former owner gave them to you—you'll just want to confirm that everything is accurate.

Then, draw up the changes you hope to implement. To make this easier, you can use an online or software program such as *Better Homes and Gardens Home Design Software* (www.homedesignersoftware.com) or *SmartDraw* (www.smartdraw.com). Such programs can help you lay out your design, determine whether a plan is realistic (for example, that you really can knock down interior walls), give you a sense of what the finished product will look like, and produce a polished set of plans for your contractor to work with.

Hiring a contractor or draftsperson. Although general contractors primarily deal with construction, they're obviously very familiar with design plans—having implemented them in the past—and some also have experience drafting such plans, potentially at low cost. On the other hand, if your contractor will also be implementing the plans, you won't have the benefit of an extra set of eyes. Also, most contractors are not formally trained or certified in design planning.

A draftsperson is trained in design planning specifically. However, he or she won't have the same level of education or experience as an architect. If your plans are relatively simple and you know what you want, however, a draftsperson may be able to draw them up for less money.

Hiring an architect or designer. Among design professionals, an architect is probably the most expensive option. While it's possible to have the architect simply draw up plans for an hourly fee, the more common approach (especially on a major remodel) is to hire the architect to both draft the plans and make sure they're implemented correctly during construction. This is expensive—as much as 10% of the project cost, with payments made regularly as the project progresses.

Nevertheless, hiring an architect often makes sense for a major remodel. An architect is highly trained in both building design and structure and is likely to think of solutions that you might not, potentially lowering your building costs. If you're moving walls, adding square footage, or changing your roofline, an architect can be an essential part of your team. And if you want to incorporate environmentally friendly features into your remodel, an architect with that expertise will understand important factors like the direction of light and sun and the toxicity or safety of chosen materials.

Your contractor, if you hire one first, may be able to recommend an architect. Also ask neighbors, especially those with similar homes who have done remodels that you like. And of course, use other contacts like friends, colleagues, and even real estate agents, who have certainly seen the work of local architects. Choose an architect with residential (not commercial) experience and malpractice insurance coverage, to protect you in case the architect's plan is flawed and something goes wrong.

Another alternative is to work with an interior designer. Though they don't have the same technical expertise as architects, they're trained to work with layout, design, and construction. Most charge hourly rates, so it may be worth it to buy even a few hours of time to generate ideas as you draft your plans.

Hiring an engineer

You may also need to hire an engineer to confirm that your plans won't compromise the structural integrity of the house or to make sure systems like plumbing, electric, and heating/air conditioning are properly installed. Some engineers will draft plans, too.

Your local building department may require you to hire an engineer to review your plans for a major project before approving them. Engineers are well worth their cost, which can be as low as a few hundred dollars. It's best to get the engineer involved early on, before you get too committed to a project that may not be entirely feasible.

To find an engineer, start by asking your architect (or other design professional) or contractor for recommendations. Also ask at the local building office. Look for an engineer who carries malpractice insurance and has experience remodeling homes of similar age and quality to your own.

Hiring a contractor

Your next step will be to hire a professional or professionals to help you implement your design plan. You may decide to hire a general contractor, who will hire and oversee the work of other specialized craftspeople, or you may hire individual contractors, like a plumber or electrician, to complete specific tasks.

Because finding professionals and drawing up agreements with them is such an important—and expensive—part of the process, we'll discuss it in detail under "Who's Going to Help? Hiring Contractors," below.

Getting permits

Most local planning departments require homeowners to get permits for at least some types of remodeling work. Permits ensure that your project complies with local, state, and federal building codes. If you're working with a licensed professional from your area, that person should know whether a permit is required for the project. But it's worth double-checking, by calling or visiting your local planning office.

To obtain a permit, you'll probably have to submit your plans and pay a fee, anywhere from an insignificant amount to several hundreds or thousands of dollars. Depending on local requirements, you may need several permits for one project—for example, one for plumbing work, one for electrical work, and so on.

You can get the permits yourself, or better yet, arrange with your contractor or other licensed professional to do it for you. That shouldn't add much to the cost, and the contractor will be able to answer detailed questions the building or planning office may bring up. As a bonus, the person listed on the permit is usually responsible for making sure it complies with local codes, so if the contractor doesn't get things quite right, he or she will be held responsible for the mistake.

As part of the permitting process, a building inspector will come out and look at the project, maybe more than once. If your project doesn't comply with building codes, the inspector may require you to bring it up to current code before the permit receives final approval.

Many a homeowner has found workers or skilled friends willing to take on a project without going through the permitting process. However, even if this saves you time and money now, your decision may come back to bite you. For example, when you sell, the buyer or the buyer's lender may insist that you redo anything that isn't up to code, or you may not recoup as much of the cost. Worse, if you later do a more extensive remodel and can't avoid the permit process, the planning department may require you to redo or repair all of your previous work. Or it may rip out walls or finished work to investigate whether the previous work was done to code.

You'll also want to ensure you comply with local zoning laws. These regulate how properties can be used (for example, for either residential or commercial purposes) as well as the dimensions of buildings, such as their height and depth. If you're planning on changing your house's roofline or adding square footage, check with your planning office to find out how your area is zoned and whether these changes are allowed by zoning regulations.

If you've got a zoning problem, you may still be able to complete the project as originally conceived, by getting special permission from the governing authority (usually, a local planning commission). This is called a variance. To get a variance, you'll probably have to present your plans to the commission and answer questions. Your neighbors may be given an opportunity to voice any objections. If the commission denies the variance, you can usually appeal. Absent that, you may have to adapt your plans to comply with zoning restrictions.

In addition, if you live in an area governed by a homeowners' association, check your CC&Rs or deed restrictions to see whether and how they limit remodeling. They may, for example, limit the types of projects you are allowed to do, or impose conditions such as permissible work hours.

TIP
Need to apply for approvals from the board of your homeowners' association? Many homeowners' associations require you to submit an application and provide things like site plans and paint samples before they'll give you the green light. Dealing with that process is normally your job, not your contractor's.

Demolishing the old stuff

Before construction begins, most projects require demolition, or ripping out all the structural parts and materials you don't want. It's unskilled labor, and you might save money by doing it yourself. But it's also extremely hard physical work, creates a big mess that you have to clean up and dispose of responsibly, and is a task others can handle relatively cheaply.

If you're living in your home during demolition, be sure that you or whoever is doing the work block off the undemolished parts of your living space with plastic sheeting and masking tape. Dust and debris get around easily. And be sure that workers don't track the mess into other parts of your home, for instance when they use the restroom. (As we'll discuss below, you can specify which restroom they'll use in your contract, as well as how much cleanup they'll do at the end of each work day.) Also, talk with your contractor to find out whether any of the material can be reused or recycled.

Finally, be particularly careful about demolition if you're working on an older home that might contain toxins such as asbestos or lead. Asbestos may be found in popcorn ceilings, old duct work, and flooring. Lead is often found in paint in homes built prior to 1978. Both are potentially harmful if you breathe the airborne fibers or dust. Hire professionals to test for and safely remove them.

And no matter the age of your home, tearing out walls in damp areas such as a bathroom, kitchen, or utility room, may reveal mold growth, which can cause health problems or allergic reactions. You or your contractor may be able to treat the problem, most likely with bleach and a fan and by stopping the moisture source. Larger problems may require specialized professional help—but ask your contractor for recommendations. Mold removal and abatement is an emerging specialty, and not licensed, so it's easy for people to call themselves specialists without much real knowledge.

Buying construction materials

You have two main options—buying everything yourself or having the contractor do the buying for you. If you do the buying, you have more control, can do some bargain shopping, and have the freedom to change your mind at the last minute.

However, that doesn't mean you'll get the best price. As regular customers, contractors often get deep discounts from suppliers. Your best bet might be to look around until you find exactly what you want, then have your contractor go out and buy it.

Another advantage to making your contractor responsible for purchasing materials is that it will save hassle later, when the project is underway. If your supply of sealant didn't stretch as far as expected or a leaky washer needs to be replaced, the contractor can go out and buy what's needed, rather than waiting around (and possibly delaying the project) until you can take care of it.

If you're interested in the environmental and health impact of the materials you purchase, look for products certified by The Greenguard Environmental Institute (www.greenguard.com), the Forest Stewardship Council (www.fscus.org), or Cradle to Cradle (www.mbdc.com/c2c). All have undergone rigorous certification procedures to test for environmental impact. Look also at environmentally friendly substitutes, many of which won't cost more than their less friendly counterparts. For example:

- **Linoleum instead of vinyl.** According to Greenpeace, vinyl is the most environmentally harmful plastic out there, and it's made with substances (dioxin and phthalates among them) that can contribute to serious health problems. True linoleum, made from linseed oil, is a better choice.

- **Low or no-VOC paints.** Regular paints release toxic volatile organic compounds (VOCs), but non-VOC paints are now readily available. Go to www.eartheasy.com/live_nontoxic_paints.htm for a list of healthier options. Also, look for low- or no-VOC sealers and caulks.

- **Bamboo, cork, or reclaimed wood instead of carpet or hardwood.** Carpet is a particularly bad choice if it emits VOCs, as most do. If you're planning on replacing carpet anyway, consider options like cork or bamboo (eco-friendlier because they both regrow quickly). If carpet is your choice, seek out products certified by the Carpet and Rug Institute's Green Label and Green Label Plus programs, which have low VOC emissions. For more information, visit www.carpet-rug.org.

For other environmentally-friendly products, check out www.buildinggreen.com.

Doing the actual construction

This is where the majority of work will get done: foundation or framing work, electrical, plumbing, heating and cooling, flooring, cabinetry, surfacing interior or exterior walls, and more. You and your contractor should schedule regular meetings (weekly or even daily) to discuss and review the progress. Writing this into your contract will make it official and ensure that both of you set aside the time.

Don't be surprised if the project falls behind schedule. If one step in the process is delayed, the rest usually are too. Late deliveries, bad weather, or a host of other surprises can throw you off track, and aren't necessarily the contractor's fault.

Finish work

The devil's in the details. After the main construction project is done, little tasks will need to be attended to, like installing fixtures or baseboards, touching up paint, or putting face plates back on the light switches. That's what finish work is.

Getting contractors to focus on these tasks isn't always easy. They've already completed the bulk of their work and may be eager to move on to their next job. You'll need to create a document, called a "punch list," that specifies all the final details and remaining work. Ideally, you'll make the last payment to your contractor conditional upon completion of the entire job, including everything on the punch list.

Alternatively, you may agree to do some of the finish work yourself. The tasks involved are usually relatively straightforward, but can take a lot of time. First, find out how much the finish work is worth. If you request a very detailed bid from potential contractors (we'll explain how in the next section), you'll know exactly how much they're charging for it, and whether it's worth your time to do yourself.

USA TODAY Snapshots®

Physical stores' advantage
Sixty-seven percent of survey respondents favor shopping at stores vs. online. Main reasons to shop at stores:
Need to see or try on item — 51%
Need to have product sooner than the time it takes to ship — 13%
Better price — 12%
Avoid shipping charges — 12%

Source: Accenture Retail & CGS Innovation survey of 602 adults 18 and older. Margin of error ±3 percentage points.

By Jae Yang and Alejandro Gonzalez, USA TODAY 2008

Who's Going to Help? Hiring Contractors

What is a "contractor"? In the broadest sense, it means any skilled person you bring in to perform services. For example, if you're completely replacing your kitchen, you may need an electrician to upgrade the wiring and put in lighting, a plumber to move pipes, a cabinetmaker to design or install cabinets, a tile setter to lay new flooring, and a trained installer to put in Corian countertops.

However, for a major remodel, someone needs to be in charge of coordinating the work of all these professionals. You don't want them doing their work in the wrong order, or stepping on each other's toes. That's where a "general contractor" comes in. The general contractor is usually a skilled craftsperson who does a lot of the work, often using workers in his or her employ, and also hires and supervises subcontractors for specialized tasks.

Hiring a general contractor is certainly convenient: You usually need to sign only one contract, versus multiple contracts with subcontractors. The overall cost of the subcontractors' work will be part of the general contractor's bid, and the contractor will ultimately be responsible for managing the subcontractors and ensuring that their work is satisfactory.

A downside to working with a contractor is that it will probably cost more than separately hiring subcontractors. You'll likely be charged for the time that the contractor spends managing the project, plus a markup on what the subcontractors charge. The contractor's profit will probably be in the range of 10%–25% of the entire project cost.

It's possible to act as your own general contractor, directing the work of others. But you'd have to be constantly available to hire and deal with workers and keep the schedule and worksite under control. If you have a full-time job or other responsibilities, this could be difficult or even counterproductive. You may also find it difficult to find and hire the best subcontractors (a general contractor knows the field and already has relationships with good workers).

This section will help you locate, contract, and work with a general contractor. The same guidance should be followed, however, in hiring any licensed professional.

Getting names of the best general contractors

Perhaps the best people to ask for recommendations are your neighbors or friends who have remodeled, especially if they have homes of a similar style. Visit and see the type and quality of work the contractor is capable of. You can also ask colleagues or local real estate professionals for recommendations. Or, if you've already started working with an architect or designer, that person may be able to suggest a contractor.

Interviewing prospective general contractors

Try to get the name of at least three contractors to interview. When you call to set up interviews, be wary if a contractor isn't available within the next couple weeks or offers to squeeze you in. It could mean that he or she is already too busy to take on your project or give it full attention. And of course, if a contractor doesn't return your call quickly, or shows up late to the interview, you can probably expect the same kind of treatment during construction.

An interview lets you ask the contractor questions about education and experience and discuss what you're hoping the contractor will do. The contractor can look at your home and any written plans you've already drawn up. He or she may offer suggestions or insights like, "We could reuse that lumber," or, "The city probably won't approve a spiral staircase."

Now's the time for both you and the contractor to see whether you are interested in working together. This person will be sawing and hammering at your most valuable possession, often while you're away or are still padding around in your robe and slippers. You want to feel comfortable with day-to-day communication, which may involve difficult decisions as surprises pop up—perhaps a denied permit or unavailable materials. And you want the job finished beautifully—and up to code—not just slapped together.

CAUTION
Make sure to meet the person who'll actually be assigned to your job. If you're hiring a contracting firm, the person who comes out to discuss the project with you may be a salesperson. Ask to interview the person who will actually supervise your job on-site before you make your hiring decision.

Here are some important questions to ask a prospective contractor:

- **How long have you been a general contractor?** Experienced contractors can often do the job better and more efficiently than newer ones. They may cost more, but it could be worth it, especially given their longstanding relationships with high-quality subcontractors. Also, an experienced contractor is more likely to give accurate estimates about how long a project will take and what will be involved—particularly important in an older home, where it's anyone's guess what's behind the walls.

- **Are you licensed?** Most states regulate contractors, usually by requiring them to pass a written exam, provide proof of insurance and adequate funding, show some degree of experience, or some combination of these. (Find your state's requirements at www.contractors-license.org.) You should work only with licensed contractors—especially because you can complain to the licensing organization if they don't perform as required. Even if a contractor claims to have the proper license, check it yourself, most likely at your state's website.

- **Do you have insurance?** Ask for proof that the contractor carries proper liability, property damage, and workers' compensation insurance. Without such coverage, you could face major out-of-pocket expenses if, for example, the contractor or any employees falls or is otherwise injured while working on your home. Follow up with the insurer to confirm that the coverage is still current.

- **How will I contact you?** Be sure that your contractor will be available to answer your questions throughout the process. A cell phone number is best.

- **What type of projects do you normally do?** The more similar the contractor's work is to your job, the better.

- **Will you do or supervise the work?** Smaller contractors often do the majority of the work themselves, but if your contractor works on several jobs at once, he or she may be jumping back and forth between job sites. That's not necessarily a deal breaker, but find out how often you'll see the contractor and where else he or she will be.

- **Will you submit a total cost bid?** Contractors can submit different types of bids. A total cost bid limits the amount you pay to the amount agreed to up front, so the contractor must estimate the overall cost at the beginning and stick to it. For reasons we'll discuss in "Getting bids," below, this is often preferable.

- **Do you have references?** Every contractor you consider should be willing to provide you with a list of references. Ask for a few—at least one in progress and one completed, so you can see how a contractor handles a current job site (how well organized it is, whether the project is on schedule, etc.) as well as what the finished product looks like. Call and ask what kind of work the contractor did, how it turned out, how the process went, and whether the person liked working with the contractor. Find out whether the contractor did work on time, kept in good contact, and used high-quality materials and subcontractors. Then ask to see the work yourself. It may feel like a strange request, but it's the only way to ensure that you're actually talking to a reference, and not just the contractor's good friend or cousin.

Getting bids

After having looked at your home and discussed your plans, the contractor will calculate how much it will cost to do the project and possibly give you a written estimate. The amount may be exactly what you expected or an eye-popping shock. Don't sign anything yet—you don't want to unwittingly consent to having the work done at the estimated price.

When you've narrowed down the field to contractors with whom you're really interested in working, ask for bids. The bid is different than an estimate, because it's the contractor's commitment to do the job for the amount of money specified. While the estimate may have been based on an informal discussion of the project plans, the bid will be much more specific. It will include all the project details, including the materials to be used.

Cost basis of bids. To arrive at a dollar figure, most general contractors estimate how much time and energy they think a project will take, including hiring subcontractors, then add in how much the materials will cost. They'll agree to do the job for that amount even if circumstances change. This is called a total-cost or fixed-price bid.

Alternatively, the contractor may offer a cost-plus bid, in which you pay the contractor for labor, materials, equipment, and a certain markup (typically 20% of the overall cost). You won't know exactly how much everything will cost, because you'll establish these costs as you go along. A cost-plus bid might be your only alternative if you're dealing with a house that has serious unknowns—for example, is very old and hasn't been updated since it was built. In that case, a contractor might not be willing to give you a total-cost bid, because the risk is too great that he or she will face unanticipated expenses and lose money on the deal. Avoid a cost-plus bid if possible—it means a contractor can submit a low estimate and woo you with the hope of saving serious cash, then increase the bottom line when unexpected "surprises" pop up during the remodel.

Finally, a contractor may want to submit a time-and-materials bid. Essentially, you agree to pay the contractor for materials, plus an hourly rate for the contractor and any workers. You don't know ahead of time how long it will take the contractor to do the job—and of course, he or she has no particular financial impetus to do it quickly. This type of arrangement makes sense for a small job with a discrete task, but it can easily become unmanageable and expensive for larger jobs with multiple workers and projects. However, it's possible to create a hybrid, by capping the possible amount you spend—in which case, if the contractor does the project for less time, you win. Or you might agree to have the contractor renegotiate with you when a certain dollar amount is reached.

Contents of a bid. To get the most accurate bid, give the contractor as much detail as possible, including which materials you want used (down to the manufacturer, product name, and model number). Ask the contractor to break the bid into as many steps as possible. For example, in a bathroom remodel, you might want a breakdown of costs for demolition, cleanup, moving plumbing, moving or upgrading wiring, putting in new drywall, inserting a new bathtub or shower and surrounding tile, building a new vanity, installing new flooring—you get the picture. This level of detail lets you compare costs between different contractors—and decide what you might want to do yourself, to save money.

Choosing the best bid. The lowest bid isn't necessarily the best bid. An inexperienced contractor may estimate too low and later cut corners to reduce costs. Or desperate contractors may bid low, maybe because they haven't managed their cash flow properly and need some quick income to cover costs on a previous job. If you get one bid that's significantly lower than the rest, be cautious about accepting it, but consider using it as a negotiating point with another contractor.

Negotiating a Written Contract

Once you've chosen a contractor and agreed to work together, you'll need to draw up a contract. Though dry legal language is no fun, it's important. The contract commits you to pay the contractor and commits the contractor to perform the work as outlined—with legal backup, since either of you can sue the other for failing to do what you've promised (unless you agree in the contract to give up this right). A well-written contract is also helpful for dealing with details like when the work will be finished and when you'll make payments.

Every contract should cover certain terms, discussed in this section. Most likely, the contractor will have a form contract for you to fill out—which probably protects the contractor more than it protects you. You can use it as a starting point, but you may need to negotiate additions or deletions, using the guidance below. Don't listen to any contractor who says the form can't be changed, even if it means you have to find a different contractor. If possible, attach additions to the contractor's standard form; if your changes are major, type up a totally new document.

Later changes should also be in writing. To make those changes, you'll create addendums to the original contract called change orders. Both you and the contractor will sign the change orders. Your contractor may have a basic standard form for this purpose.

Payment terms

The contractor probably wants as much money up front as possible—a bad idea for you, not only because you'll have to come up with cash sooner, but because it won't leave the contractor much incentive to finish the work. As a compromise, many homeowners agree to pay in three stages, including:

- **A prepayment or deposit.** This should be only for materials the contractor is buying for you that will be delivered directly to your home. Some states limit the maximum deposit amount, for example, to 10% of the overall contract cost. Be suspicious if a contractor wants anything over the cost of materials. It may mean that the contractor is using the money to catch up on payments to subcontractors or to suppliers for other jobs.

- **Smaller, regular payments throughout.** These will be paid as the contractor and subcontractors complete different stages of the work. On a small job, this might be one payment when the job is halfway through. With a bigger project, it could be several—even weekly—payments as the work progresses.

- **A final payment when the job is finished.** You want this payment to be as big a percentage of the project cost as possible, to motivate the contractor to wrap up all loose ends. Make it conditional on completion of the job and your satisfaction with it.

Whatever payment schedule you agree to, be sure it's accurately spelled out in your contract.

Other terms

Here are several other key terms the contract should include:

- **Contractor's business information.** Ask for identifying information such as the contractor's phone, address, and license number.
- **Tasks the contractor will complete.** The agreement should lay out what the contractor is responsible for doing, in the same kind of detail discussed in the bid (in fact, you could attach the bid and refer to it in the contract). It should also identify any tasks

the contractor won't be responsible for—for example, if you'll be doing the finish work.

- **Plans.** If you haven't drafted any design plans, you'll have to spell out even more clearly what the contractor is obligated to do. If you do have plans that you expect the contractor to follow, attach a copy.

- **Materials.** Be very specific about what materials the contractor must use, such as types of wood or brands of paint or fixtures. Don't allow substitutions without your express permission (avoid the words "or equivalent"). Otherwise, the contractor could simply decide that other, cheaper materials are comparable and use them instead. Have the contractor agree to contact you before using materials other than those specified in the contract.

- **Start and finish dates.** Although outside events may intervene, you should be able to set a date when work will begin and a deadline by which the project will be completed. (First, check whether your homeowners' association rules limit how long a project can take.) A contractor may agree to only a "substantial completion" date—a date by which the major work will be done, but finish work might not be. That's okay if your last payment is conditional on final completion.

- **Schedule.** You and your contractor may agree to target dates for finishing particular portions of the work. However, don't expect the contract to reward you if the dates—other than the start date and substantial completion date—aren't met. It's too hard for the contractor to anticipate problems and delays, so most won't agree to this.

- **Start and finish times.** Your contract should specify when work will start in the morning and when it will finish in the evening. Again, check whether your homeowners' association (if any) limits when work can be done.

- **Demolition.** Specify who will be doing the demolition and be responsible for disposing of the waste.

- **Daily cleanup.** Lay out how much cleanup the contractor will do on a daily basis—that is, whether workers will do things like put away their tools and sweep up piles of debris before going home. This will help ensure your house stays livable. You'll also want to limit the impact of workers in your home—for example, by specifying which restroom they can use, where they can park, and what parts of the house they won't have access to. This will protect your safety and privacy and prevent dust and debris from entering parts of the home that aren't under construction.

- **Liability.** Make sure the contract obligates the contractor to provide workers' compensation insurance for employees (and to make sure the subcontractors have done the same) as well as liability coverage to protect your property and your neighbors' property in the event of damage.

- **Responsibility for tools and materials.** The contract should state where tools and materials will be kept for safekeeping, and who will be responsible if either are stolen.

- **Subcontractors.** You'll want to know who the subcontractors on your job are, and how to reach them. This will help you stay in touch and lessen the risk of any subcontractor filing a mechanic's lien for repayment, discussed below. If the general contractor isn't prepared to give you this information, make sure the contract at least specifies that you have the right to disapprove any subcontractor with whom you don't want to work.

- **Release of lien forms from subcontractors.** Obligate your general contractor to obtain a final release, final payment, and final lien waiver from all subcontractors. This release means subcontractors have been paid and won't be able to bring liens against the property. Some states, such as California, require contractors to get releases if the consumer requests it. Check your state's contractor's licensing board for requirements where you live, and to find any standard state forms used for this purpose.

What If Your General Contractor Doesn't Pay the Subcontractors?

If the subcontractors and suppliers don't get paid for work they do, they can file what are called mechanic's liens against your property. A lien is similar to your mortgage—it's a debt, secured by your property, which must be paid or at worst, get recovered in foreclosure. Subcontractors and suppliers can file liens when they don't get paid, even if you've paid the general contractor for the work. (Your general contractor can also file this type of lien, but we're assuming you'll pay him or her and avoid this problem.)

To make sure your general contractor has paid all subcontractors and suppliers and they won't be sticking you with a lien, you can make your final payment to the contractor conditional upon you receiving a written release from each subcontractor and supplier.

Another option is to require the general contractor to get waivers from subcontractors or suppliers as they're paid. This allows you to keep track of how much the subcontractors and suppliers are getting, and limits their ability to recover by the amount they've already received.

You can also try to get your contractor to agree to accept two-party checks to subcontractors or suppliers. The idea is that you write checks that both the contractor and subcontractor or supplier must endorse, and payment goes directly to the subcontractor. Of course, this means you'll be responsible for monitoring what's happening a little more closely, which your contractor may not agree to.

- **Permits.** The contract should specify that the contractor is responsible for obtaining all permits and getting final approvals, and specify who will pay for the permits. (Permit fees may be included in the contractor's overall bid price.)

- **Price.** Whether you negotiated a total-cost bid or some other arrangement (as discussed under "Getting bids," above), be sure it's spelled out in your contract.

- **Financing contingency.** If you'll be paying for the project with financing, such as a home equity or construction loan, make sure the contract is contingent upon your obtaining the financing, so you can back out if the money doesn't come through.

- **Meetings.** You'll want to meet with your contractor periodically, ideally weekly or even daily, to discuss how things are going. Putting this in writing helps ensure that those meetings happen.

- **Contract changes.** As discussed further below, the contract should require your written permission to make any changes.

- **Warranty.** Your contractor should warrant that the work (including the work of any subcontractors) is free of any defects due to faulty workmanship or defective materials for at least a year.

- **Dispute resolution.** Many contracts specify how disputes will be resolved: for example, by arbitration or mediation. If you agree to one of these, you won't be able to sue the contractor directly for violation of the contract (and vice versa). Mediation is usually preferable to arbitration, since it means that you'll try to reach a mutually agreeable solution with the help of a third party. Arbitration, by contrast, means a third party makes a decision almost as a judge would, possibly leaving you no right to appeal.

- **Cancellation provision.** Spell out clearly the conditions under which either you or the contractor can cancel the contract. Ideally, you should be allowed to back out for any reason, as long as you give a certain amount of notice and pay for work that's already completed. (Under the Truth in Lending Act, you also usually have a right to rescind the contract within three days of signing it, as long as you sign it in a location other than the contractor's principal place of business.) Of course, if you insist on such a no-fault clause, you'll probably have to give the contractor the benefit of the same.

Making midproject changes

No matter how carefully you negotiate, unexpected expenses may arise after the project gets underway. You yourself might be one reason. Perhaps you'll decide to upgrade or change building materials, or alter a design element. Other changes may be unforeseeable, like the need to replace a deteriorating pipe.

Such job changes are normal, and the contractor should have no problem negotiating around them. Traditionally, these changes are handled with contract amendments called change orders—your contractor may have a standard form for this purpose. But there's a simpler way, particularly useful for small changes that may come along every day. Create a "Contractor Midjob Worksheet" like the sample shown below. If the two of you meet regularly, you can talk about how things are going and make notes on this worksheet. The final column is meant for both of your initials in order to show your agreement about any cost changes. Review your worksheet regularly to make sure all the issues get resolved.

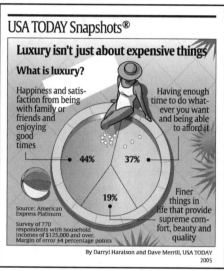

USA TODAY Snapshots®

Luxury isn't just about expensive things

What is luxury?

Happiness and satisfaction from being with family or friends and enjoying good times — 44%

Having enough time to do whatever you want and being able to afford it — 37%

Finer things in life that provide supreme comfort, beauty and quality — 19%

Source: American Express Platinum Survey of 770 respondents with household incomes of $125,000 and over. Margin of error ±4 percentage points

By Darryl Haralson and Dave Merrill, USA TODAY 2005

Who pays for the costs of the various changes (whether you or the contractor) will depend on what's in the original contract. Don't expect to hold your contractor responsible for truly unforeseeable surprises that aren't the contractor's fault. In the end, expect to spend about 10% more than the agreed-upon contract price.

		Sample Contractor Midjob Worksheet			
Date	Issue/Question	Response	Added cost?	Resolved?	Initials
7/1/08	Contractor uncovered plastic piping in the laundry room—switch to copper?	Yes	$500	Yes	IB JS
7/5/08	Spanish tile no longer available—Portuguese okay?	Yes	$200	Yes	IB JS
7/7/08	Neighbors complaining about plants being stepped on—replace?	Yes; contractor and home-owner will each pay half.	$25 to us	Yes	IB JS
7/12/08	We found a salvaged door on Craigslist—can we use instead of buying a new one?	Yes	Contractor will reduce cost of materials by $150, but charge hourly for labor to fix hinges and cracks on old door.		IB JS

Figuring Out Where the Money Will Come From

Once you have a good idea of what your project will cost—and have built in a cushion for the unexpected—it's time to figure out how you'll pay for it.

Paying with cash

If you have the cash, using it to pay for your improvement project has its benefits. You won't worry about how to pay it back, and you won't pay any interest. But you could also easily deplete your savings account. And as a homeowner, you'll want to keep about three to six months' living expenses handy, to deal with emergencies or help you pay the mortgage if you unexpectedly lose your job.

Also, you don't want to use up cash if it simply means shifting other purchases to high-interest forms of credit, like credit cards. You'd be better off borrowing money for your remodel from a lower interest credit source, like a home equity or construction loan (discussed below).

Using home equity

Depending on the amount of equity you have in your home (the difference between the home's value and any liabilities against it, like your mortgage), you may be able to finance your remodel using a home equity loan, home equity line of credit, or a refinance loan. For more information on these, see Chapter 7.

Construction loans

If you're like many new homeowners, you may not have much equity to borrow against, or the cash to make the changes you'd like. In that case, a construction loan might be the best option. A construction loan is like any other mortgage, secured by the house itself. But the main difference is, the lender's security doesn't come from the present value of the home, but instead the value of the home after you've finished construction. That means you're able to borrow against the future, higher anticipated value of your home, even if you don't have enough equity to get a loan otherwise.

TIP

Get a green mortgage. The FHA's Energy Efficient Mortgage (EEM) allows buyers and refinancers to borrow extra cash to make energy-saving improvements. The process starts with a home energy rating systems report (HERS) that tells you what improvements are needed and what they'll cost. The HERS inspection and report usually costs between $100 and $300. For more information, see the FHA's website at www.fha.com/energy_efficient.cfm.

With a construction loan, you're usually charged a variable interest rate and pay only interest until the project is completed. The interest rate on a construction loan is often higher than what's available on home equity loans or lines of credit. But the higher interest rate is usually just for the short term, because when the project is completed, a so-called "permanent" (long-term) loan will take its place. Normally you'll set up the construction loan and the permanent loan at the same time. Also, once the project is completed, you may decide to refinance or take out a home equity loan at a lower interest rate. With the improvements you've made, you're more likely to have the equity to do it.

Lenders are willing to offer a construction loan when they're confident that the improvements you make will increase the value of the property. For this reason, you'll probably be required to submit your project plans to the lender and get its approval. The lender will keep tabs on the project's progress—maybe even visit your home—and will make payments over time, too.

The cash will probably never be in your hands, though. The lender will pay the architect, contractor, or other professionals directly. You may be able to negotiate for a two-party check, requiring your signature and the professional's signature to make a payment. That would help you stay in control of the project and obtain lien releases from subcontractors.

Another loan program similar to a construction loan is the Fannie Mae Homestyle Renovation Mortgage. Like a construction loan, it lets you borrow an amount based on the value of your home after you make improvements. Unlike a construction loan, you'd select a fixed rate or hybrid adjustable rate mortgage. However, you'd need to refinance your entire mortgage, and the maximum you can borrow is currently $417,000 (in 2008; the amount changes annually). It's not a viable alternative for many homeowners. For more information, visit Fannie Mae's website at www.fanniemae.com.

Other payment options

If none of the payment options explained above work for you, consider an unsecured credit line from a bank or other financial institution. In essence, this is not that different from using a credit card. The amount you'll be able to borrow will be based on your credit history, and the interest rate will probably be significantly higher than the rate on a secured debt. Unless you expect to borrow only a modest amount and pay it back immediately, however, this option could end up costing you more than is financially wise.

USA TODAY Snapshots®

American homes

Cities with the largest and smallest average household size:

4.33 — Santa Ana, Calif.
2.07 — Cincinnati
2.60 — U.S. average

Source: Census Bureau

By David Stuckey and Alejandro Gonzalez, USA TODAY 2006

Another option is to borrow from your IRA or 401(k). However, whether you can borrow from your 401(k) will depend on whether your employer allows it, and you'll probably be able to borrow only part of it, such as 50%. Most experts consider 401(k) loans a last-resort strategy. Although you'll be paying the interest into your own account, you'll be losing the benefits of compound interest while the money's in your hands. And if you don't pay the cash back, you'll be subject to income taxes and penalty payments.

While you can borrow from your IRA, it's generally only for the short term—beyond 60 days, you'll pay the taxes and penalties of an early distribution. So while it may serve as a short-term bridge until you can obtain other financing, it probably isn't practical in most circumstances.

Living Through a Remodel

Living in middle of a construction site is no fun. However, you may have no other choice. If so, here are a few pointers:

- **Ask the contractor what adjustments you'll be expected to make.** For example, the contractor may want you to be available during certain hours or on certain days, or be out of the house by a certain time, or be willing to switch bedrooms midway, or willing to be a gofer ... you get the idea. But if you don't ask in advance, you may not find out until the last minute.

- **Remodeling a kitchen.** Prepare yourself for the very real possibility that your kitchen won't be accessible for some period of time. Budget to eat out more than usual, and consider the time of year you do the project—if it's summer, you may be happy cooking with an outdoor kitchen or barbeque. In winter, you might get creative with a hot plate or Coleman stove, indoors. Figure out where you're going to put everything currently stored in your cupboards and refrigerator. Be ready to wash the dishes in the bathroom.

USA TODAY Snapshots®

Get out the charcoal
About 74 million adults say they've barbecued in the past year. How often they cook out:

At least once a month **50.1 million**

Less than once a month **23.9 million**

Source: Census Bureau

By Alejandro Gonzalez, USA TODAY
2008

- **Remodeling a bathroom.** If you only have one bathroom, try to find somewhere else to stay while it's being remodeled. Work with your contractor to limit the amount of time you're imposing on family or friends or paying for a hotel or rental.

- **Dealing with problems and delays.** Expect both, and try to be flexible. It's easier to do this if you aren't up against a deadline—the birth of a new baby, or the influx of family for the holidays. If you are, give yourself as big a time cushion as possible.

- **Protecting your stuff.** To protect your personal items from damage or theft, put anything you don't need in storage and seal off any areas that are not being worked on. You hopefully don't have to worry too much about the workers themselves, but your home may, at times, be open to anyone who's up to no good. Construction tools and materials have become popular targets for thieves.

USA TODAY Snapshots®

Not-so-humble abodes

States with the highest percentage of homes with four or more bedrooms:

39.2% Utah
28% Maryland
26.5% Virginia
26.2% Colorado
26.2% Minnesota

Source: Census Bureau   By David Stuckey and Marcy E. Mullins, USA TODAY
2008

- **Protecting your family.** Make sure that any unsafe areas, such as demolition sites or high planks, are not accessible to children. And have a plan for your pets—you don't want to hear meowing from behind sealed walls (yes, this has really happened). Pet birds are particularly susceptible to dust and fumes—many contractors want them out of the house.

- **Plan some getaways.** When your nerves start to frazzle, it's time for a low-cost vacation—perhaps a quick road trip to an old friend who will put you up and provide hot showers and home-cooked food for the weekend.

Following these tips won't ensure that your project is trouble free, but will help you survive with some sanity.

After Damage: Who Pays?

Look What Happened! What to Do First_____242

Making a Homeowners' Insurance Claim_____245

Is the damage or injury covered under your policy?_____245

Is the damage or injury worth filing a claim over?_____246

Is anyone else liable for the damage?_____247

How to file a claim_____248

How you'll be paid_____250

Disputing a denied claim_____251

Making a Home Warranty Claim_____253

How Long Has This Been Going On? Liability for
Existing Defects_____254

Who's responsible?_____255

Do you have a case?_____256

Built to Last? Liability for Defects in New Homes_____258

Are defects covered by a builder's warranty?_____258

Can you file a builder's warranty claim?_____260

Are defects covered by a manufacturer's warranty?_____261

Does state law offer extra protection?_____261

Should You Sue? Deciding to Go to Court_____262

Are there alternatives to a lawsuit?_____262

Is a lawsuit worth it?_____263

Because you're vigilant about home maintenance, you'll avoid the worst home ownership surprises—the leaking roof that damages your hardwood, or the long-dead tree that topples onto your garage. Nevertheless, no home is guaranteed free from sudden or unexpected damage. You'll sleep easier if you're familiar with the "what ifs" and learn how to:

- respond quickly after damage happens

- file a homeowners' insurance claim

- make a home warranty claim for malfunctions in your home appliances, and

- figure out whether someone (perhaps the previous owner, the builder, or the inspector) is liable for having failed to tell you about defects.

Look What Happened! What to Do First

When you first arrive home or wake up to discover a fire, flood, break-in, or other problem, here are the top ways to protect your home and your personal safety. Try to memorize the basics now, since you won't have time to read this book in the midst of a stressful situation.

- **For emergencies, call 911.** You knew that, of course. But resist the urge to take matters into your own hands—for example, by entering your house if you don't know whether burglars are still inside.

- **Turn off utilities.** If you can safely do so, turn off the main water, gas, or electric lines if any of these are leaking or creating danger (for example, if contact might occur between electrical lines and water). If any power lines come down or gas leaks develop, report these to your utility company.

- **Protect the evidence of what happened.** Whether you'll eventually be dealing with police, the insurance company, or the home's seller, you may need to prove what went wrong and how bad it was. That means, in the event of a burglary, not touching anything, especially objects that might have fingerprints on them. And after a police visit, ask for a report, which will help if you ask your insurance company to cover a theft. Resist the urge to clean up damage until you've found out whether your insurance company wants to take a look at it first (the exception being where leaving things as-is would lead to further damage, in which case take photographs and save at least a sample of the

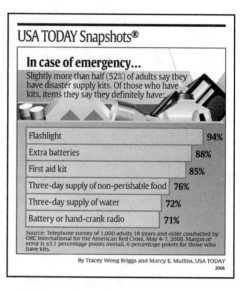

USA TODAY Snapshots®

In case of emergency...

Slightly more than half (52%) of adults say they have disaster supply kits. Of those who have kits, items they say they definitely have:

Flashlight	94%
Extra batteries	88%
First aid kit	85%
Three-day supply of non-perishable food	76%
Three-day supply of water	72%
Battery or hand-crank radio	71%

Source: Telephone survey of 1,000 adults 18 years and older conducted by ORC International for the American Red Cross, May 4–7, 2006. Margin of error is ±3.1 percentage points overall, 6 percentage points for those who have kits.

By Tracey Wong Briggs and Marcy E. Mullins, USA TODAY 2008

damaged items, such as water-soaked carpets or burnt clothing). In the case of an injured guest at your property, collect the names of and contact information for any witnesses.

💡 **TIP**

It may not be as bad as it looks. As Kip Diggs, a spokesman for State Farm Insurance, told USA TODAY's Christine Dugas, "A common mistake is to assume that waterlogged clothing and upholstered furniture are beyond repair. Homeowners should try to clean it, dry it out, and save the receipts."

- **Call your homeowners' insurance company.** Unless the damage is minor enough that you plan to keep quiet about it to prevent your premium from going up (as discussed under "Making a Homeowners' Insurance Claim," below), get in touch with your insurance carrier as soon as you can. Your policy probably requires prompt communication—they may have 24-hour phone lines awaiting your call, and may want to help you arrange cleanup and repairs. If possible, have your policy number on hand, along with a paper and pen so you can write down your claim handler's name, contact information, and suggestions.

- **Make temporary repairs to protect your home from further damage and make it safe.** Remove valuables, board up any broken windows, and do whatever else is needed to stop further deterioration of your property and possessions. Such protective measures are typically required under a homeowners' insurance policy. If you'll be living elsewhere, tell the neighbors where to reach you, and return to the property regularly to see how it's doing. The good news: If you save receipts for what you spend on temporary repairs and for accommodations if you must live elsewhere, you can submit them to your insurance company for reimbursement.

> *The three most common homeowners' insurance claims:*
>
> *(1) Fire and lightning; (2) wind and hail; (3) water damage and freezing.*

- **If someone has been hurt in your house, help them!** For example, if your dog bit someone, restrain the dog and take the person to the emergency room or provide basic first aid if appropriate. Your homeowners' insurance should cover your first-aid costs.

- **Waiting for the power to come back on?** Turn off your computer, unplug and turn off lights, and disconnect appliances to help prevent a power surge when the electricity returns. If you turn on a gas oven for heat (we don't advise it), crack a window open to prevent a buildup of carbon monoxide. Keep the refrigerator door closed as much as possible—food will stay cold for up to three days. Moving a freezer item such as a frozen turkey to the fridge will also help.

- **Cancel any stolen credit cards.** Doing so—by phone—is not only a good idea for self-protection, but may also be required by your insurance company. While you're at it, protect yourself from further identity theft by having what's called a "fraud alert" placed on your credit history. Just call one of the big three credit reporting companies, and it will notify the other two—you'll find details on www.annualcreditreport.com. Any business that checks your credit will then be told they must phone you before authorizing new credit or opening a new account in your name. But remain alert for any suspicious activity, like calls from creditors or missing mail.

Making a Homeowners' Insurance Claim

You paid the premiums, so you'll be covered for damage to your house, or for injuries to visitors, right? Probably, but don't pick up the phone just yet.

First, you need do a little research, decide whether making a claim is even worthwhile, and be ready to defend your right to coverage, as discussed in this section.

Is the damage or injury covered under your policy?

There's no getting around it. You're going to have to open your policy and read it, cover to cover, even if it makes your eyes cross. Try to identify which parts of the policy say you're covered for the damage. In general, the damage

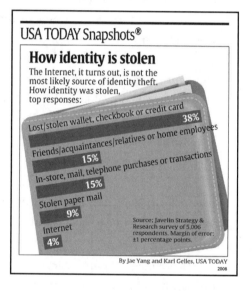

USA TODAY Snapshots®

How identity is stolen

The Internet, it turns out, is not the most likely source of identity theft. How identity was stolen, top responses:

Lost/stolen wallet, checkbook or credit card **38%**

Friends/acquaintances/relatives or home employees **15%**

In-store, mail, telephone purchases or transactions **15%**

Stolen paper mail **9%**

Internet **4%**

Source: Javelin Strategy & Research survey of 5,006 respondents. Margin of error: ±1 percentage points.

By Jae Yang and Karl Gelles, USA TODAY 2008

needs to have been sudden and accidental, such as water damage from a broken dishwasher or wind damage to your roof shingles, as opposed to being an ongoing maintenance concern, such as a leaky pipe or aging roof. And any injuries to guests or visitors at your house (or even elsewhere, if accidentally caused by members of your household) must have been unintentional.

Next, check the list of exclusions to make sure none of them cancels out the coverage you thought you had. For example, a wall that suddenly cracks would normally be covered, but not if it was a result of earthquake damage, which is typically excluded.

Finally, check on the limits to your deductible (the money you'll have to pay out of pocket, typically around $1,000) and how much you'll potentially receive after you've spent that amount.

Is the damage or injury worth filing a claim over?

If the damage is minimal—for example, $150 to fix a broken window, or $300 for a dental visit after the neighbor kid chips his tooth on your sink—you might not want to say a thing about it to your insurance carrier. The reason is simple: Insurance companies are notorious for upping your premiums or even cancelling your policy based on your past claims or your house's history of damage. One claim alone won't ordinarily do it—but if the house's history includes claims by former owners, for example because they made two claims based on windstorms and you then make a third, that might tip the balance.

How big is the problem of raised premiums after a claim? In a 2007 study, the Independent Insurance Agents & Brokers of America (IIABA, at www.iiaba.net) found that nearly three million households had lost their insurance coverage since 2003, and another 26 million had seen their premiums go up. They concluded, "Frequent claim activity, no matter how small, can impact your renewal and rate." As a homeowner, you have to be strategic, and put in claims only when the damage is high enough that paying it yourself would be painful.

If the damage amount is less than you'd have to pay to reach your deductible, filing a claim won't gain you any immediate return anyway (though you'd be closer to reimbursement if a later claim were to arise). Even if the damage is, say, $1,200 and your deductible is $1,000, having the insurance company pay the remaining $200 might not be worth the risk.

Unfortunately, you don't have much time to decide whether to make a claim. Most policies require you to give "prompt notice" of the loss or damage. The policy probably won't define prompt notice, except perhaps to say that it's within a "reasonable time" or as soon as is "practical." Up to a month is usually okay.

Of course, if the damage is so bad that you're living under a tarp or at the friend's while considering your options, don't hesitate to get on the phone to your insurance company, especially because your living expenses will probably be covered while you're out the house. In less drastic cases, get busy reading your policy, call repair people or others to estimate costs, then make your decision.

> TIP
>
> **If you pay someone's medical bills without collecting on your insurance, make sure the person can't sue you later.** Just as with minor damage, minor injuries might better be left unreported to your insurance company. Of course, the injured person should see a doctor first, to find out the full extent and cost of the injuries. And if possible, you should wait until the person has healed. Then protect yourself by having the person sign what's called a "release," acknowledging your payment and freeing you from further liability for claims based on the injuries. You can find a release form for personal injuries in *101 Law Forms for Personal Use*, by Ralph Warner, Robin Leonard, and the Editors of Nolo (Nolo).

Is anyone else liable for the damage?

Let's say your house gets damaged by a fire that was caused by some faulty wiring. Not so long ago, when you bought the house, the disclosure report you got from the seller (which was also signed by their real estate agent), as well as the report you got from your own inspector, all said the wiring was in fine shape. You might feel frustrated, and wonder whether you have any legal remedy against one or all of these people.

If you're making an insurance claim for the damage, your first step should be to simply explain the situation to your insurance company. That's because the company has a right of "subrogation," meaning a right to go after third parties to recover any amounts it ends up paying you.

Whether your insurance company actually decides to act on its right of subrogation is another matter. Many of them decide it's not worth the cost or time to track people down and possibly sue them, especially because there's no guarantee of winning. But if you paid a deductible for this damage, be sure to urge the company onward and complain to your state's department of insurance if they do nothing. You'll get paid back your deductible out of the proceeds of the lawsuit, too.

> **CAUTION**
> **You can't be paid for the same damage twice.** If your insurance company pays you for the damage, does nothing with its subrogation rights, and then you turn around and sue the former owners or others and win, your insurance company has the right to collect what it paid you out of the proceeds.

Of course, if the damage isn't covered by insurance—and plenty of types of damage aren't—you may want to take action against the responsible parties yourself, as discussed in "How Long Has This Been Going On? Liability for Existing Defects," later in this chapter.

How to file a claim

For damage or injuries that are bad enough to justify filing a claim, here are your next steps (after you've dealt with "What to Do First," above).

- **Fill out claim forms.** Your insurance company will send you these forms within a set period of time (dictated by your state's laws). You'll need to fill out and return them promptly, and keep a copy for your files.

- **In injury cases, give your insurance company the injured person's name and contact information.** Also include a description of what happened, and any legal papers you receive. You won't have to act as intermediary—the insurance company will ask the person for written proof of the loss and authorization to see medical records, and may require the person to undergo medical exams. If you're sued, the insurance company will take the lead in your defense.

- **Set up a file for documents and notes related to your claim.** That should include not only your claim forms, but receipts for any materials you buy, and your detailed notes of conversations with insurance company representatives. Be sure to write down their names, titles, and phone numbers.

- **Find your inventory of possessions.** Use it to make a complete list of anything that has been damaged or lost. Locate any receipts or proof of value you can find, to prove how much you deserve as payment. And if your power was out for a while, itemize any food that spoiled in your refrigerator or freezer.

- **Create a list of your favorite contractors, if any.** Someone's got to do the fixups, and it's in your interest to be proactive about who that will be. USA TODAY's Christine Dugas advises, "In some cases, your insurer may authorize you over the phone to hire one."

- **Expect a visit from the insurance company.** They will probably arrange for an adjuster to come and inspect your home to confirm the damage and find out what repairs are needed.

- **If your home is unlivable, find out how much your insurer will authorize for temporary additional living expenses.** Dugas says, "Some insurers will pay for you to stay in a hotel, rent an apartment, or stay in a mobile home on your property. If you're stretched to the limit, ask your agent for a cash advance." But, she warns, "You may be living in temporary quarters for a while, so find out if there are limits on the total amount your policy allows for these expenses. If you are forced to eat out in restaurants, most policies will pay only an amount above what you would normally spend on food at home."

> ### CAUTION
> **After big disasters, expect slow insurance company response.** Dugas explains, "When a major disaster occurs, insurance companies typically send mobile units to the area to help handle all the claims. But if the roads are closed or electricity is out and you are one of many homeowners filing a claim, you can expect delays. Insurers don't necessarily handle the claims on a first-come, first-served basis. They will generally deal with the worst situations first."

How you'll be paid

How and when your insurance company will pay for any damage or injuries depends not only on obvious factors like their cost to fix things, but in the case of property damage, on whether you plan to remedy the damage as opposed to living with it. For example, if the shed burns down and you decide to replace it with a vegetable garden, the insurance company won't want to pay you the full value of a new shed.

The typical scenario in the case of physical damage is that, after the company has reviewed the evidence of damage and visited the property, you're offered a settlement amount—or at least an advance against the final amount, if the damage is large. If you don't plan to rebuild or repurchase, the settlement amount will be reduced.

For repairs or rebuilding that can't be finished right away, you'll probably be given a certain length of time—somewhere between three months and a year—to finish, and then will need to submit receipts for any amounts over the advance, up to your policy limits. Alternately, the insurance company may agree to pay the contractor or repairpeople directly, particularly if they request it as a condition of working.

If both your house and your personal belongings were damaged, you may receive two separate checks. However, the structural-damage check may also be made out to your mortgage lender, which will have to endorse it, and may require you to put the money into an escrow account. That's a way to guarantee you'll make the repairs, thus protecting the lender's collateral. Unfortunately it can be inconvenient if the contractor wants up-front payments, while the lender will release the funds only in increments as the work gets done. You'll get a third check for living expenses if you have to temporarily move elsewhere.

In a personal injury case, the typical scenario is that the insurance company will start by directly paying for the injured person's medical expenses, up to your policy limit. If the injured person sues you, the insurance company will normally hire lawyers to defend your case and will pay the damages, again up to your policy limit. But it also has the power to accept a settlement or make decisions about the case without getting your consent or approval. The insurer may also reimburse you for your lost wages on days you had to attend court.

Disputing a denied claim

What if your insurer denies your claim or offers less than you believe you deserve? USA TODAY's Christine Dugas says, "Ask for a letter pointing to the policy provision that is the basis for the decision." Reread your policy, then draft a polite but firm letter explaining why you believe the decision was wrong. If you can come up with any new evidence to back up your assertions, such as contractor's estimates for repairs or appraiser's statements of the value of your damaged goods, include copies. Send the letter via certified mail with a return receipt, and keep a copy for your records.

USA TODAY Snapshots®

Garbage time
Top five foods thrown away by U.S. consumers because of spoilage:

Fresh vegetables and bagged salad — 58%
Fresh fruit — 49%
Bread — 49%
Milk, yogurt and cheese — 48%
Pre-packaged sandwich meat, hot dogs, bacon — 29%
— 19%

Source: DuPont Ipsos Public Affairs

Note: Margin of error ±3% percentage points.

By David Stuckey and Marcy E. Mullins, USA TODAY 2005

If you aren't happy with the insurance company's response (or if you'd rather someone else draft the letter in the first place), consider hiring a lawyer. Most lawyers prefer to do this kind of work on a contingency fee basis—meaning you'll pay less up front, but have to shell out a percentage of the amount you win.

It's impossible to estimate your chances of winning, but here's a legal tidbit that's good to know: If there is ambiguity in the policy language, courts will find in favor of the policyholder. The idea is that the insurer caused the uncertainty to exist, and that you had a reasonable expectation of coverage.

Ray Bourhis, a lawyer at Bourhis and Wolfson in San Francisco, also advised Dugas, "Find out what your state allows in terms of damages if you're cheated by your insurance company. It increases your leverage if you have the right to recover punitive damages." Your lawyer will be able to tell you this—or if you don't have one yet, contact your state insurance commissioner (find yours at www.iii.org, click "Directories/ Resources," then "Listings by State," then "Insurance Departments & Commissioners").

How to Avoid Rip-Offs After a Disaster

If your home has been destroyed or damaged by a hurricane or other disaster, USA TODAY's Christine Dugas advises caution in hiring contractors and other experts. She suggests (based on tips from the Insurance Information Institute):

- Don't be rushed into signing a contract with a roofer, contractor, or builder. Consult more than one, and compare written estimates for the job.
- Beware of contractors who encourage you to spend a lot on temporary repairs. Those payments will come out of your total insurance settlement, and you may not have enough left for permanent repairs.
- Check their references and find out if they have a record of complaints with the Better Business Bureau.
- Be wary of public adjusters who go door to door soliciting business after a disaster. They may settle your claim quickly for less than you deserve, and you'll have to pay them a portion— usually 15%.
- If you decide to hire an attorney, make sure the person has experience handling insurance cases.

 "Before a disaster strikes," by Christine Dugas, September 19, 2003.

RESOURCE

For more information on handling insurance claims: See Insure.com and the Insurance Information Institute's website, www.iii.org.

Making a Home Warranty Claim

In addition to your homeowners' insurance, you may have a home warranty. It was most likely purchased for you by the seller, as a way to, in the words of USA TODAY's Christine Dugas, "sweeten the deal."

Think of your home warranty as a supplement to your homeowners' insurance policy. It will provide repair and replacement of mechanical systems and attached appliances in your house, such as the furnace, plumbing and water heater, dishwasher, laundry machines, wiring, and electricity. The idea is that if one of these breaks due to normal wear, the warranty company sends a repairperson, and you pay a set fee for parts and labor, around $50 to $100.

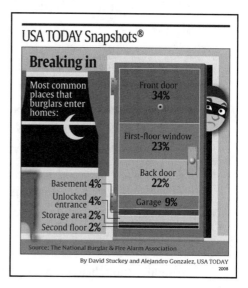

USA TODAY Snapshots®

Breaking in

Most common places that burglars enter homes:

Front door **34%**

First-floor window **23%**

Back door **22%**

Garage **9%**

Basement **4%**

Unlocked entrance **4%**

Storage area **2%**

Second floor **2%**

Source: The National Burglar & Fire Alarm Association

By David Stuckey and Alejandro Gonzalez, USA TODAY 2008

It's worth getting familiar with your home warranty policy, so that you'll know when to request services. It's certainly convenient to have the company deal with choosing and sending a repairperson. And in the best-case scenario, you'll get an expensive new home component for the mere cost of a service visit (though you'll pay for every visit, for example to evaluate the problem and then later make repairs).

But home warranty policies contain some major exclusions, like for preexisting conditions (those which arose before you got the warranty), conditions created by your failure to have an item serviced as often as recommended, problems due to improper installation, and more. The exclusions can seriously undermine your coverage—and some home warranty companies are quick to use them against you, as evidenced by the massive volume of consumer complaints.

A related problem is that it's in both the repairperson's and the warranty company's interest to do patchwork repairs (for which you pay a service fee each time) rather than simply replace whatever's broken.

If you're having trouble getting adequate coverage from your home warranty company, persistence is your best bet. Keep calling and writing letters. When phoning, write down the date, time, and duration of the call, the customer service representative's full name and ID number, as well as the call center location. Send any relevant evidence as to why you deserve coverage, such as a statement by a contractor saying that the problem looks like it developed only after you got the warranty.

If you remain unsatisfied, you could take the company to small claims court, as described in *Everybody's Guide to Small Claims Court*, by Ralph Warner (Nolo). The advantage to small claims court is that it's fast, easy, and you don't need a lawyer's help.

Also check whether a government agency in your state—probably either your department of insurance (as in California) or real estate (as in Texas)—regulates home warranty companies. If so, contact that agency to file any complaints and get help asserting your rights. Unfortunately, not all states have passed regulatory laws.

Of course, if you're not happy with your home warranty company, you shouldn't renew your coverage. And even if you've never tested the company by filing a claim, many experts feel that you're better off, in the long run, setting aside a few thousand dollars for emergency repairs instead of spending money (usually $300 to $900 per year) on a home warranty.

How Long Has This Been Going On? Liability for Existing Defects

Let's start with a caution: Homes don't come with a lifetime warranty. You buy them, they age, they decay, and it's normally your job to deal with the consequences without running back to the seller to complain. Resist the urge to sue someone every time a pipe springs a leak or the foundation cracks.

But complaining may be justified if there was something wrong with the property and someone—the seller, the seller's agent, or the inspector—should have told you about it but didn't. Ideally, you'll be able to resolve matters without going to court. But we'll start by analyzing whether a lawsuit is possible, so that you can work your way up to one, if need be.

> **TIP**
> **Will your insurance company cover the damage?** If so, there may be no need to take action on your own, as described under "Making a Homeowners' Insurance Claim," above.

Who's responsible?

Even if you think you've been wronged, you can't sue everyone involved in the sale of your home. The responsible parties might include one or more of the following

- **The seller.** Nearly every state has laws requiring sellers to advise buyers of certain defects in the property, typically by filling out a standard disclosure form before the sale is completed. (This responsibility remains even if you bought the house "as is.") The standard form usually asks the seller to state whether the property has certain features (like appliances, a roof, a foundation, systems for electricity, water, and heating, and more) and then rate or describe their condition. Some states' disclosure laws are more comprehensive than others, and if a feature isn't on the list, the seller may not be required to speak up. Also, the seller isn't usually required to scout out problems. But if there's clearly a place where the seller should have stated a problem but denied it, try to figure out whether the seller in fact knew about the problem. For example, if the seller patched over or hid problem areas, or if the neighbors tell you about the seller's efforts to deal with a problem, the evidence is on your side.

- **The seller's real estate agent.** Some states' laws make sellers' agents liable for failing to disclose problems they observed or were told of by the sellers. Again, check your state's disclosure laws and try to figure out whether the problem could have been seen before the sale.

- **Your inspector.** We're assuming—no, hoping—you got a home inspection before buying. In theory, the inspector should have spotted problems that the seller wasn't even aware of. If the inspector missed problems that an expert should have noticed, the inspector may be liable. Read over your inspection report to see what it said about the area in question. Some buyers are embarrassed to find that the problem is spelled out right in the report, which they didn't read carefully enough. Others find that the problem falls within an area that the inspector rightfully excluded from the report, for example because it wasn't visible and accessible.

Do you have a case?

Once you've figured out the possible responsible parties, you'll want to know whether their action—or inaction—entitles you to compensation. If your situation meets the criteria below, you may have a case. We've collapsed a few legal principles into this list, but it will apply to most situations in most states. (If you're dealing with a new house and think the builder might be responsible, read the next section.)

- **The defect was there before you bought the home.** Problems that started since you bought or are a natural result of your home's aging or your lapses in maintenance are yours to deal with. Of course, determining when a problem started can get complicated. For example, a blockage in your sewer line may be a new problem, or it may be a recurrence of a long-time issue with roots growing into the pipes. You may need a professional's analysis. But if the problem could have started before you bought the house, keep reading.

- **It's not an obvious defect that you could have seen yourself before buying.** If there was a huge crack running across the living room ceiling at the open house and you've only now decided to bring it up, no dice. But if it was hidden by a false ceiling, the matter may be worth pursuing. Don't worry if your inspector should have seen the problem—that just means you've got a potential claim against the inspector, too.

- **No one told you about the defect before the sale, or someone actually lied to you about it.** The responsible party may have been the seller, the seller's agent, or the inspector, as explained above.

- **You relied on the lies or nondisclosures.** This one's probably easy. If, for example, you took the seller's word that a remodel job was up to code in deciding to buy or in setting your price, you acted in reliance.

- **You've incurred monetary damage as a result.** Your costs of repairs or related damages (such as destruction of your personal property due to a flooded basement, or a decrease in your property value due to an undisclosed environmental hazard) will become, legally speaking, the "damages" that you may collect—even if you haven't paid any out-of-pocket costs yet (for example, you need a new foundation but haven't actually hired a contractor to build it). But don't expect to collect any damages that go beyond the house itself, such as for your pain and suffering.

Which States Don't Require Seller Disclosures?

As of this printing, the states of Alabama, Arkansas, Colorado, Florida, Kansas, Massachusetts, Missouri, Montana, New Jersey, New Mexico (except for condos), North Dakota, Utah, Vermont, West Virginia, and Wyoming don't require sellers to disclose material facts about the property. And in New York, sellers of single-family homes can choose to pay you $500 instead of filling out the disclosure form.

If you live in one of those states, it's "buyer beware"—meaning if you asked the seller about problems and the seller lied, you can sue, but if you forgot to ask, you're on your own.

Built to Last? Liability for Defects in New Homes

Before you moved into your new home, your local town, city, or municipality most likely inspected it and issued a certificate of occupancy. That indicated that the home was, at a minimum, livable. However, many new homeowners are unhappy to discover that the certificate doesn't guarantee that everything is in working order or even complete. In fact, *Consumer Reports* has estimated that 15% of new U.S. homes have at least one major defect.

If items in your new house simply remain uncompleted, what happens next depends on what you agreed to at the closing. Your contract may have allowed you to do a closing inspection of the home, at which time you and the builder should have created a punch list of items yet to be done. The seller has a contractual obligation to fix the items on that list, and you should keep insisting on follow-through. Don't assume that the home warranty (discussed next) covers uncompleted items—some warranties specifically exclude them.

Are defects covered by a builder's warranty?

At least a year's worth of seasonal changes are often needed to put a new house to the test. For example, only in winter may you discover that water seeps into the basement or around window frames, that the landscaping was badly graded and leads to mudslides, or that you've got a mold problem. And guess what: Your homeowners' insurance probably doesn't cover construction defects.

That's why most home builders issue their new owners a warranty (often called a "limited warranty") on their work, either within the sales contract or as a separate document. (By the way, such warranties aren't usually required by law.) The warranty's maximum term is typically broken up into one-, two-, and ten-year terms, based on the type of needed work. You'll probably get a one-year warranty for labor and materials, two years for mechanical defects (plumbing, electrical, heating, air conditioning, and ventilation systems), and ten years for structural defects. The result is that the best parts of the warranty expire quickly—your carpeting, tiles, paint, and roofing, for example, may not be covered after the first year.

If you received a warranty, read it over to determine its length, who's supposed to handle problems (the builder may have bought third-party insurance), and what's covered and excluded. Pay special attention to your own responsibilities—you may have been given a detailed list of maintenance obligations. Ignoring these gives the builder a perfect excuse to deny you protections under the warranty.

Typical exclusions from a builder's warranty include:

- **Damage owing to your own abuse, misuse, neglect, failure by you or your homeowners' association to provide maintenance** (such as cleaning the gutters, draining your water heater, touching up caulk or grout, or dealing with pests), or failure to maintain adequate ventilation and humidity levels in the home.

- **Deterioration of construction materials within expected levels,** including warpage or shrinkage within industry standards, or changes due to weather conditions, natural disasters, or soil movement or settling.

- **Damage caused by outsiders** (such as rioters, vandals, animals, or airplanes) or "acts of God."

- **Damage caused by people you hired to work on the property.**

- **Your housing costs and expenses if you have to move out while repairs are being made.**

- **All home appliances or equipment that are consumer products,** such as your refrigerator, and dishwasher, some of which may come with their own warranties (which the builder should have transferred to you).

TIP

Get an inspection before every warranty expiration date.
Some defects are hard to detect, so it may be worth paying a professional
to point out what the builder needs to fix. In fact, many builders' warranties or contracts say they'll send a quality-control inspector within
the first year to check on your house. Keep track of the date yourself, and
make sure the builder's inspectors truly seem to be scouting for trouble—
if not, hire your own. In preparation for any inspection, make a list of
every problem you've observed. Something as apparently minor as a
cracked tile could indicate a major problem, like a shifting foundation.

Can you file a builder's warranty claim?

If the defective or damaged item is covered by the builder's warranty,
read what it says about procedures for filing a claim. Many warranties
require you to send written notification to the builder, while others give
you a hotline to call. In fact, sending a letter to the builder is a good
idea regardless of what the warranty says. This shows that you're serious
about asserting your rights, and creates evidence that you might later
want to use in court. Send the letter by certified mail with a return
receipt, so the builder can't later claim not to have received it. Also,
keep notes (legible ones) on your every conversation with the builder,
including the dates. You can use this information to confirm, in your
letters to the builder, what you agreed to. And they might also be good
to show to a judge someday.

Be prepared to act quickly. Sometimes you can protect your rights
just by notifying the builder of problems within the warranty period.
However, some warranties are cleverly written to let the builder string
you along without making the repairs until the warranty period has run
out and you've lost your rights. (Don't bring in any outside contractors
to do repairs yet, as this could allow the builder to cancel the benefits of
the warranty.)

SEE AN EXPERT

Has your builder gone missing? A few builders are fly-by-night operations that close up shop, leave town, and change their name as soon as the work is done—or near to done. (Some builders have left even before finishing up amenities like a promised swimming pool or golf course.) For cases like these, go straight to a lawyer for help.

Are defects covered by a manufacturer's warranty?

If your builder isn't accepting responsibility for a problem, figure out whether a manufacturer's warranty might apply—for example, to an appliance, windows, roof shingles, or other product. You may be able to argue that the product itself failed, in which case a manufacturer that stands behind its product will provide replacements and repairs. The catch, however, is that the product needs to have been installed properly—and improper installation in new building is often the very core of the problem.

Does state law offer extra protection?

Warranty or not, you may get added protection from the laws in your state. In New Jersey, Texas, and various other states, the laws give homeowners an automatic warranty of their home's habitability and good workmanship. Some states may require you to give the builder a chance to make repairs before suing.

Laws passed by legislatures aren't your only hope (though they're the easiest to find). In most states, such as Colorado, Illinois, New York, and Washington, the "common law" (court decisions on individual cases that then set the rules for everyone else) may also protect you. Such states' courts have said that, just by the act of building you a house, the builder provides "implied warranties" that the house is habitable (safe, sanitary, and fit for use) and was built in a workmanlike manner, in compliance with local building codes. And even without an implied warranty, you may be able to sue a builder on another legal ground, such as fraud, breach of contract, or negligence.

> **TIP**
> **What if you signed a warranty saying you were waiving (giving up) your rights under state law?** Not all of these agreements are binding. Consult an attorney for an individual analysis.

You won't necessarily have to do legal research to find these laws and implied warranty rights. Many states have consumer protection agencies to help advise you on builder problems. Check whether your state agency has published an explanatory pamphlet online. However, if you're having trouble, now may be the time to consult an attorney or read *Legal Research: How to Find & Understand the Law*, by Stephen Elias and Susan Levinkind (Nolo).

Should You Sue? Deciding to Go to Court

If, after reading the information above, you think you have a good legal claim against your home seller, selling agent, inspector, or builder, you'll have to decide whether to pursue any legal remedies.

Are there alternatives to a lawsuit?

No need to rush to court. You may be able to recover what you're owed more cheaply and with less stress. Try these two steps first:

- **Send a demand letter to the responsible party.** This means a polite letter explaining the situation, requesting reimbursement, and suggesting that you're considering suing ("If I don't hear from you within ten days, I may pursue legal remedies"). If possible, include a copy of your contractor's estimate or bill for repairs. Send your letter by certified mail and keep a copy for yourself.

- **Suggest mediation.** You can propose that you and the other party sit down with a neutral, professional third party who will help you reach an agreement. This tends to be much less expensive than going to court, and ideally creates a spirit of compromise leading to a result everyone will live by. Another, less flexible option is binding arbitration (in which the third party issues a final decision, with no appeal). If your dispute is with your inspector or a builder, check your contract—you may already have agreed to mediation or arbitration.

Is a lawsuit worth it?

If you weren't able to resolve your disputes with the methods above, you'll have to decide whether to file a lawsuit. If the problem will cost less to repair yourself than to pursue in court, you might as well chalk this one up to experience. If not, however, you shouldn't have to pay for someone's outright lies or shoddy work. In legalese, you could potentially sue based on someone's failure to disclose (according to your state's statute), negligence, fraud, breach of contract, breach of warranty, negligent misrepresentation, or some combination of those. Here's how to begin:

- **Make sure you're within any appropriate deadlines ("statutes of limitation").** Every state puts limits on how long you have, from the date you discover a problem or reasonably should have discovered it, to sue someone. They don't want you dragging the seller into court 20 years after the sale, when no one recalls what happened. Most statutes of limitations are somewhere between two and ten years, but it will depend on where you are and what type of claim you have. Find your state's laws on this with either an online search, by contacting your state's housing regulatory agency, or by consulting an attorney.

- **Consider small claims court.** Filing in small claims court allows you to proceed with your case without a lot of the expensive administrative hassles of a "regular" lawsuit. You can represent yourself—in some states, attorneys are actually forbidden—the rules are not usually as strict, and your case should be resolved relatively quickly. However, every state places a dollar limit on the amount of damages you can sue for—usually somewhere between $1,500 and $15,000. To find your state's exact limit, search for the article "How Much Can You Sue for in Small Claims Court," on Nolo's website at www.nolo.com. Even if your damages are over the limit—for example, if the repairs cost $8,000 and the limit is $5,000—bringing a suit for $5,000 and forgetting about the rest might make economic sense, saving time and attorney's fees.

- **Decide whether to bring suit in state court.** If you're over the small claims court limit, your next option is filing suit in state court, most likely with the help of an attorney. Some attorneys will take this type of case on a contingency basis, meaning you don't pay a fee up front but pay a large percentage of the damage award. You may still be responsible for paying court costs and other fees, plus expenses such as the attorney's phone calls and postage. Or, the court may award reimbursement of attorney's fees as part

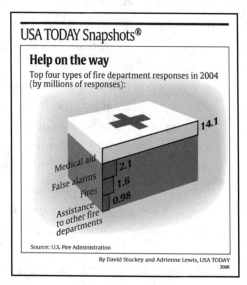

USA TODAY Snapshots®

Help on the way

Top four types of fire department responses in 2004 (by millions of responses):

14.1

Medical aid 2.1

False alarms 1.6

Fires 0.98

Assistance to other fire departments

Source: U.S. Fire Administration

By David Stuckey and Adrienne Lewis, USA TODAY 2006

of your damages. If you're suing a builder, consult a lawyer who specializes in construction litigation. Also talk to your neighbors, who may be experiencing similar problems. You may be able to band together and bring a class action lawsuit, or have your homeowners' association bring the suit.

TIP

Your homeowners' association also has responsibilities to you. For example, the directors and officers must maintain and repair the common areas properly, and can be sued if they fail in this duty. Ongoing relations between homeowners and community associations are beyond the scope of this book. If you have trouble, however, talk to homeowners in your community and consider hiring an attorney.

Movin' on Up:
Planning for Your Next House

Ready to Go? Deciding When to Move_____266

Another Paint Job!? Your Selling and Moving Costs_____267

Financial Strategies for Moving Up_____269

    Start saving for another down payment_____269

    Watch the market_____270

    Get preapproved for a mortgage_____270

    Choose the right property_____271

    Keep the cash coming: Become a landlord_____273

Maximizing Profits on Your Home Sale_____276

    Repair and inspect_____276

    Sell it yourself: Save on real estate commissions_____277

    Make your house look its best_____278

    Price it right_____280

    Take all tax breaks_____281

How to Buy and Sell Simultaneously—Without
  Getting Stuck_____282

By now, you've figured out how to maintain or improve your home, take advantage of financing and tax breaks, and play diplomat with the neighbors. All these skills will serve you well when it comes to one last task—planning for the future. For many homeowners, that means moving after they've built up some equity or the market has picked up, putting more desirable homes within their reach.

USA TODAY Snapshots®

Why people move

46%
27%
18%
8%

Housing-related | Family-related | Work-related | Other reasons

Source: Census Bureau, 2005-06 data

By David Stuckey and Veronica Salazar, USA TODAY 2008

If you hope to someday trade in for a bigger, better, or just different house, this chapter will help you:

- decide when to move
- understand the costs of moving
- strategize your financial approach to moving up
- maximize the profits from the sale of your current home, and
- learn how to handle buying another house while you sell the one you're in.

Ready to Go? Deciding When to Move

People move for lots of different reasons. Here are times you should consider it:

- **You can't afford your current home.** If your current home is simply more than you can handle financially, even after considering the refinancing or mortgage workout options discussed in Chapter 7, you may have no other choice.

- **You need to switch locations.** There's no point in staying put long-term if the location isn't working for you—whether because the neighborhood has deteriorated, you need better schools, you've changed jobs, or other transitions.

- **Your family circumstances have changed.** A new baby (maybe twins!), a child leaving for college, an elderly relative moving in, or a split with a spouse or partner are all circumstances that might necessitate a move.

- **Your need more—or less—space.** If the size or amenities of your current home don't meet your needs, and renovating or remodeling, (discussed in Chapters 9 and 10) won't solve the problem, it might be the right time to move.

USA TODAY Snapshots®

Second Street comes first

Of the USA's 5.5 million streets, the most common names:

Second Street	7,972
Main Street	7,712
Third Street	7,466
First Street	7,172
Fourth Street	6,582

Source: 2006 Tele Atlas digital map data

By Tracey Wong Briggs and Suzy Parker, USA TODAY 2006

- **You can afford to move up.** If you utilize some of the financial strategies discussed below, you may have enough cash, equity, or a combination of both to move to a better place.

Another Paint Job!?
Your Selling and Moving Costs

As a renter, you may be familiar with moving hassles like packing and unpacking boxes. But as a homeowner, the process of selling and moving involves other significant expenses, which can add up to as much as 10% of your house's overall value. You'll want to plan for these expenses carefully—and limit how often you pay them by not moving too often. You'll incur costs such as:

- **Preparing your house for sale.** Before you move, you will likely spend some money getting the place ready. This may include small improvements and repairs, storage fees, and decorative touches like new flowers on the front porch. Fortunately, many of these costs will be recouped when you sell, or may help you sell more quickly. Still, expect to spend at least a few hundred dollars—and possibly thousands if you hire a staging professional.

USA TODAY Snapshots®

Men vs. women on driving

Will stop to ask for directions: Men 42% Women 61%

Have experience with a Global Positioning System device: Men 36% Women 26%

Source: Harris survey (conducted for Lincoln Mercury) of 580 car, sport-utility vehicle and truck owners April

By Shannon Reilly and Alejandro Gonzalez, USA TODAY 2005

- **Listing your house for sale.** Unless you sell yourself, you'll incur significant expense—probably 5%–6% of the selling price—paying a real estate broker. Even if you sell on your own, you should plan to spend several hundred dollars advertising the sale and having an attorney review the documents.

- **Transaction costs.** Expect to spend at least several hundred dollars—and very possibly more —on escrow and related fees, like transferring title and purchasing a home warranty plan. The exact amount will depend on the customs where you live and what you negotiate with the buyer.

- **Moving costs.** These costs can vary depending on whether you hire a full-service mover or do it yourself, as well as how far you're moving and how much stuff you have to move. It isn't unheard of to spend a couple of thousand dollars or more on an in-town move, but you may be able to spend significantly less if you go the friends-with-a-pickup-truck route. (Don't forget to budget for the celebratory pizza afterward.)

- **Purchasing costs.** As your pocketbook probably remembers, buying a home is expensive. In addition to your down payment, closing costs usually add up to 2%–5% of the home's purchase price (including some prepaid costs, like insurance and your mortgage). (Of course, you'll avoid these if you're moving into a rental.)

Financial Strategies for Moving Up

No matter when you decide to move, there are steps you can take to prepare yourself financially. Here are a few simple strategies.

Start saving for another down payment

Unless you're downsizing, you'll most likely pay more for your next house than you did for your current one. That probably means making a larger down payment. And the more you put down, the less interest you'll pay on your next loan. If you plan to sell your current home, you'll hopefully be off to a good start—you can cash out any equity and apply it toward your down payment.

The more equity you've built, the better this strategy works—a good thing to remember when you're working hard to pay down the mortgage or make valuable home improvements. It's sort of like a forced savings plan. (For more information on whether to prepay your mortgage, see Chapter 7, and refer to Chapter 9 for advice on making improvements that truly increase your home's value.)

USA TODAY Snapshots®

Where we live in relation to our moms

21% Same house

3% Different country

31% Same country, different state

3% Same street, different house

14.5% Same city, different street

27.5% Same state, different city

Source: Harris Interactive online survey of 2,256 adults (April 14–18) for for Skype. Margin of error ±3.8 percentage points.

By Mary Cadden and Alejandro Gonzalez, USA TODAY 2006

Of course, equity isn't your only potential source of down payment money. If you see a move on the horizon soon, you might want to start setting cash aside, especially if you don't expect your equity to amount to much. Remember also to calculate in the costs of moving, discussed above, in determining how much cash or equity you have to apply toward a down payment.

Watch the market

If you have some control over when you sell your home, it pays to be aware of what's happening in your local real estate market. Conventional wisdom says it's preferable to sell in a "seller's market"—that is, when there are many buyers in the market, and you as a seller can command top price. But the rule changes a little if you're buying and selling in the same market. The very competition among buyers that drives up the price of your house will also drive up the price of the house you're trying to buy.

To understand market conditions, pay attention to what's happening around you, even down to specific neighborhoods, price ranges, or home types within that market. For example, if prices have jumped sky high, demand for higher-priced houses may decrease, but demand for comparatively affordable starter homes might hold steady. That could make it easier for you to both sell your current home and buy another one at a good price.

As we'll explain later, a real estate agent can help you understand what's happening in the local market, but you can do a fair amount of research yourself. Start going to open houses long before you think you're ready to move (but only if you're sure you can resist the temptation to make an impulse buy). Look at websites like Zillow (www.zillow.com) and Domania (www.domania.com) to tell you what has sold, at what price, in recent months. You'll also probably get a feel for what's happening in the market by reading the local paper (check the business or real estate sections) and talking with others in the neighborhood.

Also pay attention to mortgage interest rates, which can affect both the strength of the market and the amount of home you can afford. If rates are low, you'll be able to get a bigger mortgage, which can make it a good time to buy. And lower rates mean more borrowers will be able to qualify for mortgages—particularly good if your house is a true starter home, because it will be within reach for the most number of buyers.

Get preapproved for a mortgage

If you get preapproved for a mortgage before making your next purchase, you'll maximize the chances of having the offer accepted. With a loan preapproval, a lender will commit to lending you money on certain terms, based on your financial criteria. Besides offering you some financial security, this helps convince a seller to accept your purchase offer, especially if you're competing with other buyers who aren't preapproved. In some cases, sellers will accept lower offers from preapproved buyers, knowing the deal is likely to go through. (For more information about how lenders decide how much you can borrow, see Chapter 7.)

Choose the right property

Another way you can maximize your buying power is to strategically choose your next home. You have a distinct advantage this time—having done it once, you'll already know a lot about what you want. Use that knowledge to target the neighborhoods and house features most important to you.

You've doubtlessly heard the mantra "location, location, location" when it comes to finding homes with good value. And while you might not have had a lot of control over the location of your first home—it may have been the most you could afford—you can probably afford to be pickier now. If investing in an appreciating asset is part of your goal as a homeowner (it usually is!), take the mantra to heart. Here are location-specific factors that affect value:

USA TODAY Snapshots

Neighborhood street vs. Wall Street
Which do you think is the better investment?

Real estate market
Street 69%

Stock market
24%

Don't know
7%

Source: TIAA-CREF survey of 1,001 investors ages 30 and older who help make household financial decisions. Margin of error: ±3 percentage points.

By Jae Yang and Julie Snider, USA TODAY
2006

- Schools. People pay for neighborhoods with better schools. If you have children, this may also be important to you.

- Safety. No one likes high crime levels.

- Resources and accessibility. People like to reach freeways, grocery stores, health care providers, and other services easily—but don't want these in their backyards.

- **Improvability.** If you can find a home in a good location that needs improvements—now or in the future—you may get it at a bargain. For example, as architect Dennis Wedlick told USA TODAY's Craig Wilson, "If you only judge a house from outside, you may be missing out on a home that has a lot of potential and might not mean a big investment. Simply adding a porch, that can transform a home. If it has good bones, you can keep making changes."

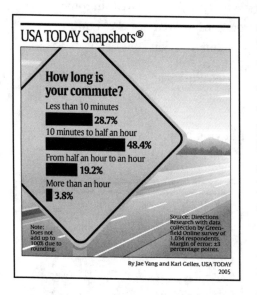

USA TODAY Snapshots®

How long is your commute?

Less than 10 minutes
28.7%

10 minutes to half an hour
48.4%

From half an hour to an hour
19.2%

More than an hour
3.8%

Note: Does not add up to 100% due to rounding.

Source: Directions Research with data collection by Greenfield Online survey of 1,034 respondents. Margin of error: ±3 percentage points.

By Jae Yang and Karl Gelles, USA TODAY 2005

The longer you plan to stay put, the less important it is to focus on the neighborhood's investment value (of course, you should like the neighborhood and location yourself, since you plan to be there for a long time). For example, a home in a brand new development isn't likely to appreciate as quickly as a home in a more established neighborhood. But if you plan to live there a long time, and it has the features most important to you, it could be the better choice.

RESOURCE

For a comprehensive resource on homebuying: See *Nolo's Essential Guide to Buying Your First Home*, by Ilona Bray, Alayna Schroeder, and Marcia Stewart (Nolo). This highly rated book covers issues of importance to all homebuyers, such as assessing the market, finding the best mortgage, choosing the best real estate professionals to work with, locating the ideal property, and more.

Keep the cash coming: Become a landlord

Perhaps you're ready to move—but not ready to sell. Or maybe, in an uncertain market, you don't want to risk bearing the monthly expenses of having the house sit unsold for an indefinite length of time.

In either case, consider renting out your current home and buying or renting another one to live in. (If, however you live in a development governed by a homeowners' association, check whether it restricts rentals before you get too far with your thinking.)

Becoming a landlord has these advantages:

- **Rental income.** With well-chosen tenants, you'll receive monthly rent checks. Ideally, these will outweigh your expenses, producing a positive annual cash flow. But run the numbers first. One issue is that you can't count on receiving rental income for 12 months out of the year. Even if your property is in high demand, transition time between tenants can take a month or two. Also understand that your rental income will not be pure profit. You'll need to subtract your projected property taxes, mortgage payments (if the house isn't yet paid off), insurance, utilities, repair and maintenance costs, and if you don't wish to spend your own time dealing with tenants, property management fees (approximately 8%–10% of the rental income). Once you've calculated your annual projected rent minus any expected vacancies, then subtracted all your likely expenses, you'll arrive at your annual profit. If it looks like you'll come out $1,200 to $2,400 ahead each year ($100 to $200 each month), you're doing well by industry standards.

- **Tax deductions.** Some landlords can claim so many deductions that it more than offsets all their rental income, resulting in what's known as a "net loss"—which you may be able to deduct from your nonrental income, such as a salary. Some of the major deductions include mortgage interest, depreciation, repair costs, travel, and home office expenses. For more information, see *Every Landlord's Tax Deduction Guide*, by Stephen Fishman (Nolo).

TIP

Keep your emotions out of the rental picture. As Jonas Lee, managing partner of real estate investment firm Redbrick Partners told USA TODAY's Adam Shell, making money as a landlord "requires a systematic approach." Unfortunately, he adds, residential landlords tend to "overestimate how much they will make." Shell further explains, "Redbrick uses a simple equation to calculate likely yield: It takes 50% of annual rental income and divides that by the property's purchase price. For example, a $1 million home that rents for $6,000 a month, or $72,000 a year, nets a rental yield of 3.6%. In contrast, a $75,000 home that rents for $1,100 a month, or $13,200 annually, delivers a heftier yield of 8.8%. Most properties yield roughly 4% [a year]."

- **Property appreciation.** The longer you wait, the more the property is likely to be worth. Many real estate investors feel that the safety of investing in real estate compensates for short-term losses or low profits and the potentially lower returns that they might get from riskier investments, like stocks.

- **Being your own boss.** Some people love the independence and the chance to put in a little sweat and creativity in search of higher returns. Who knows—this may be the start of a career change.

But there are some disadvantages to converting your home to a rental. These include:

- **Loss of the personal residence exclusion.** If you have owned and lived in your home for two of the last five years, you won't owe capital gains tax on the first $250,000 you make when you sell ($500,000 if married filing jointly). But if you convert your house to a rental and don't sell within three years, you'll lose the benefits of the exclusion.

- **Smaller down payment.** If you have equity in your current home and don't cash it out to put toward your next one, you'll have to borrow more—and pay interest. This could significantly reduce the financial benefits of renting out your home.

- **Property management responsibilities.** While you may enjoy being your own boss, it's work. Remember the days of calling the landlord when something needed to be fixed? Now you'll be receiving the calls, not making them. Fortunately, you can hire a property management company to take care of these day-to-day issues, but that usually costs 8 %–10% of your monthly income. If you can't part with that amount, have your hands full with other projects, don't have the time or inclination to learn the landlord/tenant laws, and aren't ready for ongoing dealings with tenants, contractors, and local officials, being a landlord may not be for you.

- **Costs.** You'll be responsible for the same home maintenance costs you had when you lived there, but the tenant will not have the same motivation to keep the place in good repair. And during some months, your property may sit empty. All these costs eat into your profits.

Don't Make These Landlording Mistakes

Here are five common errors people make when evaluating costs of managing a rental unit:

- Failing to factor in losses caused by vacancies and tenants who don't pay.
- Underestimating costs for property insurance.
- Not setting aside enough cash for repairs, such as leaky faucets, and major unanticipated capital outlays for replacing old furnaces and electrical systems.
- Failing to factor in higher tax burden in future, especially if sale triggers a reassessment.
- Ignoring the cost of hiring a handyman or property manager.

 "Renting out a home 'all about numbers'; Cheaper house might provide better return," Adam Shell, July 15, 2005.

RESOURCE

Helpful information on becoming a landlord: Pick up a copy of *Every Landlord's Legal Guide*, by Marcia Stewart, Ralph Warner, and Janet Portman (Nolo), which provides all the legal and practical information you need—including how to screen tenants, handle repair responsibilities, collect and return security deposits, legally enter rental property, hire a property manager, terminate a tenancy, and more. The book includes charts for the law in every state, and dozens of forms (including a lease) on CD-ROM.

Maximizing Profits on Your Home Sale

When you do decide to move on, you'll want to do it with as much cash as possible. Here are some ways to make sure you sell for high returns.

Repair and inspect

As we've discussed, keeping your home in good repair pays off in the long term. When you sell, you'll find that well-maintained systems save you from making costly repairs or negotiating a lower price.

But if you've put off any repairs or maintenance, you might want to investigate and fix matters before you sell. A good guide to ferreting out problems on your own is *Real Estate Home Inspection Checklist from A to Z*, by Guy Cozzi (Nemmar Real Estate Training). You could also hire a home inspector to prepare a complete report on your home. The idea would then be to fix any small problems that turn up. This saves the virtually inevitable hassle of the buyer discovering the same problems during the buyer's inspection and turning them into a negotiating point. For major problems that you aren't prepared to deal with, set your selling price accordingly.

However, if you do hire an inspector and discover any defects, you won't be able to sweep them under the rug—you'll probably have to disclose them to the buyer. In most states, it is illegal to fraudulently conceal major physical defects in your property such as a nonworking garage door or a basement that floods in heavy rains. And many states now require sellers to take a proactive role by making written disclosures on the condition of the property, usually on a special form that you'll have to sign and date. You'll have to decide whether the risk of a major undisclosed defect outweighs the value of hearing an inspector evaluate the condition of your home.

Generally, you must disclose only information within your personal knowledge. However, some states' laws identify certain problems that are your responsibility to search for, whether you see signs of the problem or not. In these cases, or where you could have seen a particular defect but turned a blind eye, you could ultimately end up in court, compensating the buyer for the costs of your failure to speak up.

Sell it yourself: Save on real estate commissions

Another way to maximize profits on your sale is to sell your home without hiring a real estate professional. Typically, the seller pays the broker a 5%–6% commission, who then pays half of that to the buyer's broker. You can eliminate or reduce this cost by selling the house yourself—as an estimated 20% of home sellers do.

Of course, selling yourself involves quite a bit of work. You'll have to advertise the property to potential buyers, show the home to interested parties, comply with any legal requirements (such as disclosures), choose a buyer, negotiate the contract terms, investigate whether the buyer is financially qualified, and more. In addition to having to learn some new skills, these tasks will take a significant amount of time.

Your investments of time and money are most likely to pay off in a hot market, when buyers will be eagerly looking for you, not the other way around. You can also make your task easier by using online advertising-and-support services like www.owners.com and www .homesbyowner.com. For a list of locally based FSBO sites, go to www .fsboguide.com. Of course, these services charge money for anything above basic services, usually a few hundred dollars.

Another option is to hire a broker or agent for only limited tasks, or for a reduced commission. For example, you may hire someone to advertise the property and negotiate the contract, but show the property to prospective buyers yourself. This will help you reduce costs, while still ensuring you get the services of a professional.

CROSS REFERENCE

Interested in selling your home FSBO? California homeowners should pick up *For Sale By Owner in California,* by George Devine (Nolo). It walks you through the entire process and includes legal forms to make the sale. Sellers in other states will benefit from *The For Sale By Owner Kit,* by Robert Irwin (Kaplan Publishing).

Make your house look its best

You probably toured many houses before settling on the one you now own. If you're like most buyers, you may have been swayed by professional or even amateur "staging"—the cleverly placed, attractive antiques and furniture, vases of fresh flowers, or highly manicured landscaping that the seller put in just to prepare the house for sale.

Staging works!

82% of home buyers are likely to be distracted from important issues when they go through a staged home. (Source: National Association of Exclusive Buyer Agents (NAEBA), based on a 2007 survey of brokers and agents.)

When you're ready to sell, be prepared to employ some of those same tactics yourself. Your goal isn't to trick anyone, but to present your house's positive features in the best possible light.

Professional stagers, whose services can costs thousands of dollars, may go so far as to redecorate, rent furniture, and put in new landscaping. But even if you don't hire a professional, small spruce-ups should have a positive effect on your bottom line.

Secrets That Sell

Donna Freeman of HGTV's *Designed to Sell* can help you dump your house in no time. Excuse us. Make that "sell" your house in no time. "My motto is this: The way you live in a house and the way you sell a house are totally different," says Freeman, a Los Angeles-based real estate agent. Here are ten things to do right now to assure your house will sell faster:

Get rid of clutter. "That's universal. Ask someone who won't hold back" to give you an honest opinion of what needs to go.

Wipe up dirt. "Once you live in the house, the dirt becomes invisible. I went into a house once, and dirt was literally hanging off the ceiling fan. The sellers never even noticed."

Roll on a fresh coat of paint. "Just make sure the color is neutral."

Open the curtains and blinds. "Let the sun shine in. The rooms look larger and have more energy. If the home looks small, the buyers don't think they're getting as good a value."

Pump up curb appeal. "Many times an agent will give an address to drive by. If the outside doesn't look good, well, that's that. Our goal is for the buyer to approach the house and say, 'Oh, boy!' Believe it or not, a new doormat works wonders."

Make your master bedroom a haven. Replace dingy bedding and soiled carpeting. "It's distasteful. Make the master bedroom look like a retreat, someplace they want to spend some time."

Temporarily relocate furry occupants. "Make sure all pet items are out of sight. And the odor. My word, the odor! Have someone come in and do a sniff test for you."

Box up plastic kids' toys. "You don't want buyers tripping over them in every room. And if they're pushed up against the wall, you can't see the size of the room. Bright colored plastic is offensive in every way."

Secrets That Sell, continued

Leave the house when it's being shown. "Buyers don't want you to stay. They can't see the wonderful fireplace because they're too nervous the seller is there."

Finish the projects that you've started. "The buyer sees all this work he'll have to do. Floors unfinished. Molding around windows. They'll (want to) patch a hole, not paint over it. The buyer will wonder what happened. It's a red flag."

 "Make yours a happy sales experience; De-clutter, repaint, and 8 other good ideas," by Craig Wilson, May 27, 2005.

 RESOURCE
For more tips on dressing up your home for sale, see:

- Elizabeth Weintraub's articles on http://homebuying.about.com (click "Selling a House")
- *301 Simple Things You Can Do to Sell Your Home Now and for More Money Than You Thought: How to Inexpensively Reorganize, Stage, and Prepare Your Home for Sale,* by Teri B. Clark (Atlantic Publishing Company)—we especially like that it has photos—and
- *Fix It, Stage It, Sell It, Quick!,* by Robert Irwin (Kaplan Publishing), a compact and informative guide.

Price it right

To set the sales price of your home, you'll need to know a little bit about what's selling in your neighborhood, how quickly, and for how much. Quick sales at or above asking price mean the market is "hot," and you may be able to set a relatively high price. (In the hottest markets, it's not uncommon to get offers well above asking price.) But when there are many homes on the market that sell well below their asking price and take a long time, the market is "cold," and you'll want to employ a different strategy. In that case, you might want to price your house lower, engaging the interest of buyers who have lots of other options.

Setting your asking price accurately from the beginning is smart for a couple of different reasons. First, it means your house will probably sell faster. Keep in mind that every month you spend making a mortgage payment is another month you're not applying that same payment to your next home. (This is a particularly tough position if you've already purchased that other home and are paying two mortgages.) Second, the longer your home sits on the market, the more potential buyers will start to wonder whether there is something "wrong" with it. They may think it's overpriced, that it must have some undisclosed flaw, or that you're desperate and will accept a lower price.

If you hire a real estate agent, he or she will be able to show you a list of comparable homes ("comps") and tell you their asking and actual sales prices. A real estate agent will also advise you on a good asking price, taking market conditions into account. Many will do this for free, in hope of getting your business. Just be aware that some may set an artificially high price to convince you that hiring them will actually yield such stellar results. (You can always ask them to show you the listing and sales prices of homes they've sold in recent months, to get an idea for how realistic they are.) And as explained earlier, you can do some research yourself.

Take all tax breaks

When it comes time to sell, if you've owned and lived in your home (as your principal residence) for two of the last five years, you can exclude the first $250,000 of gain ($500,000 if married filing jointly) from capital gains tax. The gain is the selling price, reduced by the price you paid ("the basis"), minus any allowed adjustments. If you think you may have this much gain, make sure you keep careful track of those adjustments that can reduce your basis, such as closing costs and the cost of home improvements. For more information, see Chapter 8.

How to Buy and Sell Simultaneously—Without Getting Stuck

Selling one home while buying a new one can be a juggling act. If you buy a new house before selling your old one, you risk having two mortgages and may sell for a lower price because you're desperate to get your equity out. If you sell first, you may be left without a place to live when the sale closes.

Here are a few ways to make this work:

- **Make a contingent offer.** If you are in a buyer's market, you can make the sale of your current home contingent on you finding a new home to buy. In a seller's market, when you place an offer on a new home, you can make the offer contingent on selling your current home. The seller may insist on a "wipe out" clause, which means that the house is left on the market and if another offer comes in, you have a limited amount of time, such as 72 hours, to wipe out the contingency (even if you haven't sold your house). If you don't, the seller can accept the other offer.

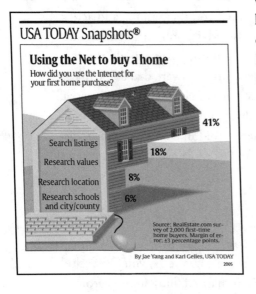

USA TODAY Snapshots®

Using the Net to buy a home
How did you use the Internet for your first home purchase?

Search listings — 41%
Research values — 18%
Research location — 8%
Research schools and city/county — 6%

Source: RealEstate.com survey of 2,000 first-time home buyers. Margin of error: ±3 percentage points.

By Jae Yang and Karl Gelles, USA TODAY 2005

- **Extend escrow.** When you contract to sell your home, negotiate a long escrow period so that you'll have adequate time to find and put an offer on a new house (with a shorter escrow period, of course).

- **Rent back.** Include a provision in your sales contract allowing you to rent your current house back from the buyer for some period of time, so that you can complete the process of buying a new property without having to move all your stuff out. Expect to pay a little more than you would for a "regular" rental, to cover the buyer's expenses.

- **Get bridge financing.** If you are going to briefly own two homes, make sure you have enough cash by either borrowing the money (perhaps from family, friends, or by taking out an equity line of credit on your current home) or by getting a "bridge loan" from a financial institution. A bridge loan is a short-term loan and a last resort—because fees tend to be fairly high and won't be spread out over a long time (you'll be refinancing as soon as you sell and get a permanent mortgage).

> **TIP**
> **Save money by using the same agent for both buying and selling.** As USA TODAY's Thomas Fogarty suggests, buying and selling in the same market gives you some leverage. Your selling agent "will be interested in representing you as a buyer, because that'll give them a piece of the commission on the house you'll be moving to. Suggest that if they knock a point or two off the price of selling your home, you'll also let them represent you as a buyer."

It's best to figure out a strategy before you sell your home, so that if you're confronted with a promising offer, you'll be ready. Likewise, you'd hate to agree to purchase a new home and find it difficult to sell the old one. In such a situation, you might accept less for the house than you would have if you'd planned ahead.

> **RESOURCE**
> **Looking for more information on selling your house?** See:
> - *House Selling For Dummies*, by Eric Tyson and Ray Brown (For Dummies)
> - *Seven Steps to Sold: The Secrets to Selling Your Home for Big Bucks … Fast!*, by Donna Freeman, Shannon Freeman, and Craig Boreth (Three Rivers Press)
> - Articles at Real Estate ABC, www.realestateabc.com/homeselling.

Index

A

Accessibility, 271, 272

Actual cash value insurance, 61, 62

Adjustable-rate mortgages (ARMs), 116, 118–119, 120–121, 122, 133

Adjustment period for interest rates, 122

Adverse possession law, 97

Age of home, 46, 192, 215–216, 254–255

Agreement granting permission to use property, 98

Ahluwalia, Gopal, 212

Air-conditioner maintenance, 50, 69–70

Aker, Scott, 79

Alarm systems, 16

Alternative Minimum Tax (AMT), 165

American Council for an Energy-Efficient Economy, 72

America's Best Lost Recipes, 111

Angie's List, 206

Animals, laws regarding, 106–107

Annual fee for HELOCs, 166

Annual percentage rate (APR), 155

Appeal of tax assessments, 184, 186–187

Appliance expenditures, 41–42, 192, 203

Appliance installation, 196

Appraisals, 126–127, 162

APR (annual percentage rate), 155

Architects, 213, 214–215

ARMs (adjustable-rate mortgages), 116, 118–119, 120–121, 122, 133

Asbestos, 218

Attorney for state court lawsuit, 264

Automobiles and green driving, 84–86

B

Babysitting co-ops, 94

Bailout with potential buyback scam, 139

Bait and switch scam, 139

Balloon loans, 118, 120–121

Bamboo floors, 220

Banking gap, generational, 163

Bankruptcy, 138

Banks, 6, 158. *See also* Loans

Bargain shopping, 38–42, 192, 202–203, 219. *See also* Money-saving tips

Barker, Olivia, 94

Base rate, 155

Bathroom maintenance checks, 50, 52

Bathroom remodeling, 192, 193, 212, 213, 238

Beauty products, the environment and, 75–76

Bedroom remodeling, 213, 279

Better Business Bureau, 252

Better Homes and Gardens Home Design Software, 214

Bids from contractors, 224, 225–227

Blighted property, laws against, 106

Block, Sandra, 61, 85, 149, 170–171, 176–177, 178, 179, 181

Books on home improvements, 200

Bourhis, Ray, 251

Break even point in refinancing, 150–152

Bridge financing, 283

Bridge loans, 283

Budget
  adapting to circumstances, 32–33
  financial goals, 22–25, 34
  fiscal exercises, 43
  home furnishing expenditures, 38–40
  income, 25–26
  for maintenance, 46
  overview, 22, 32
  prioritizing expenditures, 33–38
  for renovation projects, 201–204

spending plan, 25–31, 33
  See also Money-saving tips

Buie, Elissa, 43

Builder's warranty, 258–261

Building inspectors, 217, 256, 260, 276–277

Building permits, 108–109, 216–218, 231

Bullwinkle, Alice, 33

Burglaries, 16, 242–243, 253

Buyer's market, 281, 282

Buying your home, 2, 271–272

C

Campaign for Safe Cosmetics, 75–76

Cancellation fee for HELOCs, 166

Cancellation provision in contracts, 232

Capital gains tax, 176, 180–183, 274, 281

Carbon monoxide detectors, 52, 64

Carpenter ants or bees, 54–55

Carpet and Rug Institute, 220

Carpet for floors, 220

Carpooling, 85, 94, 130

Cauchon, Dennis, 186

CC&Rs (Covenants, Conditions, and Restrictions), 107–108. *See also* Homeowners' associations

Ceiling fans, 90

Cell phones, 43

Certificate of occupancy, 258

CFL (compact fluorescent) lights, 88–89

Chalkboard paint, 13

Change of address notifications, 4–6

Change orders, 227, 232, 233

Charitable contributions, 10

Chatzky, Jean, 28

Childproofing your home, 19, 239

Children, 6, 24, 28, 37, 69

Chimney maintenance, 50

Chocolate-Filled Cookies, 111

Chu, Kathy, 59, 60–61, 62

Circuit interrupter maintenance, 52

City planning office, 109

Clark, Bill, 101

Clarke, Betsy, 94

Class action lawsuits against builders, 264

Cleaning products, green, 69, 72–74

Cleaning tasks, 48, 51

Climate change and gardening, 78–79

Climate zone map (USDA), 78

Closing costs for HELOC, 166

Closing documents, 8

Clothes dryer vent maintenance, 50

Clothing, the environment and, 75

Coffee mugs, reusable, 83

Communication

  with contractor, 220, 223–225, 232, 233–234, 238–239

  with lenders, 130–132

  with neighbors, 108–110, 112–113

Community activities, 93

Community associations, 9, 69, 107–108, 217–218, 264

Community supported agriculture (CSA), 82

Commute times, 272

Compact fluorescent (CFL) lights, 88–89

Comparable property, 186, 270, 281

Compost, 79

Condominiums, 9, 69, 107–108, 217–218, 264

Construction loans, 235–237

Construction projects. *See* Contractors; Remodeling; Renovations

Consumer protection agencies, 262

Consumer Reports, 258

Contingency fee basis, 251, 264

Contingent offers, 282

Contract for remodeling, 220, 227–233

Contractor Midjob Worksheet, 233–234

Contractors

  change orders, 227, 232, 233

  communicating with, 220, 223–225, 232, 233–234, 238–239

  contract with, 220, 227–233

  for drafting plans, 214

  employee vs., 208–209

estimates and bids from, 224, 225–227

and finish work, 220–221

hiring, 216, 222–227

overview, 221–222

for purchasing materials, 219–220, 229

and subcontractors, 222, 230, 231

Cork floors, 220

Cost-plus bid, 226

County recorder, 97

Covenants, Conditions, and Restrictions (CC&Rs), 107–108. *See also* Homeowners' associations

Cradle to Cradle, 219

Crawl space maintenance, 50

Credit cards, 23, 159, 244–245

Credit score, 131, 147, 156, 159–160

Crime prevention, 15–17

CSA (community supported agriculture), 82

Curb appeal, 279

D

Daily cleanup by contractor, 230

Damage prevention, 8, 12, 18–19, 54–55

Database of State Incentives for Renewable Energy, 90, 180

Deadbolt locks, 15

Debt-to-income ratio, 158–159

Deck building and maintenance, 50, 196

Deductible for homeowners' insurance policy, 64–65

Deed in lieu of foreclosure, 137

"Defensible space" around your home, 19

Degen, Francis, 170

Demand letters, 262

Demolition prior to remodeling, 218–219, 229

Design. *See* Interior design

Designed to Sell (TV program), 279–280

Diapers, 76

Diggs, Kip, 243

Disability insurance, 125

Disasters

damage prevention, 8, 12, 18–19, 54–55

insurance coverage for, 59–62

inventorying goods prior to, 14–15, 49

personal possession replacement, 62

tips for recovery, 252

See also Emergencies; Homeowner's insurance policy

Discount stores, 41

Dishwashers, 70

Dispute resolution provision in contracts, 232

Disputes with neighbors, 110–113

Do-it-yourself jobs, 195–197, 204–209

Down payment on next house, 268, 269, 274–275

Downspout maintenance, 50, 52

Drafting plans, 213–215, 229

Draftspersons, 214

Drain trap maintenance, 49

Driveway maintenance, 51

Driving green, 84–86

Dry rot (fungus), 54–55

Dugas, Christine, 14, 243, 249, 251, 252

E

Earthquake insurance, 59

Earthquake-prone states, 6, 12

Easements, 98–99

Education, saving for your children's, 24

EEM (Energy Efficient Mortgage) from FHA, 236

Electrostatic filters, 69–70

Emergencies

  defects in new homes, 258–262

  fires, 18, 19, 60–63

  first tasks when discovered, 242–245

  home maintenance vs., 48–52

  home warranty claim, 253–254

  insurance claims for, 245–252

  lawsuits for damages, 262–264

  liability for existing defects, 247–248, 254–257

  saving for, 23–24, 34, 125

  See also Disasters

Employees, IRS laws on, 208–209

Encroachment on neighbor's property, 95–98

Energy audits, 87–88

Energy Department, 86

Energy Efficient Mortgage (EEM) from FHA, 236

Energy-saving tips, 27, 35, 68–69, 70, 71, 77. See also Greening your home

Energy Star rating, 41, 89, 90

Engineers, 197, 215–216

Environmental Protection Agency (EPA), 68, 87

Environmental Working Group, 76

Environment-friendly products, 69, 72–74, 82, 84, 219–220. See also Greening your home

Equifax, 159

Equity skimming scam, 139

Escape routes, planning, 19

Escrow impound accounts, 119, 127–128

Escrow period, 282

Estimates

  and classes on construction, 200

  from contractors, 224, 225

  for cost of tax preparation, 170

  for home equity loans, 163

  for mortgage, 149, 156–157

  See also Bids from contractors

Evacuation practice, 9, 19

Expenditures per household, 145

Expenses
  appliances, 41–42, 192, 203
  discretionary spending vs. goals, 32
  home furnishings, 38–40
  home improvement projects, 193,
    194, 195, 198
  and life insurance, 125
  prioritizing, 25, 33–38, 129–130
  for services, 209
  spending patterns, 27–31
  See also Living expenses
Experian, 159
Exterior wall check, 50, 51

F

Fair Isaac Corporation (FICO),
  159–160
Fannie Mae Homestyle Renovation
  Mortgage, 236–237
Farmer's markets, 80–81
Faucet maintenance, 50, 51
Federal Housing Administration
  (FHA), 133, 236
Federal Trade Commission's
  Mortgage Shopping Worksheet, 154
Fences, laws on, 102–103
FHASecure, 133
FICO (Fair Isaac Corporation),
  159–160
Filing system. *See* Organizing your
  records
Financial goals, 22–25, 34

Financial priorities, 125
Financing contingency, 232
Financing for remodeling, 145,
  232, 234–238. *See also* Refinancing
  your house; entries beginning with
  "Home equity"
Finish work after remodeling,
  220–221
Fire department responses, 264
Fire extinguishers, 19, 52, 64
Fireplace, outdoor, 77
Fireplace dampers, 27
Fires, 18, 19, 60–63
Fiscal exercises, 43
Fitzpatrick, Laura, 186
Fixed-price bid, 225–226
Fixed-rate mortgages, 116, 118–119,
  120–121, 148
Flannagan, Madelyn, 61
Flood zone precautions, 8, 59
Flowers, edible, 58
Fogarty, Thomas A., 193, 194, 283
Food and the environment, 80–84
Forbearance of lender, 135
Foreclosure, 128–133, 137, 138
Foreclosure-rescue scams, 138–142
Forests, living near, 17
Forest Stewardship Council, 219
For-sale-by-owner (FSBO), 268,
  277–278
Foundation wall maintenance, 51
401(k), 24, 28, 34, 124, 237
Fraud alert on credit history,
  244–245

Fraud in mortgage applications, 162

Fraudulent scams, 138–142

Freecycling, 75

Freeman, Donna, 279–280

Front porch, 13, 196

Fruit trees, 104

FSBO (for-sale-by-owner), 268, 277–278

FTC's Mortgage Shopping Worksheet, 154

Fuel efficiency, maximizing, 85, 86

Furniture, quality of, 38–39, 77

Furniture liquidators, 39

G

Garage, locking interior door to, 16

Garage-door opener maintenance, 52

Garage sales, 101

Gardening, 56–57, 58, 77–80

G Diapers, 76

General contractor. *See* Contractors

GFE (Good Faith Estimate), 149, 156–157

Gifts, recycling, 94

Goals, 22–25, 32, 34, 35–37. *See also* Budget; Savings

Golden, Matt, 87

Gomez, Alan, 105

Good Faith Estimate (GFE), 149, 156–157

Government agencies, notifying, 6

Government help for mortgages, 132, 133

The Greenguard Environmental Institute, 219

Greening your home
cleaning products, 69, 72–74

driving green, 84–86

easy changes, 68–72

eating green, 80–84

floors, 219, 220

gardening and lawn care, 77–80

and maintenance, 86–90

overview, 68

personal care products, 75–77

remodeling tips, 215, 219–220

renovations, 86–90, 198

sustainable materials, 77, 198, 199, 219–220

and value at time of sale, 199

Green mortgage from FHA, 236

Green Power Network, The, 90

Green power programs, 90

Green remodel guides, 198

Grilling, gas or propane vs. charcoal, 79

Gross income, 26, 159

Gross-up, 176–177

Guaranteed replacement insurance, 60–61

Gutter maintenance, 50, 52

H

Hammer for home toolbox, 47

Hauck, Dennis William, 19

Haunted houses, 19, 20

Hazard insurance, 58–62

Health and gardening, 57

Health products, 75–76

Heating system maintenance, 51

HELOC (home equity line of credit), 164–166, 235

HERS (home energy rating systems report), 236

Hill, James, 57

Hiring professionals, 197, 206, 215–216, 219, 222–227

Hiring unskilled labor, 206–209

Holiday lights, 105

Home appraisals, 126–127

Home-based businesses, 10, 175–176

Home energy rating systems report (HERS), 236

Home equity, 160–161, 164, 235, 269

Home equity debt interest deductions, 175

Home equity line of credit (HELOC), 164–166, 235

Home equity loan, 146, 162–166, 235

Home furnishing expenditures, 38–40

Home improvements

how-to information, 199–200

IRS list of examples, 182

loans for, 145, 146, 163, 174

notifying insurer of, 61

prioritizing, 24, 35–36

record keeping for, 10, 11

and resale value, 36, 191–194, 280

saving for, 24–25

and tax basis, 181

See also Refinancing your house; Remodeling; Renovations

Home inspectors, 217, 256, 260, 276–277

Home loan documents, 8–9

Home office, 10, 175–176

Homeowners' associations, 9, 69, 107–108, 217–218, 264

Homeowner's insurance claims

burden of proof on insured, 14

for damage dispute with neighbor, 113

denial disputes, 251

denials for specific dog breeds, 64

for emergencies, 245–252

filing a claim, 248–249

maintenance considerations, 53

most common, 244

payment for, 250

policy increase or cancellation from, 64–65

practicality of, 246–247

for workers injured at your home, 206–207

Homeowner's insurance company ratings, 58

Homeowner's insurance policy
and alarm systems, 16
maintenance considerations, 53
notifying insurer of damage, 9, 243
organizing your records, 7–11
organizing your worldly goods, 11–15
penalty for not paying, 34
reviewing, 58
saving money for payment, 22
updating information on, 35
verifying coverage, 58–65, 245–246
See also Homeowner's insurance claims

Homeowners' Protection Act, 126

Homestyle Renovation Mortgage from Fannie Mae, 236–237

Home warranty policies, 253–254, 268

Hope for Homeowners program (FHA), 133

Household emissions tally, 68

Household Spending Plan, 25–31, 33

Housewarming party, 7, 93

Housing and Urban Development Department (HUD), 132, 133, 135

Housing counselors with HUD approval, 132

Housing market problems, 132, 133, 136

How-to information, 199–200

Hybrid cars, 177

Hybrid car tax credit, 179

Hybrid loans, 118–119, 120–121, 237

I

Identity mortgage fraud, 162

Identity theft, 244–245

ID number for expensive items, 15

Impound accounts, 119, 127–128

Improvement receipts, 11

Impulse shopping, 32–33

Income, 25–26, 29, 273

Independent contractors vs. employees, 208–209

Independent Insurance Agents & Brokers of American (IIABA), 246

Index (interest rate), 122

Inflation guard for insurance policy, 60

Injuries to guests at your home, 243, 244, 247, 248, 250

Injuries to workers at your home, 206–207

Inman, Bradley, 194

Inspection reports, 9, 214, 256, 260

Insulation
in attic, 35
and energy efficiency, 89

installing, 196
for pipes, 49
for water heater, 70
weatherstripping, 50, 52
Insurance
architect's, 215
contractor's, 224, 230
engineer's, 216
life and disability, 125
notifying of new address, 6
PMI, 10, 124, 126–127, 173–174
See also Homeowner's insurance
claims; Homeowner's insurance
policy
Insurance adjusters, 249
Insurance Information Institute, 15
Interest-only loans, 118, 120–121
Interest rates, 119, 122, 145, 165,
236, 270
Interior design
bargain shopping and, 38–40
organization considerations, 11–15
painting, 13, 38, 51, 107, 196,
204, 279
preparing to sell, 267–268
in space-challenged homes, 204
usage considerations, 37
Interior designers for remodel, 215
Internet resources
for bargain hunting, 35, 38,
39–40, 41, 270
for budgeting, 25
for buying a home, 282

calculators, 36, 122, 153
for eliminating carpenter ants, 55
on energy efficiency, 72, 86
green remodel guides, 198
homeowners insurance company
ratings, 58
for household emissions tally, 68
recycling, 70
for regional gardening information,
56
tools list for home maintenance,
46–47
toxicity ratings for products, 76
Interviewing contractors, 223–225
Inventory of your possessions,
14–15, 49, 249
Irrigation system, 57
Itemizing tax deductions, 169–172

J

Jones, David, 129
Jouzaitis, Carol, 109–110
Junk mail, 71

K

Kids' party, 95
Kill-A-Watt power meter, 87
Kitchen remodeling, 193, 196, 213,
238
Knox, Noelle, 46, 48, 138

L

Landlord, becoming a, 273–276

Landscaping
gardening, 56–57, 58, 77–80
learning about your area, 78–79
maintaining records of services, 10
overview, 56–57
plants and shrubs, 17, 51, 56–57, 77–80
trees, 51, 77, 103–104
value at time of sale, 193, 194, 278

Land surveyors, 96

Langdon, Libby, 204

Late fees for mortgage payments, 121, 173

Laundry, energy-saving methods, 68–69

Lawn, 77

Lawn care, 77

Lawsuits
for failure to disclose defects, 256–257, 262–264, 277
in small claims court, 113, 127, 254, 263–264
in state court, 264

Lead in homes (pre-1978), 218

Legal Research (Elias and Levinkind), 262

Lending institution mortgages, 157–158

Level for home toolbox, 47

Liability for damage, 247–248

Liability for defects in new homes, 258–262

Liability for undisclosed defects, 247–248, 254–257, 262–264, 276–277

Liability insurance, 59, 63–65

Liability of contractor, 230

Licensing, checking on, 53, 224

Lien release from subcontractors and suppliers, 230, 231

Life insurance, 125

Life-of-the-loan cap, 122

Line of credit, 164–166, 235, 237

Linoleum vs. vinyl, 219

Lirof, Willow, 38, 40

Living expenses
if house is damaged, 61, 247, 249, 250
and life insurance, 125
and moving, 176–177
saving three–six months worth, 23–24, 34, 235

Loan modification, 135

Loan officer at banks, 158

Loan payoff, 119

Loans
balloon, 118, 120–121
bridge, 283
choosing, 154–158
construction, 235–237
credit cards vs., 23
home equity, 146, 162–166, 235
home loan documents, 8–9

hybrid, 118–119, 120–121, 237

interest-only, 118, 120–121

life-of-the-loan cap, 122

modification of, 135

option, 118, 120–121

qualifying for, 158–161

two-step, 119, 120–121

See also Refinancing

Loan to value ratio (LTV), 127

Local laws, 102–106, 109, 110, 217, 258

Local property taxes, 174

Location-specific factors, 271

Locks, changing, 15

"Loss of use" insurance policy provision, 61

Low-E coating for windows, 89

Loyalty to lender, 150

LTV (loan to value ratio), 127

M

Mail forwarding by postal service, 4

Maintenance

do-it-yourself, 195

and environmental awareness, 69–70, 86–90

obligations under builder's warranty, 259

overview, 46, 49–52

in preparation for selling, 276–277

preventing emergencies with, 48–52

as protecting your investment, 193

recognizing pest problems, 53–56

record keeping, 10–11

by tenants, 275

Maintenance checklist, 49–52

Maloney, Jim, 186

Manning, Anita, 17

Manuals and warranty information, 10–11, 49

Manufacturer's warranties, 10–11, 49, 261

Margin over interest, 122, 165

Market conditions, 117, 191, 270, 280–281, 282

McBride, Greg, 124

McCollum, Jeff, 62

Mechanic's liens, 231

Mediation, 112–113, 262–263

Medical bills resulting from injuries in your home, 63

Mice and rats, 54–55

Minimum draw or loan balance, 166

Mold growth, 218–219, 258

Money-saving tips

bargain shopping, 38–40, 41–42, 192, 202–203, 219

dining in, library books and DVDs, 32

for driving, 85–86

energy efficiency, 27, 35, 68–69, 70, 71, 77

financial diet tips, 43

for home furnishing shopping, 38–40

housewarming party, 7

for property taxes, 183–187

for renovation equipment and materials, 202–203, 219

See also Greening your home; Refinancing your house

Mortgage application fraud, 162

Mortgage Assistance Solutions, 140–141

Mortgage banker at banks, 157–158

Mortgage boom and consequences, 117

Mortgage brokers, 156–157

Mortgage interest tax deduction, 172–173

Mortgages

adjustable-rate, 116, 118–119, 120–121, 122, 133

alternative payment arrangements, 134–136

calculators for comparing, 153

finding the best loan, 154–156

fixed-rate, 116, 118–119, 120–121

Good Faith Estimate, 149, 156–157

inability to pay, 128–133, 137, 138

interest and points, 9, 152

interest rates, 119, 122, 145, 165, 236, 270

keeping costs down, 123–128

overview, 116–119

points, 9, 152, 153, 155, 173

preapproval, 270–271

reviewing, 119–122

scams to avoid, 138–139

second mortgage, 134, 163–166

selling property before foreclosure, 136–137

working with a broker, 156–157

working with a lending institution, 157–158

See also Loans; Refinancing your house

Mortgage Shopping Worksheet, 154

Moving cost tax deductions, 176–177

Moving to another new home

buying and selling simultaneously, 282–283

choosing the right property, 271–272

deciding when, 266–267

financial strategies for moving up, 269–276

maximizing profits from sale, 276–281

overview, 266

selling and moving costs, 267–268

Mulch, 79

Multiuse spaces, 12

Musty odors, 49

N

Nasser, Haya El, 101

National Association of Professional Organizers, 12

Negative amortization, 118

Neighborhoods, 191–192. *See also* Community associations; Local laws

Neighborhood watch group, 16

Neighbors

 dispute resolution, 110–113

 as joint owners of a fence, 102–103

 as joint owners of trees, 103–104

 meeting and greeting, 93–95

 overview, 92

 and property lines, 95–99

 and remodeling projects, 108–110

Neighbors-only party, 93

Net income, 26

Noise, laws against excessive, 101–102

Northern American Insulation Manufacturers' Association, 89

Notice of Default, 131, 136, 141

Notini, Jill, 41

Nuisance laws, 100–101

O

Off-site protection

 for documents, 8

Open houses, 270

Option loans, 118, 120–121

Organic Consumers Association, 76

Organic products, 75–76, 82

Organizing your possessions, 14–15, 49, 249

Organizing your records, 7–11. *See also* Record keeping

Origination points mortgage fees, 157

Outdoor art, 13

Outside lighting, 16–17

Ownership records, 8–9

Owner's manual for new homeowners, 1–2

P

Packaging-to-waste ratio, 83

Painting, 13, 38, 51, 107, 196, 204, 279

Paints, low or no-VOC, 220

Paper consumption, 71

Parking permits, 6

Patio, 13, 196

Pay It Down! (Chatzky), 28

Payment terms, contractor's, 228

Periodic cap, 122

Permits for remodeling, 11, 205, 213–218, 231

Personal care products for green living, 75–77

Personal liability insurance, 63

Pest control professionals, 53, 55

Pesticides, 77

Pest threats, 53–56

Pets, 37, 63, 64, 76, 106–107, 279

Phantom rescue scam, 139

Phipps, Ron, 46

PITI (principal, interest, taxes, insurance) payments, 159

Plans for remodeling, 11, 205, 213–218, 229

Plants and shrubs, 17, 51, 56–57, 77–80

Plat map, 96

Pliers for home toolbox, 47

PMI premiums, 10

PMI (private mortgage insurance), 10, 124, 126–127, 173–174

Points, 9, 152, 153, 155, 173

Police reports, 243

Powderpost beetles, 54–55

Power purchase agreement (PPA), 90

Power strips, turning off, 71

Prepaying your mortgage, 119, 123–125

Prepayment penalties, 119, 148

Prepayment penalty tax deduction, 173

Prescriptive easements, 99

Pricing your house, 280–281

Prime interest rate, 165

Principal, interest, taxes, insurance (PITI) payments, 159

Prioritizing expenditures, 25, 33–38, 129–130

Private mortgage insurance (PMI), 10, 124, 126–127, 173–174

Private nuisance, 100

Project Lifeline, 131

Property appreciation, 274

Property lines, 95–99

Property management, 275

Property rights, 99–107

Property taxes, 10, 22, 32, 174, 183–187

Protecting your family and possessions, 239, 244

Punch list for contractors, 221, 258

Purchase and ownership records, 8–9

Q

Quality-control inspectors, 260

Quitclaim deed, 137

R

Rain barrels, 79

Range hood maintenance, 51

Ratcheting screwdriver with multiple bits, 47

Rats and mice, 54–55

Real estate agent fees, 181, 268, 283

Real estate agent liability for failure to disclose, 256

Real Estate Home Inspection Checklist from A to Z (Cozzi), 276

Real Simple (magazine), 12

Reassessment of property, 184

Rebates, 35, 41, 203

Reclaimed wood floors, 220

Record keeping
  builder's warranty claim, 260

Household Spending Plan, 25–31, 33

income, 25–26, 29, 273

for insurance claims, 248–249

mortgage loan documents, 162

organizing your records, 7–11

for tax deductions, 168, 172

See also Expenses

Recycling, 70, 75, 83, 94

Redmond, Kelly, 78

References for contractor, 225

Refinancing your house

alternatives to, 162–166

application process, 161–162

calculating costs and benefits, 148–153

choosing the right loan, 154–158

overview, 144–147

qualifying for a new loan, 158–161

Refrigerator maintenance, 51

Remodeling

communicating with neighbors, 108–110

delays and problems, 220, 229, 239

demolishing old areas, 218–219, 229

determining cost vs. value, 36, 192

financing, 145, 234–238

finish work, 220–221

hiring for, 197, 206–209, 215–216, 219, 222–227

informing insurer of, 61

materials for, 219–220

midproject changes, 233–234

overview, 212–213

permits and plans for, 11, 205, 213–218, 231

personal survival, 238–239

and property lines, 95–99

protecting your family and possessions, 239

refinancing based on, 145

See also Contractors; Renovations

Renovations

DIY projects vs. hiring a pro, 195–197

greening your home, 86–90, 198

hiring unskilled labor, 206–209

increasing value with, 190–194

informing insurer of, 61

overview, 190, 197–200

project budget, 201–204

record keeping for, 10, 11

scheduling your project, 202, 204–205

See also Remodeling

Rental income, 273

Rent back clause, 282

Renting out a room in your home, 26

Reorganization bankruptcy, 138

Repair receipts, 11

Repayment plan for mortgage, 134

Replacement cost insurance, 60

"Replacement value" insurance, 62

Resale value, 36, 191–194, 280

Retiree debts, 137

Retirement savings, 24, 28, 34, 124, 125, 237–238

Return policies, 40

Reupholstering, 39

Rodents, 54–55

Roof maintenance, 19, 51, 194

Roof replacement, 193, 196, 212

S

Safety and security
carbon monoxide detectors, 52, 64
crime prevention, 15–17
damage prevention, 8, 12, 18–19, 54–55
evacuation practice, 9, 19
fire extinguishers, 19, 52, 64
and home maintenance, 48–52
smoke detectors, 18, 50, 64

Savings
automatic deduction programs, 34
for down payment on another house, 269
for emergencies, 23–24, 34, 125
overview, 22–25
paying for remodel with, 235
for retirement, 24, 28, 34, 124, 125, 237–238
See also Expenses; Money-saving tips

Sawistowski, Steve, 17

Scams, 138–142

Scharin, Bob, 178

Schedules for home improvement projects
with contractor, 229
DIY jobs, 202, 204–205

Screwdriver for home toolbox, 47

Seller or seller's agent's failure to disclose, 247–248, 254–257, 262–264, 276–277

Seller's market, 270, 277, 280, 282

Selling your home
buying and selling simultaneously, 282–283
before foreclosure, 136–137
FSBO or minimal Realtor use, 268, 277–278
preparing your home, 267–268, 278–280
See also Moving to another new home

Seo, Danny, 13

Service providers
cost of, 209
employees' insurance benefits through, 207
licensing of, 53, 224
maintaining files on, 10
notifying of new address, 6
trading with, 43

Shipping or delivery costs, 40, 42

Short sale, 137

Showerhead, low-flow, 71

Shutoff valves, 18–19

Siding as a home improvement, 193

Sliding glass doors, 15

Slobs and home decor, 37

Small claims court, 113, 127, 254, 263–264

SmartDraw software, 214

Smoke detectors, 18, 50, 64

Software for home designers, 214

Solar energy, 90

Solar lanterns, 13

Solar tax credit, 179

Space-challenged housing, 204

Space design, 12

Spending plan, 25–31, 33

Spite fences and houses, 102, 103

Sprinkler system for fires, 18

Staging your home, 278–280

State court lawsuits, 264

State laws
    adverse possession law, 97
    on contractor requirements, 224
    on disturbing the peace, 102
    on fences, 102–103
    on home warranty companies, 254
    on insurance company cheating, 251
    on lien release from subcontractors, 230
    on seller's disclosure requirements, 255–256, 257, 276–277
    on warranties and implied warranties, 261

State property taxes, 10, 174, 183–187

Statutes of limitation, 263

Storage areas and storing items, 12

Storm doors and windows, 89, 194, 196

Stroller, Michael, 140–141

Subcontractors, 222, 230, 231

Subrogation, 247

Sump pump maintenance, 49

Sustainable materials, 77, 198, 199, 219–220. *See also* Greening your home

Sweat equity, 201. *See also* Remodeling; Renovations

Swimming pool maintenance, 50

T

Tape measure, 47

Taxable income, 176–177

Tax assessments, 126–127, 183–187

Taxation
    amended returns, 178
    for capital gains, 176, 180–183, 274, 281
    first time itemizers, 169–172
    property taxes, 10, 22, 32, 174, 183–187
    record keeping for, 9–10
    tax assessments, 126–127, 183–187
    taxpayer's top worries, 168

Tax benefits for green choices, 90

Tax credits, 177, 179–180, 203

Tax deductions
and Alternative Minimum Tax, 165
documenting, 168, 172
for interest, 163, 172–173,
174–175
for moving expenses, 176–177
overview, 9–10, 168–169
for PMI, 173–174
for points, 9, 173
for prepayment and late payment
penalties, 173
for rental expenses of landlord,
273–275
for state and local property taxes,
174
Taxpayer Relief Act (1997), 180
Tax preparer, choosing, 170–171
Tax rates for property, 185–186
Tax refunds, 172
Termites, 51, 52, 54–55
Terms, contractor's, 228–232
Thermostat, programmable, 90
Time-and-materials bid, 226
Title insurance, 96, 98–99, 149
Title transfer, 268
Todora, Jim, 186
Toilets, low-flow, 71
Tongue & groove pliers, 47
Tools, 46–47, 57, 203, 205
Torpedo level with magnetic strip, 47
Total cost bid, 225–226
Toys, choosing green, 76

TransUnion, 159
Trash-covered property, laws against,
106
Trees, 51, 77, 103–104
Two-step loan, 119, 120–121

U

U.N. Intergovernmental Panel on
Climate Change, 78–79
Underinsured home statistics, 60
Uniform Residential Loan
Application, 161–162
U.S. Department of Agriculture
(USDA), 75–76, 78, 82
U.S. Postal Service, 4
Utilities, 5, 11, 18–19, 27, 242
Utility companies, 86, 89, 90, 98
Utility knife, 47

V

Vally, Norma, 46
Variance from local planning
commission, 217
Views, laws on, 105–106
Vinyl vs. linoleum, 219
Volatile organic compounds
(VOCs), 220
Volunteering in your children's
school, 94
Voter registration, 6

W

Waggoner, John, 34

Walking, environmental benefits of, 84

Warranties and implied warranties, 261

Warranty information and manuals, 10–11, 49, 261

Warranty of contractor, 232

Water bottles, reusable, 83

Water damage, looking for, 49, 50

Water heater, tankless, 89

Water heater maintenance, 49, 70

Water heater timer, 70

Water valve maintenance, 49

Weatherstripping, 50, 52

Wedlick, Dennis, 272

Weekly expenses, calculating, 28

Weise, Elizabeth, 60

Wholesalers, 203

Wiener, Debbie, 37

Wild animals, living near, 17

Wilson, Craig, 272

Windows and storm doors, 89, 194, 196

Wipe out clause, 282

Women's fears, 53

Wooden furniture, 38–39

Work From Home Handbook (Fitzpatrick and Fishman), 85

Workout assumption, 137

Workout options of lenders, 134–136

Y

Yard. *See* Landscaping

Yard sales, 101

Yield Spread Premium (YSP), 157

Yuhus, Mary Thurman, 13

Z

Zoning laws, 217

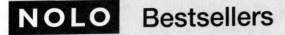

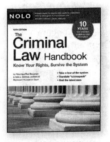

NOLO Bestsellers

Plan Your Estate

$44.99

How to File for Chapter 7 Bankruptcy

$29.99

Form Your Own Limited Liability Company

$44.99

Deduct It!
Lower Your Small Business Taxes

$34.99

Retire Happy

$19.99

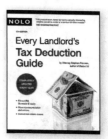

Every Landlord's Tax Deduction Guide

$34.99

Get the Latest in the Law

Nolo's Legal Updater
We'll send you an email whenever a new edition of your book is published! Sign up at **www.nolo.com/legalupdater**.

Updates at Nolo.com
Check **www.nolo.com/update** to find recent changes in the law that affect the current edition of your book.

Nolo Customer Service
To make sure that this edition of the book is the most recent one, call us at **800-728-3555** and ask one of our friendly customer service representatives (7:00 am to 6:00 pm PST, weekdays only). Or find out at **www.nolo.com**.

Complete the Registration & Comment Card ...
... and we'll do the work for you! Just indicate your preferences below:

- -

Registration & Comment Card

NAME _____ DATE _____

ADDRESS _____

CITY _____ STATE _____ ZIP _____

PHONE _____ EMAIL _____

COMMENTS _____

WAS THIS BOOK EASY TO USE?   (VERY EASY)   5   4   3   2   1   (VERY DIFFICULT)

☐ Yes, you can quote me in future Nolo promotional materials. *Please include phone number above.*

☐ Yes, send me **Nolo's Legal Updater** via email when a new edition of this book is available.

Yes, I want to sign up for the following email newsletters:

    ☐ **NoloBriefs** (monthly)
    ☐ **Nolo's Special Offer** (monthly)
    ☐ **Nolo's BizBriefs** (monthly)
    ☐ **Every Landlord's Quarterly** (four times a year)

☐ Yes, you can give my contact info to carefully selected partners whose products may be of interest to me.

Send to: **Nolo** 950 Parker Street Berkeley, CA 94710-9867,
Fax: (800) 645-0895, or include all of the above
information in an email to regcard@nolo.com with
the subject line "US-OWN1."

US-OWN1

NOLO